MODERN LOSS

MODERN LOSS

Candid Conversation About Grief.
Beginners Welcome.

REBECCA SOFFER *and*
GABRIELLE BIRKNER

ILLUSTRATIONS BY PETER ARKLE

HARPER WAVE
An Imprint of HarperCollins*Publishers*

HarperCollins books may be purchased for educational, business, or sales promotional use. For information, please email the Special Markets Department at SPsales@harpercollins.com.

FIRST EDITION

Designed by Bonni Leon-Berman

Library of Congress Cataloging-in-Publication Data
Names: Soffer, Rebecca, author. | Birkner, Gabrielle, author.
Title: Modern loss : candid conversation about grief : beginners welcome / Rebecca Soffer & Gabrielle Birkner ; illustrations by Peter Arkle.
Description: New York, NY : Harper Wave, [2017] | Includes bibliographical
   references.
Identifiers: LCCN 2017052727 (print) | LCCN 2017048796 (ebook) | ISBN 9780062499226 (E-book) | ISBN 9780062499189 (hardcover) | ISBN 9780062499196 (pbk.)
Subjects: LCSH: Grief. | Loss (Psychology)
Classification: LCC BF575.G7 (print) | LCC BF575.G7 S6266 2017 (ebook) | DDC
   155.9/37--dc23
LC record available at https://lccn.loc.gov/2017052727

ISBN 978-0-06-249918-9

18 19 20 21 22   LSC   10 9 8 7 6 5 4 3 2 1

For our parents
and our children.

Shelby & Ray   Ruth & Larry   Roni & Allan
Noah & Elliot   Saul & Hank

The opposite of war isn't peace . . . it's creation.

—JONATHAN LARSON, *RENT*

CONTENTS

INTRODUCTION

HI. WE'RE REBECCA AND GABI. We wish we never had a reason to meet in the first place, but we're so glad we did.

It was the spring of 2007, at a dinner party for six women in their twenties and early thirties, held in a cramped Manhattan walkup with no dining room and weak AC. After a round of awkward greetings, we arranged ourselves in a rough circle with plastic plates full of baked ziti teetering on our laps. The host was a mutual friend, but the rest of us were total strangers to each other. And we had no idea whether we had anything in common other than (a) we all seemed to love cheese, (b) we all clearly had functioning sweat glands, and (c) we were all facing a life without at least one of our parents.

That last reason was why we had all shown up in the first place.

The first few minutes were spent quietly blinking across the room at each other. Finally, someone started speaking. Then someone else. Soon stories came pouring out of us, unfiltered, like the Two Buck Chuck we'd been nervously sipping. As we worked our way through that pan of Italian red sauce, we fed our collective desire—no, our *need*—to share our experiences, our fears, and our outrages.

The result was massive relief. Relief even in the face of knowing that important relatives would be conspicuously and infuriatingly absent for all the hoped-for milestones that lay ahead: dog-adopting, home-buying, marriage, kids, career changes . . . exciting successes and idiotic missteps. And also proof that we weren't going crazy for struggling well beyond the mythical the-first-twelve-months-is-the-worst period or wanting to slug the next person who innocently asked, "No . . . really . . . how *are* you?" Everyone else had assured us "time would heal" or we'd "get past it," but how did they know?

It had been surprisingly difficult to find other people our age who understood what we'd been going through, or who could at least stick around to talk through our honest answers (after all, they'd asked). Even in a metropolis like New York, where you can easily get a guy in a bear suit to give you a hug.

Three years before that pivotal dinner party, Gabi, then twenty-four, was in the newsroom of the community newspaper, where she wrote obituaries—yes, for real—when she learned that her father, Larry, and stepmother, Ruth, had been murdered. The fatal connection: a frozen pipe and a call to a local plumbing company, which sent a methamphetamine addict with a long rap sheet to do the repair. That man would show up at their home about a month later, amid a four-day meth binge, intending to rob them. He ended up beating them to death inside their unassuming southwestern split-level. The house had a view of the Sedona, Arizona, red rock formations that people were always saying was "to die for"—and here they were, dead. Two thoughtful, soulful, industrious humans with an energy, resolve, and sense of adventure that made them seem younger than they were, dead.

Just six months before that first ziti dinner, late at night on Labor Day 2006, Rebecca's parents, Shelby and Ray, dropped her off in New York City after their annual Lake George Adirondack camping trip, before continuing down the highway toward their hometown of Philadelphia. Less than an hour after a round of good-bye kisses and hugs, a murky object on the darkened road led to a violent car crash that left Shelby lifeless and Rebecca motherless. The accident was on the very turnpike that had always brought them safely back to each other.

Barely four years after Shelby's death, Ray was on a Caribbean cruise, trying to eke out something resembling enjoyment after losing the love of his life. Late one night in his cabin, his heart gave out. The nightmare Rebecca had been dreading became reality. Suddenly, she was orphaned—a term she'd always associated with very young Dickensian characters clutching dented pails.

This whole grief thing we were experiencing decades earlier than most of our friends? It was a total shit show. At the time, Rebecca spent her days (and some nights) producing political satire pieces for *The Colbert Report*. During the show tapings she'd paste on a perma-smile while wondering how everyone could be laughing so hard when her beautiful, beloved mother was dead. After her father's death, she couldn't comprehend how people could happily order fries with that, while she floated through the Twilight Zone, untethered from everything she'd known.

For Gabi, the two obituaries she drafted the day after she received her Really Bad News—one for her dad and another for her stepmother—would be among the last of her obit-writing career. A merciful editor moved her onto the transportation beat after she returned to work on the heels of an epic shiva. There were fewer triggers covering the commuter railroad, to be sure. But during those early days, her grief found a way to seep out, regardless of where she was or whom she was talking to. That included, on one occasion, the tractor-trailer driver she happened to be interviewing for an article about big rig safety on the I-95 corridor. Some people, like that truck driver, rose to the occasion; others were clearly, and understandably, out of their wheelhouse. The same went for her friends.

Looking for kindred spirits, Rebecca attended a grief support group for people who'd lost their parents. Everyone was nice enough, but she was the only one who didn't qualify for AARP. Feeling isolated, she left after one session without a real connection (though with a great mushroom barley soup recipe). Rebecca searched for solace in her parents' friends but quickly learned everyone—including many of her own good friends—eventually had to get back to their lives and problems. She found a wonderful and warm grief counselor with a vested interest in helping her live a quality life, but still . . . something was missing. She needed to meet other people who'd been dumped onto a similar path.

Gabi had more luck on the support-group front. Every other week, she met with a group of people who had also lost loved ones, mostly young adult children, to homicide. These women—and one guy—understood her in a way most others could not. They never suggested "moving on" after a year or two or twenty. It was a forever trauma, and everyone in this group knew that.

At night, though, we were both alone with very loud thoughts. We opened our laptops in search of comfort, but those searches (often containing phrases along the lines of "Still grieving after two years am I pathetic?" or "How many days in a row is it okay to eat only mac and cheese?") yielded gently flickering e-candles, religious and mindfulness blogs, and *Psychology Today* articles that seemed to suggest that we might actually be going crazy. (Word to the wise: Stay away from the *DSM-IV*.)

The truth was, we didn't always want to be mindful or tend to a Zen garden. We didn't want to hear that "everything happens for a reason" or that "heaven needed another angel" or any other phrase suitable for embroidering onto a throw pillow. We were pissed and lost and wanted to know that someone else understood that when life decks you where it hurts the most, everything is a potential trigger. That it's perfectly acceptable to ugly-cry on the subway en route to work. Or hear crickets on a date once a dead parent is mentioned. Or avoid Halloween because people dress up like murder victims for fun.

It took a while. Longer than we would have preferred. But we slowly pulled ourselves out of our personal caves. And it happened because we decided not to be apologetic or embarrassed about our grief.

The sweaty little cheese lovers our friend gathered for that first awkward dinner party began to meet once a month. Because we didn't feel like using the term *support group*, we called ourselves Women with Dead Parents, or WWDP, which felt more badass (we later learned this also stands for wet-to-wet differential pressure, which is a lot less sexy than it sounds).

We shared our backstories—the good, the messy, the melancholy, and the darkly hilarious. Turns out we weren't the only ones skipping friends' wedding ceremonies in order to avoid watching proud fathers walking their daughters down the aisle. We weren't the only ones finally drifting off to sleep two hours before our alarm was set to go off, only to be awakened by dreams in which our dead parent makes a cameo. We weren't the only ones left to sort through the pieces of our parents' unfinished lives—framed photographs and colanders and half-used bottles of shampoo—and wondering how we could possibly part with any of it. We weren't the only ones in a cold war with relatives over the likes of some crappy old rocking chair with little monetary value but priceless sentimental weight.

The women of WWDP didn't question the motives of the person who'd overly decorated her surviving parent's home with the dead parent's photos when the surviving parent's new "friend" suddenly started hanging around more frequently. We exclaimed "What the fuck!" in tandem when someone revealed that LinkedIn had suggested she connect with a dead loved one's smiling face. We resented knowing that when we eventually met the people we'd marry—that is, *if* anyone would ever want to marry such damaged goods—our parents would never get to embarrass us by asking them indelicate details about their political inclinations over dinner. And when we found people who *did* want to marry us, we accompanied each other on gown searches and danced together at weddings, trying our best to fill the void left behind by lost relatives.

The experience of sharing within our little community was so powerful, and the lack of outlets that resonated with us so frustrating, that Rebecca and Gabi—we had become fast friends, then close friends, and had a couple decades of media experience between us—finally decided to create a platform together.

Enter *Modern Loss*, an online publication we launched in November 2013, when each of us was hugely pregnant with the babies who would be born shortly thereafter. The site is driven by candid storytelling and supported by a backbone of practical advice for navigating the churning waters of surviving a loss.

Modern Loss has helped to demystify a process with a long

arc. News flash: you live with grief 24/7, forever, and endure endless triggers along the way. But we wanted people to realize, along with the stark realities of having to go through life without someone important, that they aren't broken, that life goes on, and that it can actually be quite terrific—even if it's impossible to believe in the moment. And trust us, neither of us believed it for a long time.

When we told people what we were planning ("Yep, a site about living with loss, you heard that right!"), we heard comments like "That's dark," or "Sounds like a total downer," or "You'll never make any money doing something like that." Not that we asked or anything. We wanted to scream "We swear, we're not creepy!" but that probably wouldn't have helped our cause.

Naysayers aside, we knew from our own experiences we'd be filling a real need. And we were motivated by many, many people and organizations who quietly encouraged us to keep going, connected us with other people who had candid stories to share, and offered us free office space and free technical support so that we could focus our energy on working instead of on figuring out which cafés offered free Wi-Fi in the Flatiron (shout-out to Argo Tea on 22nd and Broadway). They were so energized by our mission that we were certain *Modern Loss* would be the opposite of a downer. It would be about resilience. Thriving instead of surviving, as the therapists say. Or, as Rebecca's mom said, making chicken salad instead of chicken shit (which doesn't really make sense, but damn if it's not colorful).

Since our launch, we've quickly built up a digital community of people we'd be thrilled to meet for a round of drinks one day. A community large enough that we wouldn't want to pay for that round. A community of wide-ranging stories that transcend borders and backgrounds of all kinds. A community of people turned off by platitudes, who want to be honest when they talk about grief in the same way they're honest when they talk about their jobs or their dating lives or how they're secretly kind of sick of millennial pink. A community who'd rather eat a steaming bowl of chicken soup than read an entire book's worth of metaphors for it.

In our time online, we've published hundreds of original personal essays—by people whose names you might know, and by a range of compelling new voices, too. They've told us what it feels like when Facebook knows about your dad's death before you do (pretty shitty, as it so happens!) and what it feels like to be broken up with when you are still reeling from a loved one's death (also pretty shitty!) and what it feels like to celebrate Mother's Day—in your own way—for the first time since your mother's death years earlier (okay, pretty good). We also talk about stuff that many people don't consider polite conversation. Need to manage someone's postmortem social media presence? Advice for sorting through a certain dead someone's belongings? We've got you covered. Ideas for marking the dreaded deathiversary, for going back to work after the funeral, or for a memorial tattoo that doesn't scream "cliché!"? We have all that, too.

But *Modern Loss* is more than an online publication; it's become a movement to change how we talk about grief and loss—a universal experience, if there ever was one, but still a surprisingly taboo one, at least as we've experienced it in the United States. This movement has caught the attention of many kindred spirits, some of whom we've met at our events, which have included film screenings and live storytelling gatherings where you can expect to laugh and cry over Scotch on the rocks. Others have joined in through our attempts to offer creative ways to support each other, such as something we think could go into *The Guinness Book of World Records* as "Largest Loss-Based Gift Swap,"* when nearly 150 people for whom Mother's Day is a trigger in some form gave and received gifts and cards to and from total strangers feeling the same way. The national media and like-minded organizations have also taken notice, featuring us on their pages and airwaves, and inviting us to speak and teach across the country and in the United Kingdom. Turns out the need was even greater than we'd realized.

Which leads us to today.

Modern Loss was always envisioned as a community anyone could access, no matter where they're from, who they've lost, or how long it's been (as we say, beginners are welcome). It's a community open to those grieving someone they love (including someone they might have had a complicated relationship with) *and* those who love someone who is grieving. That's why we wanted to write our first book together, and with a group of people who have their own varied insights on what it means to live with loss. Bottom line: this stuff is always more fun with friends, and also more impactful. The wide-ranging experiences in this book will prove that, just like at Thunder Road, the rules of grief are, there ain't no rules. (Yes, we quoted *Grease*, what of it?) And we're really hoping that the next time you meet someone living with loss, you'll pause

---

* Okay, this probably wouldn't be a huge competition.

and figure out a way to pull them in and connect with them. There's always a way.

Here's the thing: social mores surrounding death and grieving are shifting. People are starting to engage with loss on their own terms, not the ones society has traditionally set for them. We're living in a moment in which Paul Kalanithi's memoir *When Breath Becomes Air*—about losing and embracing life with terminal lung cancer—was a finalist for the Pulitzer Prize and a national best seller. In which there is actually a Tumblr entitled Selfies at Funerals (judge that as you will, but it exists). And in which US vice president Joe Biden, invoking his late son, Beau, looks straight into the camera at the Democratic National Convention and quotes Hemingway with tears in his eyes: "'The world breaks everyone, and afterward, some are strong at the broken places.' I've been made strong at the broken places."

Just as important, we are at a critical moment when much of the country's population is connecting over tragedies, private and public: a death of a parent, a school shooting, a friend's suicide, a terrorist attack, or a police brutality incident. We connect with these stories through social media streams, in between posts on the latest pop culture meme or #tbt memory. We may "like" or comment, or we may not, but we're certainly not pushing them away. When it comes to these platforms, we get that grief is, well, complicated. That an emoji doesn't take the place of really being there for someone who has suffered a loss. But that emoji, that comment, that PM that leads to an e-mail exchange, is not nothing either, and social sharing goes a long way toward raising awareness of who in our networks is suffering. These stories stay on our minds as we mourn public figures and national tragedies with RIP hashtags, and we're having an increasingly open conversation about them.

Loss happens, and it can happen earlier than we'd like to think it can. One in seven Americans will lose a parent or a sibling before turning twenty. As many as 15 percent of pregnancies end in miscarriage, and there are some 23,000 stillbirths a year in the United States alone. In 2016 an estimated 700 to 900 women died from pregnancy-related causes. In 2013 there were more than 41,000 suicides in the country, the shocking equivalent of about one every thirteen minutes. Meanwhile, each year hundreds of thousands of Americans are widowed; many of them will be younger than forty when it happens.

Our grief can't just be buried alongside the ones we love. Even years after our losses, we still have moments of gut-wrenching sadness. We're still annoyed by a wide variety of major and minor Hallmark holidays. We still get pissed thinking about the hand we've been dealt. But guess what? These days, we're tagging family members on Instagram. They're just not the ones we thought we'd be tagging—and ones that in our darkest moments we never thought would be in our lives.

Eventually, we're all going to lose people we love. Eventually, we're all going to die. This is true whether or not we admit it to each other. So there's value in building a community where there's no stigma to talking about death and the countless ways it impacts our lives. And with this book, and the candor of those who contributed to it, we hope to open up the conversation so that, ideally, in the future, nobody has to hear crickets in the face of a loss.

MODERN LOSS

COLLATERAL DAMAGE

But Wait, There's More?

INTRODUCTION

by Rebecca Soffer

Eight hours after I'd learned my mother, Shelby, had been killed on the New Jersey Turnpike, my best friend's husband, Paul, found my vibrator.

It was 2006, the day after Labor Day. While the rest of the country was getting ready for a busy fall season, we were in my Manhattan apartment getting ready to plan my mother's funeral. Paul and his wife, Taifa, attempted to pack a bag for me. I was single, freshly thirty, and suddenly motherless. And all I could do was curl up on my college-era Jennifer Convertibles sofa at 7:30 a.m., watching an old *Scrubs* episode while my friends quietly organized around me.

My mom had stood in this very living room only nine hours earlier, happy and healthy. She and my dad had dropped me off en route to Philadelphia, my hometown, after our yearly camping trip on Lake George in upstate New York. They'd popped in to use the bathroom, grab some water, and give me a quick round of good-bye hugs and kisses. I showed my mom a thirtieth birthday card I'd received that played a tinny version of "The Final Countdown," by the Swedish rock band Europe. We laughed, having no clue that it really was.

A few minutes after they left on that holiday Monday night, I was settled onto the sofa, straddling a bittersweet divide between freedom and the looming reality of workday-morning responsibility. I was still dressed in my camping clothes, with a daddy longlegs crawling out of my fleece jacket pocket and the sweet, dried scent of the lake lingering on my skin.

After a busy year acclimatizing to a brand-new job at a brand-new daily television show, I'd spent more time with my mom that week at Lake George than I had all that past year, and being around the person I loved the most allowed me to emotionally exhale. I normally told her nearly everything, and over that past week we'd talked through my worries during daily swims off a baking rock in the golden hour. In typical Shelby style, her attitude on the advice she provided was take-it-or-leave-it—but truth be told, she always knew just what to say.

"Bec," she said, laughing lightly, when I told her about my angst over my career and over being single at thirty, "things change. Glasses break. Plans are derailed." But, she said, "You pick yourself up, brush off the glass, and keep moving. I'm here for you."

Her advice buoyed me up, and as I got comfortable on the couch and caught up on e-mail (which included an introduction from a guy who was a setup by way of my mom's best friend), I soon felt energized and ready to dive into fall.

Then the phone rang. It was my half brother—my father's much older son—who'd been camping with us and had taken over the late-night driving shift. "Bec, there's been an accident." He described a large piece of debris in the lane, our Subaru Outback's sudden swerve, and my mother lying on the side of the turnpike, near exit 8A. My father screamed unintelligibly in the background. "Is she alive?" I yelled. "Yes, but it's bad," he said. The unspoken order: Come now.

I called Paul and Taifa, and they pulled up in their car within twenty minutes. I scrambled into the back seat, and we rushed south toward her, me still in my hiking boots caked with Adirondack dirt.

Ten minutes from the hospital, a wave of nausea slammed into me, and I broke my own horrified silence. "Tai, I don't feel her anymore." I knew in my gut I'd been lied to, that she was dead. I ran into an eerily silent emergency room and found my father in a hospital bed, his scrapes lightly bandaged. "I'm so sorry, Bec," he cried. "She's gone."

My only clear memory of what followed is wildly thinking, *Where the hell is the toilet?*, then running to the bathroom and sinking to the floor, unsure of what I had to do more urgently: pee or pass out. In that moment I did not give a crap that I was lying in invisible hospital filth, reminding myself over and over that I'd just told my mother I loved her two hours beforehand. Neither did Taifa, who lay there next to me.

Early the next morning, back in New York, my brain strained to understand the enormousness of this sudden void. Not only was my mother, the woman who had provided me, her only child, with thirty years of deep, unconditional love, encouragement, and fierce protectiveness, suddenly no more, but so was this person, this individual, gone. Shelby—the woman who was raised in a Northeast Philadelphia row house; who used the *Hair* soundtrack to teach her Mexican immigrant students English in the 1960s and '70s in San Francisco (where after work she'd fix her shag to go hear Janis Joplin); who, years later, back in Philly after marrying my dad, founded an innovative parenting and education magazine—was gone.

My mother pushed me to be aware. To explore the world, and to go well beyond the affluent suburb where I was raised. She cheered my decisions to study abroad in Italy and Spain, and to spend nearly two years working in Caracas after college, even though I've come to realize how nervous that must have made her. She remained closely involved in my adult life as well; months after a painful breakup I had early that very summer, she (not so) subtly suggested she just might create a JDate profile for me if I didn't create one myself, thanks. Some of those dates were monumentally awful, but it was of course just what I needed.

She was the most positive force of nature I'd ever known. She had my back. She had the best laugh and the biggest smile. She was only sixty-three.

I didn't know how I could possibly survive without my mother. But surely the world would be gentle with me as I stumbled around for the answer. Right?

Wrong. What I learned almost immediately is that the universe doesn't give a fig about you, dead mother or not. It will still mess you up, in matters large and small. You'll have to argue over creative upcharges from the funeral home. You'll scramble to find your footing within your circle of family and friends, without your loved one to provide backup. And you'll toe the line between keeping your shit together and having a panic attack when one of grief's many tentacles taps you on the shoulder during an important work presentation. The indifferent universe, in other words, will add insult to injury. Or, in my first experience with these aftershocks, embarrassment.

Taifa and Paul were squeezed into my apartment, packing for me and tidying up so that I wouldn't return to a rat's nest after the funeral. While I was fixating on Zach Braff's hair, Paul opened my underwear drawer in a kindhearted effort to ensure I'd have a few clean bras. He reached in and pulled out a few items. One of them happened to be my vibrator.

Paul froze, and all three of us stared at it as the *Scrubs* credits scrolled. Then we burst into laughter.

I felt my cheeks blazing red. In theory it wasn't a big deal: every female New Yorker bought one of those things when *Sex and the City* was on the air. But it felt weird to be so mortified by watching my friend's husband flail around trying to put my Rabbit away when there was clearly a much bigger emotional event taking place.

Collateral damage is defined as "injuries or other damage inflicted on an unintended target." In a death, anyone who isn't the actual deceased can be one of those unintended targets. I implored the universe to let up on these secondary whacks. But the moonscape this explosion created in my new life kept revealing craters of varying sizes—some unsurprising, and some completely so.

It was collateral damage that robbed me of a peaceful moment before my mom's funeral, for instance. When the funeral guy opened my mother's coffin "backstage," my reaction was not to throw myself on her lifeless body and sob, but rather to stare at the weird coral shade on her face and yell "WHAT THE FUCK LIPSTICK DID YOU PUT ON HER?" So as 350 mourners waited in the synagogue sanctuary, I scrubbed the lips of the alien being that was formerly my mother, determined it would not go to its final resting place looking like Tammy Faye Bakker, dammit.

The collateral damage also showed up in the guise of my body shedding fifteen pounds over the next year, regardless of what I ate, only to regain that (plus interest!) the next year, also regardless of what I ate. It dispatched me to get a brain MRI after the neurologist couldn't explain the dizzy spells screwing with my ability to look at a computer, get up from the sofa, or walk down the subway stairs. Verdict: no tumor. Just grief spinning my world upside down.

Collateral damage also visited me as PTSD nightmares even worse than my childhood one of a cookie-man slowly eating his hand while staring straight at me. It's hard to imagine any worse dream than that, but try this one on: I desperately search for my mother, but she does not want to be found. When I do find her she is emotionally distant. I frantically beg her to look at me, but she is not interested—she is completely unmoved by my distress. The prospect of experiencing that time and again made me petrified to fall asleep.

As destructive as they were, weight loss, headaches, and bad dreams didn't come as huge surprises. But the complete rejiggering of my family dynamics did. Suddenly there was no buffer between me and my father, a stubborn man I loved very much but with whom I had few comfortable ways to directly relate. Or between me and his other children, with whom I'd always had strained relations for reasons predating my birth. My mom's mere presence had encouraged people to chill out, take themselves less seriously, be nicer. Without her I felt raw, exposed to more misunderstandings and arguments. I had to come up with new ways to communicate with people I'd known for decades. And I still haven't come up with the right ways for all of them.

Collateral damage can come fast or it can come slow. Four years after my mom's death, it came knocking again one early December morning. Still in my bathrobe, I tried to absorb the news that my father had suffered a fatal heart attack while out of the country. Suddenly, I also needed to figure out how to get his body home from a port a hundred miles away. Oh, and fulfill a surprising demand from his new lady friend's family to arrange a private car home for her, too.

Another explosion had altered my moonscape, and I braced myself for staggering through its craters, trying to dodge the next bit of debris.

A WAKE

by Anthony King

My mother looks fat in her coffin. Her head is tilted forward on the satin pillow so that all of her chins are thrusting upward, and the formaldehyde has her bloated to where she's just a little bigger than she should be. It's not ridiculous, just swollen enough to make you think, *My god, was she really that fat?*

Before she went into surgery, she asked my father to tilt her head back in the coffin if she died, "so she'd look pretty for the wake." Now Dad and I are jostling for armholds to lift her dead body and shimmy it toward the closed end of the coffin, so that we can angle her head back on the pillow and alleviate some of the chin doubling. She's very heavy, and since all of her blood's been removed, her skin feels clammy and slick like an oyster at room temperature. I touched her in the hospital right after she died, when there was still the ghost of warmth. Now it doesn't feel like skin at all.

We're working to shimmy her, and I keep thinking that if we push too hard, or make some kind of sudden movement, she might pop and gush embalming fluid into the bottom of the coffin. How would we explain that? My father, my brother, and I, greeting all those sympathetic mourners, trying to pretend the deflated, wet corpse in the box beside us is completely status quo. *She wanted it this way!*

But we're not making much progress. Apparently coffins aren't made for bodies to be slid around inside them, so we push her down as best we can and tilt her head. But it tilts right back. We shimmy again, tilt, and her head creeps forward, the chins slowly rising from her neck like mountain ranges at the dawn of time. Here I am in a funeral home, my arms wrapped around my newly dead mother, and I'm thinking about the dawn of time. Death is so dramatic.

Dad decides we should give up. "Sorry, dear, that's the best we can do." He says it like they're sharing a private joke that no one else would understand but that they think is hilarious. Then he walks away and stares at the wallpaper.

My brother, Bryan, is at the other end of the room entertaining my cousin Jerry's blond daughters, four and seven, who think everything he does is the funniest thing that has ever been done by anyone. They clearly shouldn't be laughing so loud and so often in a funeral home, but the person who'd tell them to shut up is lying dead in front of me.

Aunt Nancy got here early this morning and did Mom's makeup and hair. Her eye shadow seems thicker than I ever remember her wearing it, but it's probably good to look extra beautiful when you're the centerpiece. She's wearing the same blue dress she was wearing a few years ago when I told her she looked pretty and she burst into tears. I had come into her bedroom while she was getting ready to go to church and gave her an offhanded compliment. I don't remember why I thought to say it, but she broke down crying—ridiculous sobs—and said, "When you get married someday, you tell your wife you love her every day, every single day."

Donald Bradley (who told us to call him Mr. B) runs the funeral home. Mr. B inherited it from his father when he died, which must have been a hell of a first day at work. "Keep it down or take it outside," he tells Bryan and the girls. They opt to stay and snicker on their bench, alternately poking each other and covering their mouths. The oldest one thinks this is especially hilarious. She laughs and bounces, her face bright red, but never makes a sound. Bryan sees me watching them and crosses over.

"What are you doing?"

"I don't know."

We stand in front of our mother like people stand in front of a fireplace. There have been so many of these long periods of silence in the last forty-eight hours—tense stretches when two people stand close to each other but don't speak either because they don't know what to say or because saying it is too horrible. My eyes blur, not from tears but because for some reason I keep having to remind myself to blink. Blink. Blink. Speak:

"She looks fat."

"She is fat."

We laugh, and it feels good.

"It's weird that she's dead." Is it weird that she's dead or weird that she died? Die. Died. Dying. It's such a small word for something so definite. Or maybe it's exactly the right size word for something so brief. You always hear about people who are "dying," sometimes for years and years, but they're not actually moribund, they're *fighting, praying, making amends*. We *DIE*—big D, big I, big E—in an instant, and we're gone.

Bryan thumps the side of the casket. "How much longer do we have to stay here?"

Mr. B and my dad come over. It's time to go into Mr. B's office and pay the bill for the coffin and the funeral service and all the other things that no one has any desire to itemize. We chose the sleek, aerodynamic stainless-steel coffin my mother will be buried in from all the other coffins in the showroom because it is reddish pink and Mom liked reddish pink. And because it is neither the cheapest coffin (which would be embarrassing!) nor the most expensive (which would be ridiculous!). Mr. B outlines an installment plan for the whole shebang at a low, low interest rate, which he is very excited about, but which my father nixes immediately. Dad never buys anything on credit.

Then Mr. B tells us a "hilarious" story about a man whose wife died a few weeks ago. When this man started to write the check to pay for the funeral, he broke down sobbing and had to stop. Then he collected himself and said, "I'm sorry, I always cry when I spend this much money."

We smile, but none of us laugh. Dad peruses the bill, and I read, reread, and read again the framed certificate on the wall behind Mr. B's head.

National Funeral Directors Association
presents
DONALD P. BRADLEY
with a certificate of excellence
in
Embalming & Preservation

I wonder if Mr. B learned his story of the cheapskate crying man at a convention in some horribly bland city where funeral directors gather to sample new technologies, drink themselves blind at happy hours, sexually harass the one or two female funeral directors who must exist in the world, and listen to poorly tailored experts in the field of the funereal arts share bits of wisdom like "When you force grieving people to overpay for your services, it's best to ease the unbearable atmosphere with a humorous anecdote." Everyone loves an anecdote!

My dad asks why we will need two cars to take us to the funeral, and Mr. B gives some sort of answer, but I'm too tired to listen. My throat is savagely sore from tension and snot. I force myself to swallow.

Back out by my dead mother, Jerry is using her as a visual aid to explain death to his daughters.

THE FOUR-YEAR-OLD: So she won't wake up?

THE SEVEN-YEAR-OLD: No, stupid. It's just like MeeMaw.

JERRY: Kelly! Stop it! Jess wasn't alive when MeeMaw passed. (*to the four-year-old, softly*) No, she won't wake up.

THE FOUR-YEAR-OLD: Why?

THE SEVEN-YEAR-OLD: 'Cause she's *dead*!! Dead! Dead! Dead! DEAD!

There's nothing like hearing a seven-year-old say a word four times in a singsong voice to make it meaningless. I mean, she's right. My mother is dead! Dead! Dead! Dead! DEAD! Now, who wants some ice cream? This funeral needs a pony!

Jerry notices us in the doorway and immediately ushers his kids out of the room, flashing his eyes toward us, his mouth taut with both embarrassment and anger. I watch them exit, rolling the word *dead* around on my tongue. Big D, big E, big A, big D.

The seven-year-old looks back at us, screaming, "Why do we have to leave?"

I choose to hate her. I hate my seven-year-old first cousin once removed, who I have only met once before today. And she will never know.

THE WOULD-BES

by Eileen Smith

I used to call my almost in-laws the would-bes. It sounded like their last name was Woodby, and it made me smile. It was also a shortcut for explaining how I was related to them, since my partner was a woman, and at that time gay marriage was a rainbow-painted thing in the distant future.

Her parents, who *would be*—I reasoned—my in-laws if same-sex marriage were legal, accepted me reasonably well. It took a couple of years before they teased me like they teased each other, beat me at gin rummy, and served me their watery, awful coffee first thing in the morning on our occasional trips to their mountain town in North Carolina. In return, I coined this affectionate term for them, their anglicized Italian name being significantly less WASPy-sounding. I never told them about their nickname, as it was mainly a shortcut to talk to other people about them. "What are you doing this weekend?" "Going to see the would-bes."

In addition to the Murphy-bed hospitality, they gave me a family—realer-than-TV, expansive, and multigenerational. When they posed for a photo under a flowering cherry tree on a long bench in the Washington, DC, Arboretum, there were so many of them that there was standing room only. My family, on the other hand, couldn't even fill up a picnic table. My tribe was small by design and attrition, the attrition due mostly to death, including that of my own father when I was a child.

Ten years after my ex and I fell in love, we fell out of it. It was sadder and slower than that, but in retrospect it seems staccato and swift. We moved to Chile together, hoping that maybe if we changed fields, we'd play better. But Chile couldn't hold us together; it didn't fix the ways in which we at thirty-three couldn't fulfill what our twenty-three-year-old selves had promised. The breakup was made both easier and more difficult by our relocation. I couldn't speak the language particularly well, but had no close friends nearby to talk to about it anyway. I mostly kept my feelings inside, churning and uncomfortable, and sustained myself with equally churning rations of a greasy bread called *dobladitas* and Diet Coke.

My ex and I kept in touch for a while, and occasionally I would see members of her family as they filtered down to visit her in Chile. I was not sure exactly how to divorce the would-bes, and I didn't particularly want to. So while she and I were in touch, if they invited me along, I went.

The last time I saw my ex-would-have-been father-in-law—white-haired and joking, the happiest father of three daughters, the slow-dancing Roman Catholic Vietnam veteran, the electrician with less schooling than street smarts, the most to-hell-with-everyone-who's-not-on-your-side kind of guy—was at a café. It was on a corner close to my apartment in the now hip Bellas Artes section of Santiago, and it was about a year after the breakup. On this day, I looked into the bright blue eyes of someone I once believed would be a part of my extended family forever, but who I suspected I would never see again. The distance between my ex and me was becoming too great to continue our own friendship, as we both became more occupied with our separate futures than our shared past.

I knew in a way that this was it. You break up, and you lose. You lose the would-have-beens, and the much older sisters, and their three kids—people who had made me an aunt before my own sister had children. I wished I could've kept them, but the would-have-beens weren't mine anymore. When I last saw him, my ex-would-have-been father-in-law chose a hug over a handshake as a hello. Then, after milky coffee served out of glasses fitted into little metal stands, he hugged me tight and close and sad, and we said a wordless forever good-bye.

My ex and I have no friends in common in Santiago, and were it not for a trip up to her neighborhood one day for work about a year ago, we might never have seen each other again. She was wearing a blue jacket trimmed with red on a wintry day, and little white puffs of air came out with our spare words. I wondered if she remembered when we were so short of cash that first year living together that we waited until we could see our breath at the kitchen table before turning on the heat.

Months later, when the guidebook I'd been working on that winter day when I saw her came in the mail, I googled her anglicized Italian name. That's how I found out that the happiest father of three daughters, the slow-dancing Roman Catholic Vietnam veteran, the electrician with less schooling than street smarts, the most to-hell-with-everyone-who's-not-on-your-side kind of guy, had died of cancer a few months earlier. Shortly before he died, I read, he told the people who took care of him that they should go out and live a good life, because he'd already lived his.

I felt a bitter, cold knot, the whoosh of something forever gone. And I wept. For his suffering, for his wife's suffering. For the sisters and their husbands, for my ex and her not-so-new wife, for his grandkids, who were my first niece and nephews. And for me.

He hadn't been my would-be for years, and all this time after our breakup, he'd been my never-was for almost as long. But he was the person who taught me how to put up drywall, yet left me to finish the bathroom tiling project myself. He left me a bag of grout and a bucket and walked away whistling. He was never my father, but he was a father I knew, and he treated me like one of his own, and those were two of the things that made him precious to me.

I had lost him so long before, twice even—once because of the breakup, once at that café. But knowing that he had died hit me hard, the third and final loss.

Where do you go to mourn someone you no longer have any connection to? If I still owned the house with the tiles and the tub, I'd have gone to that bathroom to cry. Because bathrooms are good for crying, and because that was a place I could feel his presence, even as he'd left me there, alone.

The saddest thing about the sadness I have over his death is that I have no place to put it. I can't go back to that bathroom, and I can't go back in time. His death becomes part of the interconnected web of people and relationships I no longer have access to, because this is the present, and that was the past.

THE SECOND THIRD CHILD

by Eric Meyer

My wife Kat and I tell ourselves we'd love another child for who they are, not for who they replace. We even believe it. But we can't be sure of it—and that keeps us from shutting our eyes, jumping back into the adoption process, and hoping it will turn out okay. We know all too horribly well that sometimes, it doesn't.

For years we'd planned to have a family of two children. We each grew up with a single sibling, so it felt right. We saved up to buy the right house as our first house, a center-hall colonial with three bedrooms in a neighborhood we loved. We tried to get pregnant, and when that didn't work out, we started the adoption process.

Within five years we had two daughters, Carolyn and Rebecca.

To our mutual surprise, it wasn't long before we realized that we wanted to add another child to the family. So we started the process of adopting a third child. Two years later, our son Joshua came home. And it felt great. It felt right. The joyful tumult of a house that was full of life, a house we expanded to accommodate the change, lifted our hearts even on the most stressful of days. We had finally uncovered the family we were always meant to be.

Three years later we buried Rebecca, killed by an untreatable brain tumor on her sixth birthday.

We were a family of two children after all.

As we emerged from the first, worst wave of grief, Kat and I talked about adopting again. Without Rebecca, the house seemed filled with too many rooms and not enough use. Two children could never create the kind of joyous chaos that three produced. Especially those three.

The effect was magnified by the fact that Rebecca was the middle child. Before, we had two sisters who were a few years apart, and a sister and a brother even closer together than that. After, we had a sister and brother who were seven years apart.

It wasn't even a matter of going from three siblings to two. In a very real sense, we'd gone from three siblings to two only children.

They each have their own lives, after all—lives we're more determined than ever to let them live. When Carolyn has sleepovers or after-school commitments, Joshua is left with us. There's no best-friend big sister to play with him, giggling as they wrestle or shrieking as they play tag. And when he's out doing something or stays late at preschool, Carolyn says, "Wow. It's so *quiet* when Joshua isn't here."

It was never quiet, before.

Carolyn and Joshua are close in their own way, but the silent chasm their sister's death opened up sometimes feels too wide to bear. And I hate it.

I can't tell them how much I hate it. Especially not Carolyn, who'd feel guilty about going to friends' houses or to play rehearsals. I can't stifle her because her sister died.

But there's still a huge hole blown in the center of the family—and so my wife and I talked about adopting once more. We wanted so much to hold a baby again, soothe it to sleep, watch it grow. We discussed it over and over, trading off between arguing for it and against it, sometimes changing positions within the same discussion. In the end, we decided not to.

The surface reason is that we both feel too old. In our mid-forties now, we'd be close to fifty by the time we finished the adoption process. While that certainly would be exhausting—much more so now than it would have been, say, ten years ago—the real barrier of age is that we'd be trying to raise a teenager in our sixties. And quite possibly, given our respective medical histories, condemning that child to bury one or both of us before they left high school.

But the true reason, the one we eventually forced ourselves to face and accept, was that the child could one day ask us, "Did you adopt me because your other child died?" And we would have to say yes, because we wouldn't have adopted again, if not for Rebecca's death. We were happy with three.

There are already enough risks of identity and abandonment issues with adopted children. Kids naturally ask, at some point, "Why did my birth parents give me up? What did I do? Wasn't I good enough?" My wife, who was adopted, went through it. Carolyn has gone through it, and we fully expect Joshua to as well. If she had lived long enough, Rebecca would have, too.

But in our case, on top of "Why didn't my birth parents want me?" that child would think, "My adoptive family only wanted me so they could replace their dead child." We would have given them all the love we have. But they would feel that way at some point, and we couldn't bring ourselves to put that on them.

That child, whoever it might have been, deserves a life filled with love and free of our burdens. They deserve to live *their* life, not be forced into an open wound in ours. We still mourn that decision. And that's the worst part: you can make the right decision, the very best decision you know how to make for yourself and your family, and still have cause to mourn.

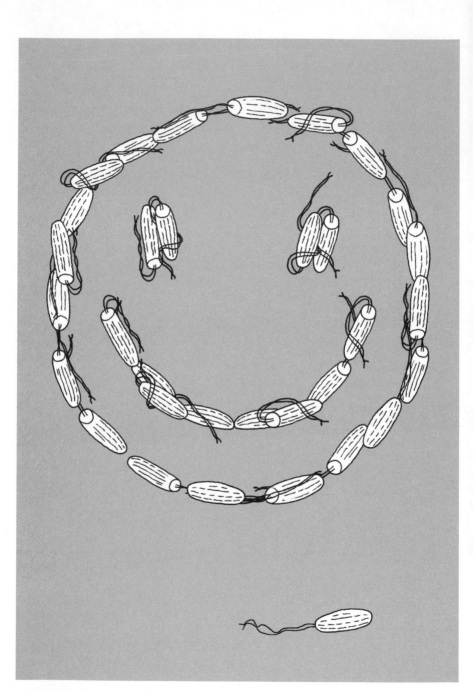

THERE WON'T BE BLOOD

by Ruby Dutcher

I find something very comforting in bleeding every month.

It's reassuring. "Everything's fine down here," says my uterus with a nod and a thumbs-up. "You've got plenty of iron, you're definitely not pregnant, and you're probably not dying! Just let us take care of this, and you keep on doing that great job you're doing being you!"

Over the past few years I've been comparison-shopping different methods of birth control, and I've found myself having to justify this desire to continue menstruating to multiple gynecologists, some of whom have been utterly lovely, and some of whom have been bizarrely insistent on prescribing me the kind of hormonal birth control that has the potential to stop your period entirely. It has been difficult for me to explain to these doctors exactly why the idea of not getting my period for years at a time freaks me out so much.

See, back when I was nineteen, the year my mother died, I didn't get my period for nine whole months.

As far as anyone could tell, there was nothing physically wrong with me. I wasn't starving myself, and several doctor's visits and panicked home pregnancy tests reassured me that I definitely wasn't "with child." I was eventually told that it was probably due to extreme levels of stress, combined with a bad reaction to my brief experimentation with the birth control shot. My family doctor reassured me that my period would come back. Told me it wasn't unheard of. Told me to wait it out.

Part of me was sure that I had brought this on myself. My mother's death left me numb. In theory, I felt sad, shattered, but in reality, most of what I felt was nothing. I cried the night my mom died, but after that the tears were rare—almost coveted. After the memorial I returned to school in a wintry New York, and the gray skies, brown slush, and freezing winds of the city were less than helpful. So when my period failed to return after three months, then six months, then longer, I thought, Of course. With my callousness, my neglect of my body, my withdrawal from friends and family, I'd somehow managed to kill whatever it was that had been alive inside of me.

It was like the opposite of a pregnancy. I felt barren in every sense of the word.

After a few months, I resigned myself to this new mode of existence. I struggled through school. I found something akin to joy in naps, Netflix, and ice cream from the downstairs deli.

When put into writing, this time of my life is edited down to a few short paragraphs. In retrospect it seems shorter still, a confusing blur that I prefer not to think about. But it felt like forever while I was living it. This was the winter that spanned 2013 and 2014, one of the longest and coldest in recent memory. I had a hard time believing it would ever end.

Eventually winter did end. Eventually, after almost nine months of absence, my period did come back. There was no fanfare, no change to indicate it had ever been gone. There was only surprise, some cramps, and a ruined pair of underwear that I was all too happy to throw out. I reveled in the return of its rhythm and regularity, in the rich smell of iron that reminded me that I was alive. I felt something inside me start to warm up.

I also appreciated the return of PMS. That's not a joke. Even at the best of times, I'm not good with emotions. I'm good at understanding them, and I can describe and analyze them with surprising insight and clarity. What I'm not at all good at is actually feeling them.

The mood swings that accompany PMS meant the occasional return of sadness, a feeling I'd desperately been trying to access for months. Sure, this sadness still came out in strange ways. I wept on the subway when I found out Supreme Court justice Antonin Scalia had died because, as I later tearfully explained to a friend, "Who will go to the opera with Ruth Bader Ginsburg now?" But tears over unexpected, sometimes nonsensical things were infinitely better than no tears at all.

I don't want to imply that the return of my period meant I was fixed. It was another year before I began to act like a functioning human. I don't think I'll ever feel completely normal again. But for me, bleeding was a much-needed confirmation that there would be such a thing as a new normal—an undeniable and sometimes painful sign that life, whether we want it to or not, keeps happening.

And life did keep happening. I was on my period the first time I let myself have sex after my mother died. It was unplanned, the kind of spontaneous event that was only able to take place once I left my own bed and began engaging with the world again. It was hard to touch someone else. It was weird. It was messy. It was really, really fun.

When I got up to leave just before dawn, both of our hands and bellies were red with blood.

"We look like we just murdered someone together," I said, looking down at myself, feeling a little ridiculous. I thought back to what the nuns in high-school health class taught me about the evils of condom use. Then I laughed. "Though maybe, from a Catholic perspective, we just did."

He looked at me as I laughed at my own terrible joke, wary of this war-painted, potentially crazy woman he had just let into his bed.

I didn't care. I was covered in blood, and I smelled like life.

It was good to smell life again.

MOTHER FIGURE

by Elizabeth Percer

The morning after my friend Rajna died, I found myself in her kitchen standing in front of the open refrigerator door, staring at the uncooked broccoli she'd meant to serve with dinner earlier that week. I couldn't shake the urge to do something, to find a way to help her small family get through the next few days, even the next few hours. But instead I stood in the artificial air and cooling light, undone by the broccoli.

A few days before, Rajna had been at a choir rehearsal with her two young children when she collapsed without warning. An aneurysm had erupted at the base of her brain, rendering her immediately comatose. She lingered unconscious for less than a week. *A tragedy*, we told ourselves. *Thank goodness she didn't suffer*, we said. *It could have happened when she was driving there with the kids*, her husband tried. But these were just words skirting the surface of our collective, bottomless grief.

The shock of her death was magnified by the fact that she seemed to have figured out how to live so well. I don't mean champagne holidays and caviar cruises; I mean the actual living of life, the way we spend most of the unremarkable moments that wind up defining our lives. A few years earlier, after discarding an academic career in music that had devolved from a passion into a duty, Rajna chose to devote herself entirely to her home and family. Her last two years were spent gardening or volunteering in the morning, cooking dinner and helping with homework and getting dirty with craft projects

in the afternoons. This is usually the kind of maternal shift that makes me sniff around suspiciously for signs of impending martyrdom, but Rajna seemed to derive so much joy from these activities, and had such a wicked funny bone around the chaos of child-rearing and homemaking, that my admiration for her only grew.

But even before all that, she'd taught me how to love her. Next-door neighbors in Northern California, we shared a fence for seven years, and we helped each other get through the crazy-making time of raising young children. Thanks to Rajna, I know there is really no greater gift one mother can give another than showing up unannounced to take your children off your hands, something she did several times a week. Sometimes she called to invite them over during the witching hour before dinner, when tired young children and uncooked food seem interminably at odds with each other. Sometimes she came to the door midmorning, just after breakfast and before lunch—when I'd just changed my sixth diaper of the day but hadn't quite finished my first cup of coffee—on her way to the park. We learned to share each other's joy over the children and to watch out for each other, to cobble together a semblance of family where one might not otherwise exist.

But there was something else behind this, something unspoken and sad and true. Like many nuclear families, Rajna and I were raising our children without the steady presence of older, more experienced relatives. With the exception of her in-laws, who adored her but led separately busy lives, there were no aunts or sisters or invested elders for miles around for either of us. But we were both more willing than usual to fight for the sort of life that prioritizes the bonds that keep us all afloat—maybe because Rajna, a native of Sarajevo, grew up around a deeply loving family shattered by war, and because I was the granddaughter of Ashkenazi Jews who'd fled their homeland.

My husband and I trusted and believed in Rajna and her husband so much that, in our will, we listed them as primary guardians for our children. In the weeks and months following her death, this made it easier to explain to people why I felt compelled to be there for her kids to the degree that I did. But that was only because I couldn't find a way to articulate the more profound explanation, which was that I hadn't just lost a friend; I'd lost a friend whose motherhood had been inextricably tied up in my own.

Almost immediately, a powerful circle of support collected around the family, a hive of friends and neighbors and teachers and classmates, with her two children at its dark, protected core. But for the most part, all we could do was wring our hands as the kids walked around emptied from the inside out, their bodies self-consciously awkward, as if they'd lost their sense of how to move through the world, perhaps their very sense of the world itself. And everything in me wanted to sweep in and absorb them into whatever kind of mothering nest I could fashion, to take these children I loved almost as much as my own and show them that there was a mother nearby, willing to do whatever she could to stem the tide of their grief.

But I loved them well enough to know that this would have been a selfish act, a way that they could resist the deep pain that came with the awareness that Rajna was gone. This was something I had to help them see, as a friend could, rather than something I might protect them from, as a mother might. So when Conrad—who usually waited until after school to eat most of his lunch, settling happily on his mother's lap with both legs around her waist while she took inventory of his day and leftovers—ran into his dad's arms when the bell rang, I forced myself to only mention the lunch box before walking away. And when Sophia got her ears pierced, I held back my tears of grief and pride and offered her my hand to squeeze as tightly as she wanted if it helped with the pain. And although I thought I'd have to go to therapy over the fact that their dad was not putting them in therapy, I made sure to meet them wherever they were when they wanted to talk about their mom, even if it was only to reflect on her great cooking, or the abundance of curious things now flourishing in her garden.

A few months after Rajna's death, Conrad contracted pneumonia and Stevens-Johnson syndrome, a life-threatening disorder that causes a blistering rash over the entire body. Perhaps it was a run of extraordinary bad luck, perhaps the result of a physical and emotional depletion that few young children could withstand. Visiting him in the hospital, before any of us knew whether he was out of the woods, I stood at the foot of his bed, watching as his father and a team of nurses struggled like gentle marionettes to combat his almost feral, half-conscious refusal to take his medication. I have never battled more painfully with my maternal instincts, which in this case were to take him into my arms, kiss him, hold him down like a mother lion would her cub, and tell the professionals to get their goddamn jobs done and get out of there. To do what Rajna would have done. What she would have wanted to do for any one of my children.

Instead, I stayed at the foot of his bed and silently cheered him on as he growled and whined, my hand resting lightly on his ankle, the bedsheet between us the thinnest barrier between his wild thrashing and the surety I was silently communicating to him, that he was loved beyond measure, beyond the limits of grief and fear. And as painful as it was not to mother when the ache for mothering was so palpable, I found a different sort of rightness in how I was with him just then, a new awareness of how love can flood beyond the definitions we have for it.

Usually, when we reflect on how love doesn't play by the rules, we are referring to its poor timing, or its unrequited victims, or its failure to sustain anything beyond the rush of infatuation. But maybe when rules falter or even collapse, we aren't just left in a free fall—we are also in the presence of unusual windows of opportunity. The modern world doesn't allow many of us to raise our children as we should, in clusters and groups so that while love is abundant, the sense that one person is indispensable is not as powerful as the sense that others will always be there. Because just as death can come in unexpected and life-changing ways, so too can care. There is, after all, no reason why a person cannot be both a mother and a mother figure, why we can't both fully grieve a mother and still continue to be fueled by what she showed us all how to do so well—to weather suffering and emerge with the joy of being even more connected after the worst has passed.

THINGS TO KNOW BEFORE SCATTERING ASHES

By Tré Miller Rodríguez

1. There will be bones.

SOFT CAMPFIRE ASH IT'S NOT. BRACE YOURSELF FOR SEVERAL POUNDS OF CEMENT SAND MIXED WITH SHARP BONE FRAGMENTS.

2. Portion it out.

UNLESS THIS NEEDS TO BE A ONE-AND-DONE CEREMONY, DON'T RELEASE ALL THOSE ASHES AT ONCE. YOU MIGHT THINK OF ANOTHER MEANINGFUL PLACE LATER, WANT TO HOLD ONTO SOME FOREVER, OR GIVE SOME TO LOVED ONES.

3. Handle with care.

THIS PROCESS CAN TRIGGER STRONG EMOTIONS. ASK A CLOSE, NON-SQUEAMISH FRIEND TO HELP YOU PUT THE ASHES INTO SEALABLE PLASTIC BAGS.

4. When traveling, always carry on.

YOU

YOUR BAG

5. Scout out a location in advance.

YOUR FIRST CHOICE MAY NOT PAN OUT. HAVE A COUPLE IN MIND.

6. Stop to smell the roses. Then pick them.

HEADED TO A BODY OF WATER? BRING SOME DE-STEMMED FLOWER HEADS IN WET PAPER TOWELS TO TOSS WITH THE ASHES; TAKE PHOTOS AS YOU TRACK THEIR PROGRESS.

7. Stand upwind.

COUGH!

MEMORIES FROM THIS DAY SHOULDN'T INVOLVE ASH IN YOUR EYES OR LIP GLOSS. AND WIND OR NO WIND, ASH STICKS TO SKIN. BRING WET WIPES.

TRIGGERS

What Sets Us Off Might Surprise You

by Gabrielle Birkner

My father, Larry, and stepmother, Ruth, were murdered inside their Sedona, Arizona, home on February 16, 2004. Earlier that winter, they had called a plumber to fix a pipe that had frozen. The man sent to do the repair was a methamphetamine addict who had recently been released on parole after ten years in prison. He returned about a month later, knocking on the door to my father and stepmother's home as dinnertime approached. Ruth answered, and the man pulled out a BB gun that appeared to be a firearm and ordered them into the garage. They did as they were told, offering up the keys to their cars (the theft of which was the crime's apparent motive) and the contents of their safe.

Before he left, the man, twenty-eight years old and high on crystal meth, bound and beat to death my dad and Ruth. The murder weapon: a nineteen-pound, pineapple-shaped plaster cast that was being used as a doorstop. When a household employee found their bloodied bodies two days later, the chicken they had not lived to eat was thawed on the counter, next to a partially chopped onion.

A year and a half earlier, my dad and Ruth had moved their environmental health and safety consulting business from suburban Los Angeles to Sedona—a resort town best known for breathtaking red rock formations, healing vortices, and New Age spiritual seekers. In their annual holiday letter, dated two months to the day before they were killed, Ruth wrote:

"We've spent many hours hiking, biking, exploring, and—oh—working in an environment surrounded by the Coconino National Forest. The night skies are so dark you can almost touch the stars. . . . Not too much yard work—all grounds are cacti and red rocks! We try to tiptoe through the cacti."

For the first couple of years after my dad and Ruth were murdered, the most mundane things set me off: The Kia Sedona minivan that happened to pass me on the street. The casual mention of a plumbing mishap. Doors propped open. Chicken. But these triggers were only sometimes obvious (e.g., poultry) or predictable (e.g., the third Sunday in June). More often, they seemed to emerge from the depths of my subconscious.

"It's so curious," the French novelist Colette wrote in a letter to a recently widowed friend, "one can resist tears and 'behave' very well in the hardest hours of grief. But then someone makes you a friendly sign behind a window, or one notices that a flower that was in bud only yesterday has suddenly blossomed, or a letter slips from a drawer . . . and everything collapses."

I'd be on a date, and all of a sudden, I'd imagine my father begging for mercy. I'd imagine what the crime scene looked like, what it smelled like. I'd remember how a special clean-up crew had to be hired, and how the blood-soaked carpet had to be pulled up. I'd think about the woman who did office work for my father and Ruth and had the misfortune of finding their bodies. I heard from the county victims' services coordinator that the woman was undergoing a form of psychotherapy to diminish traumatic memories.

No, I've never been to a Phish show.

Sure, I'll take another beer.

Even if that particular date hadn't googled me, and found pages of search results about the crime and the subsequent court proceedings, or excerpts from my excruciatingly raw victim impact statement, I was clearly too distracted to be any good at getting-to-know-you.

Yeah, it sucks about Bush.

The lines at Shake Shack are something else.

I had planned to read my victim impact statement in person at the murderer's sentencing, but I ended up skipping court and sending a video in my stead—explaining in my recorded statement that I couldn't bear to see the murderer's hands. "There is still a lot I can't bear to know," I said, addressing the perpetrator, "about what you used your now-shackled hands to do on the evening of February 16, when you brutally murdered two people who used their hands, their heads, their hearts, only for good."

The murderer was sentenced to two consecutive life sentences without the possibility of parole—our family's strong preference to the death penalty prosecutors originally sought. (I oppose the death penalty, as did my father.) The sentencing was a relief, I guess, but I was just as haunted after it as I was before.

Besides being disruptive in social situations, intrusive thoughts about the crime—hallmarks of post-traumatic stress disorder, my therapist at the time has since explained to me— were totally exhausting. Which is something nobody tells you about grief and trauma, and, especially, their intersection: it tires you out like nothing else (including thirty hours of labor, I can now tell you). Living in a constant state of high alert, being frequently ambushed by triggers that I hadn't antici-pated, my body was in chronic fight-or-flight mode. If the bear wasn't chasing me one moment, he would surely be on my tail the next.

I lived through that most tiring and triggering of years thousands of miles from Sedona. Just days before the murders, I had moved into my first solo apartment since graduating from college two and a half years earlier: a shabby 200-square-foot walkup in Manhattan's Murray Hill, with a barely functioning kitchenette, Pepto Bismol–colored bathroom tiles, and a view of the Chrysler Building that made the rent seem kinda-sorta worth most of my editorial assistant salary.

It's impossible to say what prompted the shift from living with constant triggers to living with fewer, from avoiding things that had once made me happy to reacquainting myself with many of those things. There were years of therapy, some trial and error with antidepressants, and a new roommate that came in the form of a frisky brown labradoodle named Rafi. Moving a year after the murders into a new apartment—this one with a full-size refrigerator in a building with some safety features that made me feel a little less exposed—has long felt significant. So, too, has falling in love and finding happiness with the man who is now my husband, as has giving birth to and mothering my children.

Then there's the passing of time, which hasn't so much healed as it has taught me how better to coexist with my grief. No longer do most days present an overwhelming number of triggers. February 16–18, since they were killed on the six-teenth and found on the eighteenth, are exceptions. That's when I'm likely to descend into the most melancholy, anxious, easily triggered version of myself—*fuck you, Kia Sedona mini-van.*

Most other days, my triggers are fewer and more idiosyncratic. Like erasing voice mails. Because I wish I had one from my dad, and that I hadn't, on occasion, sent his calls to voice mail when I thought myself too busy to pick up. Like avoiding anything I remember doing in the days leading up to the murders, fearful of what reprising those seemingly innocuous things—milling through Restoration Hardware, ordering Thai takeout, cleaning out my wallet—could portend. I'd like to say that I've found healthy ways to avoid the avoiding, that I've outsmarted my triggers and related superstitions. But a voice mail box often too full to leave a message and a wallet too stuffed to zipper belie that I am still tiptoeing through the cacti.

A LITTLE TO THE LEFT

by *Amanda Palmer*

I just sprinkled some cilantro on a potato frittata that my husband threw together for dinner. There was nothing in the kitchen but eggs and some leftover potatoes.

(And a handful of cilantro.)

Anthony came to my mind. He does that, often. And I had The Cilantro Thought:

Was it parsley he couldn't stand? Or was it cilantro?

It was one or the other. I can't remember.

The Cilantro Thought used to be something trivial, barely worth lingering on for more than a millisecond. Now it's covered in the hard shellac of grief, bronzed like a baby shoe; it's a thought pattern that grooves itself deeper over time.

The story of Anthony (the fresh wound, hardening by the minute): he moved in next door when I was nine, befriended me, raised me like the child he'd never had, and stood in for the father I'd always craved. He trained me in compassion and yoga and meditation, in the music of Fugazi and the way to deal with a hangover or a junkie college boyfriend. He didn't judge. Not much. He taught me how to love; how to have mercy on myself. He was like a priest: I brought him my confessions on a weekly, sometimes daily, basis. He was not like a priest: moments after my deep, dark confessions, we'd be cracking stupid fart jokes.

The relationship was impossible to categorize. He was the first call when I found out I was pregnant. Several times. He was the first call when I got an abortion. Several times. He was the first call when the relationships would begin and end. Anthony, the alpha and omega. We spoke almost every day.

I used to play a game with myself in high-school theater productions, a poor man's version of method acting. If I ever needed to cry on command for any reason, I had a trick:

I would just think about Anthony dying.

It never failed. I'd burst into tears.

I got the call while I was at a yoga retreat on an island seven thousand miles away. He was sick and given a death sentence, which was lifted weeks later; then he came crashing back down weeks after that. There were more false alarms and false hopes than a daytime soap. I canceled whole eras of my life, canceled moving, canceled tours with my band, canceled making any real plans that committed me to being far away from him for too long. I sat in the middle space of unknowing for years, in and out of that eighth floor on the hospital that I got to know like the back of my hand, while the chemo dripped.

I was always certain he'd make it. That he'd beat the cancer. He didn't.

All in all, he spent four years dying of leukemia.

When I was pregnant with the first child that I would actually *have*, I didn't call him first. He wasn't even the first person I told. We barely spoke on the phone anymore. Our friendship was dying, even though I'd never committed myself more to another human being; our friendship was dying along with his body, on a schedule neither of us wanted to discuss.

I told him during chemo one day, as we sat there next to the drip-drip-drip—and I felt strangely detached and scared. His illness had made him allergic to news, even good news, and selfishly, I didn't want to be disappointed by his reaction. He mustered a smile and said something kind, but distant. I can't even remember what he said. Whatever he said, I wanted more. I missed my friend.

Maybe he did say something that I've forgotten. Maybe he dispensed some loving wisdom that I don't remember. I wish I'd recorded it. I recorded hours and hours of monologues from his goddamn doctors.

He'd watched me struggle with this decision for the previous five years, struggling with a poisoned-by-antibiotics pregnancy and a prescribed miscarriage, getting thrown into panics by my own indecision, being pulled to the left and to the right.

I was seven months pregnant when he died at home, held by his friends and family. His wife, Laura, had her arms around him. I stood beside him, with my husband's arms wrapped around me, my hugely pregnant belly swelling into Anthony's back, pressing my womb as close as possible to an imaginary spot where I'd decided his soul resided, trying to herd his soul into the soul of my unborn baby like a clueless parking director in a random grassy field on baseball day: no idea where the cars go, they don't really *go* anywhere, they just have to park *somewhere*. A little to the left, back it up, whatever, a little to the right, stop.

I don't even really believe in a soul.

I believe in something. A soul-thing.

A few things occurred to me in the year after his death.

1. *I was done grieving before he really died.*

I assume this is common for those left behind by a drawn-out death-by-illness, but I'd spent so much time grieving *before* he died that I didn't have a lot of grief left over for the aftermath. The foremath had sucked out the sadness.

I'd cried for twenty-four straight hours the day I first got the news, four years before he died.

I'd cried in dressing rooms on three different continents after unwisely checking texts for blood-test updates right before hitting the stage. I'd cried in my husband's arms night after night as he lay helpfully and helplessly beside me.

I'd cried and cried. I remember feeling the deepest, darkest pit of grief when our mutual friend, my deathbed wingman/harbinger Nicholas, called to tell me that the end was pretty nigh. "Probably time to come home," he said.

How much of my reaction was due to the huge belly of pregnancy? How much was the stress of leaving London just days after we'd arrived, canceling all of our shows and plans and commitments to rush back to a deathbed? How much was just the plain, unadulterated grief that comes when you let go of that final, thin straw? I'll never know. But I rushed out of bed to the bathroom, simultaneously sobbing and vomiting into a toilet with such emotional and physical force that I surprised myself.

I looked at the vomit blarshing in the water and had thoughts that didn't follow any logic. It was like that moment of shock when you're hit by a large object and the pain hasn't been assessed; just giant, violent spatterings of black-brown grief, followed by the sharp searing of a human-size red raw wound. A physical pain that made me understand those stupid metaphors—"a sword through the heart," and all that. It actually *hurt*.

But a few days later, when Anthony was breathing his final,

labored breath and I held him in my arms, trying to convince that soul-thing to make a five-inch jump into a brand-spanking-new, conveniently placed human container, there was no searing wound, no splatter of pain. I was just a painting of myself in a pietà.

A little to the left, a little to the right.

2. *There was a bizarre yet shitty silver lining.*

I didn't notice it until about five months after the baby was born (a boy, named for Anthony, because it was too ridiculous not to, but called Ash for short, because the wound was too fresh to keep saying The Name over and over again).

I was walking down the street, feeling an incredible lightness, and I started reflecting on why it was that I was in such a wonderful mood. I had two thoughts, bam-bam, like thunder and lightning.

I'll never need to decide whether or not to have a child again.

As hard as it may be to take responsibility for the infant in my arms, I thought, it'll never be as hard as weeping uncontrollably under a tree outside an abortion clinic, wondering whether or not to go in. I'd kind of known this relief was coming if I took the plunge and had a child—the kind of relief, I believe but cannot prove, that would never come in as neat a package if I'd chosen just To Not Have Kids. And that relief had finally arrived.

And then.

I'll never have to worry again about whether or not Anthony is going to die.

This thought surprised me, because I'd never anticipated having it, or wanting to have it. It just occurred to me that as bad as it was to have him dead, he'd *never die again*. The profound simultaneous morbidness and lightness of that thought struck me as *extremely silly*. Instead of thinking about it further, I just found myself feeling relief, and allowing the relief of that thought to replace the grief.

3. He was perfect. Perfected.

I remember my beloved Latin teacher explaining the beauty of the word *perfect* as it related to grammar, and how *perfect* technically means "finished."

It struck me, shortly after Anthony died, that his story was never going to continue. We'd tell his jokes, we'd mimic his voice, we'd keep him alive in memory, his advice and his imitations of his abusive mother and his leather jacket and knife gifts. His very is-ness would live on like an eternal spirit, but he would never add to his own story.

He was done, perfect, FINITO, that last breath like the tiny, definitive black period on the final page of a novel.

Perhaps the only perfect things are dead.

4. The person who died wasn't really my friend.

I remember us sitting on the porch, him talking about his will. "You're always gone. You don't need me anymore. You're always away. You have Neil. You have your huge life. I think I'll leave the Contents of the Study to someone else." The Contents of the Study was the Stuff of His Life, his secret therapist's cave, the place we'd had a million late-night rendezvous, the place that had filtered and collected the debris of his childhood and his wanderings in the world: knives, Buddhas, boxing gloves, hundreds of books on Kafka and Jesus.

I had wanted to leave him, then. I'd *sacrificed* so much. He was *punishing* me.

What was I, Catholic?

He was Catholic. Maybe I caught it.

He was also on 20 daily milligrams of prednisone. The prednisone made him an asshole.

He stopped answering his texts.

I kept trying.

I wondered what he would have done in that hospital bed, all those hours, if he hadn't had his text-machine, so many days, driving himself to the distraction that he raised me to resist. My vegan mentor. My holy Buddhist meditating role model, gone in a poof of rare steaks, ice cream sundaes, complaining, and texting.

I couldn't believe it.

We circled around him, at the end, waiting for that last breath. We didn't want to miss The Moment.

I didn't cry, because I'd already cried, because my friend had left me months before.

The person who died was already gone.

5. *Was it parsley he couldn't stand? Or was it cilantro?*

He really hated one. Hated it. The same way he would demand his second glass of wine in the glass in which his first had been served (he despised dishwasher soap residue, you see), he would inquire of the waiter: "Is there cilantro in the dish?"

or

"Is there parsley?"

"I despise it."

I was there. But I forgot.

I could text his wife, Laura. She'd know, she'd remember.

But it's more perfect this way.

Perfect because it isn't perfect; perfect because if I don't know, there's room to wonder. Perfect, known, is dead. Unknown, maybe, is alive.

Because if there's a question, maybe there's an answer.

An answer . . . waiting there. And in that, there's always something to look forward to.

The baby grabbed a handful of cilantro off the table.

Or was it parsley?

WHEN MOM KAN'T KEEP UP WITH THE KARDASHIANS

by Kate Spencer

The thing about having a dead mom is that everyone assumes you miss her most during milestone moments.

"I'm sorry your mom is missing this!" guests shouted at my wedding, as my college roommates swayed arm-in-arm to "Sweet Caroline." "I wish your mom could meet her," friends cooed about my newborn daughters while bringing us lasagnas and flowers. And they're right, of course. There isn't a day that goes by where I don't think of all the things I long to share with her.

But the truth is, the real reason I wish she was still here is to discuss the Kardashians with me. Because holy shit, my mom would love the Kardashians.

She would hate them, too, and she would love to hate them. Dissecting their overdocumented moves would be our favorite thing to do together, along with shopping for soft, loose-fitting cotton tees and sitting on the kitchen counter together, washing cheddar sandwiches down with white wine.

Just the thought of Kris Kardashian getting a face-lift before Kim's first wedding would have sent my mom into a feminist rant. "This is why I don't dye my hair!!!!!" she'd have slowly hammered out in a text message. "She is beautiful she should love herself as she is!!!!! Love, Mom." Minutes would pass, and then another note would pop up on my phone: "Which one is dating the One Direction guy? Also, can I throw out

your old poetry journals from tenth grade?" I would roll my eyes and sigh and then type back "Kendall, and NO" with a smile. I secretly loved all her messages to me, no matter how silly.

She would loathe Kim and her airy voice and vapid narcissism. Above all my mom valued self-deprecating humor and sensible shoes, two things Kim knows nothing about. But she would connect with Khloe's brashness, wit, and family loyalty—finding in her that fiery something often stewing within herself.

My mom would sign up for Twitter and then call me, confused about how to use it. But once she had it figured out she'd follow just me, Michelle Obama, Howard Stern, my best friend from college, a bunch of local Boston weathermen, and every Kardashian on earth. "Khloe just unfollowed LamLam!" she'd tweet, and then delete it because she'd meant to send it to me as a direct message. She'd be shocked by his drug use. "He just didn't seem like the type!" she'd gasp over a cup of tea in her kitchen. But when it came to his cheating, she'd just roll her eyes. "Of course he did," she'd say with a shake of her head, reaching for her secret stash of Good & Plentys in that cabinet filled with random things that no one dared touch. "All men are disgusting." From somewhere over on the couch my dad would object. "All men but you, Jim!" she'd reply, then twist her brow at me, knowingly.

This belief would lead her to loathe Scott Disick. "I just can't stand his face," she'd say to me as we'd catch him walking in Gucci loafers across a tabloid cover at the grocery store. But she would tear up watching Kourtney give birth, applauding as she pulled her own baby from her vagina during delivery. "That's just what I did with you and your brother," she'd say, turning to me with pride. "No pain meds—"

I'd finish her sentence for her, "—just ice chips."

Always the progressive, she would applaud Caitlyn Jenner for coming out as a trans woman. She'd do her research on gender pronouns, correcting my dad every time he mistakenly called Caitlyn "he." "Your dad's not woke yet," she'd say with a roll of her eyes. "I'm working on him."

Her love for the Kardashians would push her into uncharted waters, like Snapchat. It would take her months to figure it out—"Why does it keep making me look like a dog?!"—but following the Kardashians would be the ultimate payoff. "Lamar is at their Easter celebration!" she'd squeal over the phone, marveling at how the family came together following his overdose at the Love Ranch brothel. "Oh, and don't be mad but I bought you one of those Kylie Lip Kit things."

More than anything, she'd love Kris's relationship with her daughters the most. "See how protective she is of her girls?" she'd say, pointing at the TV. "That's how I feel about you guys. She'd do anything for her kids."

"It's just too bad you didn't think to use my sex tape to elevate our family name," I'd reply.

"You don't have a sex tape!" she'd shriek. "Wait, do you?"

"Mom." I'd whack at her arm, hidden somewhere in her lumpy old bathrobe. "Ew."

"I'd be okay with it," she'd say, turning back to the TV. "Just as long as you didn't let him pee on you."

"You're ridiculous," I'd tell her, leaning over the coffee table to refill our wineglasses.

"I know," she'd say.

"That's why I love you," I'd add, and snuggle my feet under her legs.

Then we'd both turn our attention back to the TV, laughing at all the same moments until the credits rolled.

BRAIN GAMES

by Chamique Holdsclaw

My maternal grandmother raised me like a daughter in her modest apartment in the Astoria housing projects of Queens, New York. My alcoholic mother, who would pass out on park benches, and my father, who suffers from schizophrenia, weren't exactly up for child-rearing. So my grandmother gave my brother and me the structure and discipline that my parents could not, and she always showed up when it mattered.

She was at almost every one of my basketball games—in high school, in college, and ultimately in the WNBA, where I was the No. 1 draft pick in 1999. I had one goal for my new-found salary and the modicum of fame that comes with being a pro athlete: to support the woman who had sustained me for the many years that surely lay ahead of her. But in 2002, Grandma had a fatal heart attack. She was sixty-four.

I had always struggled with anxiety and with controlling my temper. Things only worsened after my grandmother died. Despite my love for basketball, I considered quitting the game. Because without her cheering me on, I struggled to find a reason to play. More than that, I struggled to find a reason to live. Acute grief mixed with what would later be diagnosed as mental illness, and the combination was toxic.

I quickly began ping-ponging between two states: sleep and hysterics. I played for the Washington Mystics, in DC, at the time. I would pull it together just long enough for practice or a game. Then I'd come home, draw the curtains, and shut myself in. Weeks would go by like this—until I finally missed a practice. A concerned friend with an extra set of keys to my apartment came to check on me. It was dark and messy inside. She said I smelled like I had just played a game. I hadn't. She got me to shower and we went outside for some fresh air. I attempted to reassure her that I was okay.

I didn't want my teammates and the public to know how depressed, despairing, and dysfunctional I'd become. I didn't want to let down my fellow players, coaches, fans, or family. Most of all, I didn't want to let down the woman who raised me and would have hated to see me so distraught. So I convinced myself I'd never again let my mental health hinder my professional life.

But four years later, it did. At that time I was playing for the Los Angeles Sparks. I thought the change in scenery—and a generous dose of California sunshine—would save me from myself. But the extreme moods and the suicidal thoughts returned. As I suffered, so too did my game, because I couldn't focus, and my relationship with my teammates, because I pushed them away.

I went home to visit my family, as my dad was struggling with schizophrenia and my stepdad with esophageal cancer. It was an overwhelming trip, and one that made me feel helpless in the face of their illnesses. One night, after I returned to Los Angeles, that helplessness turned to hopelessness. I wanted to be with my grandmother more than ever. That time, I overdosed on prescription pills and woke up in the hospital, on suicide watch. Which is when I wondered: Was I going to let my grandmother's death kill me too? How she would have despised the thought.

That realization was enough to finally get myself diagnosed (with bipolar II disorder), go to therapy, and start taking medication. It wouldn't be my last episode. In fact, my third was worse than my first two. But I always returned to treatment, with the knowledge that Grandma would not have allowed herself to be the reason that I ended my career—or worse, my life.

I'm retired from basketball now, living my truth without shame. I've become a passionate advocate for others who struggle with mental illness. Grandma's death triggered my breakdown. But her legacy would catalyze the breakthrough that has allowed me to thrive years on. I owe that to her. I owe it to myself, too.

THANKSGIVING AFTER JACK

by Anna Whiston-Donaldson

When I talk about "the first Thanksgiving," I'm not talking about *that* first Thanksgiving—the one with the Pilgrims and the Wampanoag. I'm talking about the first Thanksgiving following the death of our son, in 2011. It comes just weeks after another Thursday, the one when twelve-year-old Jack went out to play in the rain and was swept away in a raging creek behind our neighbor's house.

Just about everything about that first Thanksgiving after Jack's death feels wrong. The first road trip with three people in the car, not four. A day reserved for giving thanks and celebrating family, when ours feels severed, and our shocked brains cannot yet understand that this isn't a warped joke.

My cousins fly in from across the country. How much easier would it have been for them to stay away and try to enjoy a long weekend at home, watching football and taking walks around the neighborhood? But the pull to be together is strong, even though no one knows what to do. So we just show up, piling our coats in the corner of my aunt's kitchen, stomping the cold off our feet.

My cousin Angela, here from Colorado, begins to share how she got the call from a friend in Washington, DC, who had heard the news of Jack's accident on TV. I am hungry for details of her experience, to know that phone lines were burning up late into the night, to know that we were not the only ones suffering. But my husband, Tim, cannot bear it. He doesn't want to be transported back to that night—with its soaking rain and its smell of mud, with its fear and helplessness as teams searched for Jack, and as our ten-year-old daughter, Margaret, wailed, "But I don't want to be an only child!"

Tim leaves the room.

It will be an early indication of our differences relating to our loss. No one loves Jack more than the two of us, but we will have to show each other patience and grace again and again as we mourn the same child differently. Tim will stay busy, filling the empty hours with exercise, activities, and new friends. My circle will tighten, as I process the loss in writing and with others who mourn for Jack. I will want specifics about the accident, to know what could have been done differently. Tim will keep the main thing the main thing: Jack is gone. Our son's lime-green bedroom is empty, and no details or tearful discussions will change that. After twenty years together, with patterns long ago set, Tim and I will have to cobble together a new way of relating to each other.

And there's Margaret to think about. She wants this Thanksgiving to be no different from any other. Seeing her parents going through the motions, mustering up a laugh now and then, or giving each other a pat on the shoulder in the kitchen, is the assurance she needs that we are still able to take care of her in this frightening world where brothers disappear.

My aunt pulls the turkey from the oven. Tim returns, and he and Angela fold and cut paper into frilly lace coverings to put on its legs. This has been their job each year since another first Thanksgiving, the one where I introduced my boyfriend to my extended family. Tim was playful, and Cousin Angela was no older than Jack is now. *Was*.

We learned at that Thanksgiving nineteen years earlier that

those paper ruffles are called "papillotes." We would laugh to discover the word anew each year, as Thanksgiving would be the one day out of 365 that held any significance for us. Now, grief is introducing us to a whole new vocabulary, with common words that will never seem natural to us again: Son. Drowned. Dead.

We try to keep things light, navigating around each other in the small kitchen, beginning to carry things into the dining room. We joke about how Thanksgiving was Jack's least favorite holiday because the meal was made up of his least favorite foods. What kid doesn't like mashed potatoes?

Pulling a candle out of my bag, I place it on the table, saying, "A friend gave this to me, to light at Jack's place. I hope that's okay. It has kind of a strong scent." My cousin Eric quickly responds, "Well, Mom's sensitive to perfume, so maybe we should light it after dinner instead."

The moment feels awkward and raw.

He regrets the words as soon as he speaks them. Tears spring to my eyes. It's clear I can't do anything right, as a mother or even as a mourner. I am the one who let my kids play in the rain, and only one of them came home. I can't even choose a damn candle that won't offend. I grab it off the table and thrust it back into my bag. "It's okay. Never mind," I say.

There is backpedaling, "No, no! I'm sorry. The candle is fine." But it's not. Nothing is fine. I don't want a candle, I want my son. And I don't want to be thankful, even though through the pain and horror I can't help but be grateful that Jack was mine, even for just twelve years.

During our nighttime snuggles in the dark, he would sometimes get down on himself, saying his friend Parker was smarter, more athletic, and even had better hair than he did. I'd smile at the hair remark and list all the things that made Jack so special. I'd end with how I felt downright *sorry* for Parker's mother because she didn't get to be Jack Donaldson's mom.

"That's ridiculous," Jack would say. "You're only saying that because you're my mother. If you were Parker's mom, you would feel the exact same way about him." Sheesh. Logic. But I did feel like the lucky one, winning the parental lottery with this skinny, sensitive, hilarious kid.

I don't know how we will get through this meal or the next—or a lifetime of Thanksgivings ahead—without shattering into a million pieces. I don't know how to memorialize the very real boy who was here with us and the papillote-clad bird last year.

Maybe the right thing is lighting a candle—or maybe it isn't. Maybe it's sharing stories of Jack, with laughter through tears. I don't know.

Perhaps it is just a tattered family mustering a strength we do not have, getting in a car, pointing it west, and deciding to show up.

THE BARREN FIELD

by *Helen Chernikoff*

When I lost my babies, I didn't just want a baby like other women had. I wanted them to lose their babies, too.

I lost the first one when I was twenty-three weeks pregnant, in October, at the end of a gorgeous autumn, right before winter set in. That one—Jack, for my father's father—was the result of six months of fertility treatments. Then that next summer, I got pregnant naturally, and the following gorgeous autumn, right before winter, I lost that pregnancy, too, at seventeen weeks. Henry, for my mother's father. I went to my doctor for a routine ultrasound and there was no heartbeat. I turned my head and saw the baby floating lifelessly inside me. I can never unsee that.

After these back-to-back losses, I wasn't so much jealous of the pregnant women I knew and encountered. Jealousy, as I saw it, is minor-league; it just means you want something someone else has. Who doesn't feel that from time to time? No, I was envious, and envy is the real deal—as in not wanting other people to have the thing you want, either.

I learned that life in the immediate aftermath of a loss feels perverse. You realize what the poet W. H. Auden meant when he begged the world to stop all the clocks and cut off the telephone after his lover died. You understand that control is an illusion, and that the illusion is gone forever. Terror takes over. If this can happen, anything can, and if this did, anything will. "Nothing now," Auden wrote, "can come to any good."

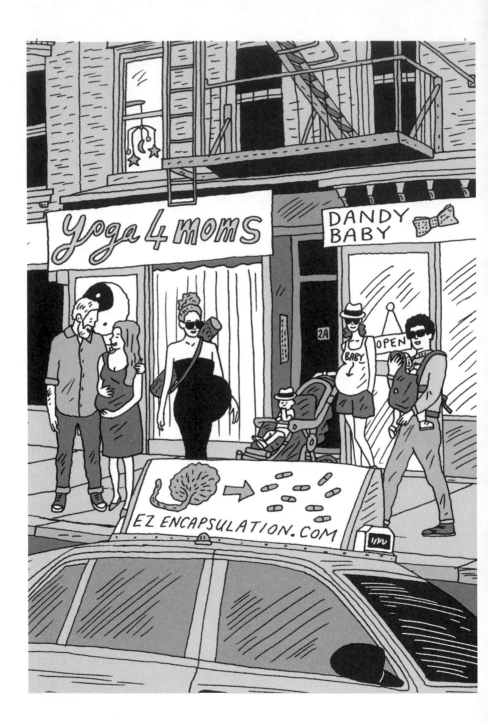

To make things worse, my Brownstone Brooklyn neighborhood is known for its hipster breeders. Doulas everywhere. Pre- and postnatal Pilates. Baby-friendly bars. Tiny fedoras. One morning, not long after I lost Henry, I saw three pregnant women on the five-block walk between my building and my favorite café, and one more when I staggered inside. The good people of the world didn't know it, but I was the angel of death. I wanted to sidle up to them and hiss: "Don't get too comfortable. Your baby could die. Your baby could die!"

It was a secret shame, because I knew in my bones that nobody else could be so evil as to wish her misfortune on her neighbor. And outside of envy's grip, I'm the kind of person who ponders and purchases just the right birthday present for a friend, who is careful not to interrupt people, who cancels a meeting to comfort a teary colleague. So what I felt after losing my babies was new and scary and lonely.

I didn't reveal even to my mother the depths of my vindictiveness, but she knew what a mess I was. She suggested, not for the first time, that I find a support group. I'd always resisted: Who would want to be a member of such a club? But this time my desperation overcame my denial.

Every Tuesday night, for eight weeks, we gathered along with three other couples in the no-frills conference room of the nonprofit that ran the program. At the front of the room stood a whiteboard on which the dedicated facilitators, themselves products of the group, sketched out things like the stages of grief. To the side was a rolling cart that contained the small literature of infertility, miscarriage, and stillbirth. The room was so cramped we had to contort ourselves and mutter "Excuse me" several times to make our way around the table. We took turns bringing snacks. We all shared our anguished stories. There was a lot of raising hands, urging others to speak first, and reflecting on what empathy is and isn't.

One of the many things I learned there: If you use the sentiment or the words "at least" in response to someone's suffering, you're diminishing their feelings, probably because their pain makes you anxious. *At least you didn't have to give birth to a dead fetus. At least you didn't have to raise a child with special needs.* That's not empathy.

My husband and I both liked and admired the people in our group, beyond feeling a bond of shared suffering with them. But I felt a connection to one woman in particular, I wasn't sure why, and impulsively reached out to her individually one night while she and our husbands were walking toward the subway. I gave her my business card and said she could call me anytime; I mentioned a possible coffee date. I felt a little puzzled by the intensity of my enthusiasm, but it was such a welcome change from envy. Taking an interest in another human being—how novel!—took the edge off my own pain. I felt benevolent, generous, warm. A Fairy Godmother to her Cinderella.

Until she got pregnant. Then the Evil Stepmother in me returned. There's a reason Cate Blanchett, as the stepmother in the movie *Cinderella*, is costumed in so many lurid shades of green and says she hates her stepdaughter because she is good. My generosity shriveled.

Please don't misunderstand me. I didn't do anything cruel to her. I just didn't do anything. I didn't call her or intimate that she should call me. We did not meet for coffee. Two years on, I don't know anything about her life.

It's especially sad, because with the passing of time, I finally feel better. Opening Facebook to find a portrait of a newborn can still be startlingly painful, but now my sadness finds its focus not on that baby's existence but on my babies' absence. I recover more quickly from those triggers, reaching a baseline at which I can again take pleasure in everyday life and others' happiness. I have fewer friends, though. The woman I met at the support group isn't the only friend I failed to make, or lost, these past few years. I miss them. Sometimes I tell myself I should go back to them now, that maybe they would understand. But my ambivalence is wrapped up in my shame.

Envy is a scorched-earth campaign: It leaves behind a barren field.

THE DOS AND DON'TS OF BUILDING YOUR CREW

Loss screws with your social circle. But your tribe is out there. Here's how to find them.

DO: Be specific about what you need —and what you don't.

IN A PERFECT WORLD, YOUR CLOSE FRIENDS WOULD KNOW WHAT YOU'D NEED AT ANY GIVEN MOMENT. BUT THEY PROBABLY DON'T HAVE A CLUE. HELP THEM OUT. THEY WANT TO BE USEFUL.

Can you come over to silently watch bad TV with me?

DO: Build something new (and they will come).

"FIELD OF DREAMS," BABY. SOMETIMES YOU'VE GOTTA MAKE THE EFFORT. START A MONTHLY DINNER, RUNNING GROUP, OR HOLIDAY GIFT SWAP FOR OTHER PEOPLE WITH SIMILAR LOSS. IF YOU DON'T KNOW THEM YET, CAST A WIDE NET. YOU'LL FIND THEM.

INVITATION
WHO: You
WHAT: Pizza, alcohol, brutal honesty
WHEN: Monday, 7:30PM
WHERE: My place
WHY: Dead boyfriend
RSVP

DO: Be open to support coming out of the woodwork — online and IRL.

KINDRED SPIRITS MIGHT COME FROM A SUPPORT GROUP, FACEBOOK PAGE, SIXTH DEGREE OF FRIENDSHIP, OR EVEN A RANDOM COCKTAIL PARTY CONVERSATION.

NEW CHAT:
2:15 PM
ENRIQUE POSITANO
Anyone else been there?
2:16 PM
MAYA ZANE
Hell, yes! PM'ing you now.

DO: Cut people a break when they don't show up.

SOME PEOPLE MAY VANISH FROM YOUR LIFE, BUT THINK HARD BEFORE WRITING OFF THE RELATIONSHIP FOREVER. YOU CAN ALWAYS SHARE YOUR FEELINGS LATER WHEN THINGS AREN'T SO RAW.

DON'T: Give up on friends who do show up but aren't helpful.

EVEN PEOPLE WHO LOVE YOU SAY DUMB THINGS WHEN THEY DON'T KNOW WHAT ELSE TO SAY.
SET THEM STRAIGHT KINDLY, BUT GIVE THEM A PASS. THEY'RE PROBABLY REALLY TRYING AND WILL WANT TO DO BETTER NEXT TIME.

DON'T: Be afraid to get real.

FOR EACH PERSON UNCOMFORTABLE WITH YOUR GRIEF, THERE'S ANOTHER ONE READY TO RISE TO THE OCCASION, LISTEN, AND CONNECT OVER THE PAIN THAT MAKES US HUMAN.
IT'S NOT A PERFECT SCIENCE, BUT WITH TIME YOU'LL GET BETTER AT SPOTTING THEM.

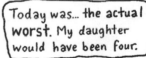

INTIMACY

$$1 - 1 + 1 = ?$$

INTRODUCTION

by Rebecca Soffer

When I think of romance, I imagine a cemetery in Upper Darby, Pennsylvania, where my mom is buried. My dad is standing at her grave. As are two of my ex-boyfriends, dozens of her best friends, and many of my own as well.

I'm not a goth, nor am I an exhibitionist. I'm way too uncool for either of those lifestyles. But to me that cemetery suggests love, and even hope, because it's where I realized the guy I was casually seeing might actually be the guy I'd marry.

It happened in October 2007 at my mother's unveiling. That's the Jewish ceremony during which the grave marker is uncovered about a year after a death. It marks the end of the intense mourning period, after which grief supposedly* moves into a slightly less painful phase.

The service was beautiful. I'd worked hard to plan it, and it was a productive way in which to channel my why-am-I-still-so-messed-up? energy. I'd invited people I loved. But I hadn't imagined Justin would be there until he showed up.

We'd only been seeing each other for two months, after meeting at a benefit where we both found ourselves standing at a silent auction table filled with such coveted items as a celebrity-signed white electric guitar and a gift certificate for storing umbilical-cord blood. He asked me about my life while looking directly into my eyes. He made me laugh. And he didn't slowly back away with *you-cray!* eyes when my eating-

---

* *Supposedly* being the operative word.

messy-appetizers-while-standing skills more resembled a tod-dler's than an adult's.

"I'm damaged goods," I told him that summer. I braced myself for rejection, but he didn't flinch.

"Well . . . I just want to be around you," he said. "Is that okay?"

Weirdly, given my fear that he'd ditch me, I wasn't sure that it was. I'd been so unsure, in fact, that on our eventual first date, a month after meeting, I buffered myself with a group of twenty friends to serve as chaperones for the Brooklyn Cyclones game on Coney Island. And for weeks I'd only go out with him on Wednesday nights. I was terrified to have anything to do with him. The way he embraced my sadness was a stark contrast to the men I'd been frantically dating in the months after my mother's death. Those swings-and-a-miss seemed part of a simple equation: woman in deep grief searching for loving comfort + guys who didn't sign up for that = nobody wins. I'd spent months feeling like a taxi nobody wanted to hail.

The first jittery suitor was Sam.* We met through a friend and went out on fun dates mercifully containing zero deep conversation. Over a casual dinner weeks later, he asked where my parents lived. I felt queasy. It was the first time I had to tell someone new what had happened. I grabbed a French fry and matter-of-factly stated the truth, that Mom had just died, and I was still very much grieving. Within minutes Sam had ushered me into a taxi, mumbling something about an earnings call in the morning, slammed the door, and *double-tapped the window* to signal the driver to hit the gas and take me far, far away. Only after I got home did the sting of what had occurred

---

* Name has been changed. Though he doesn't deserve it.

sink in. I felt like a grief hooker doing the walk of shame. And I didn't hear from Sam again.

Then there was Antonio,* or, as my friends called him, "Caracas," as their furiously nonblinking eyes communicated that they thought he was a Very Bad Idea. We'd connected—really reconnected—in early 2007 during my week-long trip to Venezuela. I had been there trying to recapture some of the happiness I'd had in the place I'd lived and worked right after college, and he was certainly a part of that picture. He'd been in my circle of friends there, and he'd met my parents when they came to visit. At the end of that return trip, "Caracas" ended things with his girlfriend, and we soon found each other in New York and Bogotá. Then he unended things with her, which of course ended things for me.

There was Evan,† the potential setup who'd introduced himself in an e-mail a few minutes before my mom's accident. We went out a month later. We had easy rapport and kissed in NoLIta. I assumed that because my mother's best friend had instigated this, he wouldn't end up being a dick. I also hoped my mom might somehow serve as my guardian angel and send someone to take care of me, because yeah, I really wanted someone to take care of me then. But after three dates, radio silence.

Guardian angels and dates weren't the only ones to, well, ghost me. Even though I was careful not to let my burden fall to others, the mere *idea* of grief scared away several friends I'd long defined as really good ones. They simply faded away from

---

* Name has been changed. Though again, doesn't deserve it.

† Name has been changed. Though yet again . . . you know where I'm going here.

my life. I'd been unwittingly waiting for people to prompt me to open up, and I think some just didn't want to know what I'd say. All these vanishings were extremely bad timing, because if grief does anything, it makes you feel alone.

Death is the ultimate breakup. And like a breakup, but to the nth degree, its reverberations can either emotionally slam you shut or crack you open in unimaginable ways. It's often both, at varying times. In the years since my parents died, I let fewer people in and ditch the bad seeds. I also try to prioritize meaningful relationships with real friends over nonurgent work commitments; as the ultimate Dad-ism often reminds me, "No one ever said on their deathbed they wished they'd spent more time at the office."

And there *are* real friends. My lonely, dark days were buffered by truly intimate encounters with unexpected people. Like the casual acquaintances who invited me for a drink or a walk because they'd had loss in their lives, and who let me cry in their arms without saying dumb-ass things like "It takes a year." Or the girlfriends who met at my mom's funeral and started planning monthly Sunday-morning bacchanalias (with a side of food) to ensure I wouldn't socially atrophy in some tiny corner of my sofa. "Brunch Club" was one of the best things to ever happen to me, and by extension, them, because it created enduring friendships.

Or my old college friend Brett, who called in response to a bleak voice mail I'd left him one December evening, three months after my mom died. "Rosenbeeeerg! Meet me at 70th and Broadway in fifteen minutes!" he boomed into the phone. I wanted to go home and drink myself into oblivion, or, frankly, worse. But I forced myself to walk through the snow flurries to meet him. When I did, he was bear-hugging an enormous

Christmas tree and wearing a huge smile. "I got something that we're gonna work on all night together! Yeah! Oh, and can I borrow twenty bucks?" And so, two Jews indeed spent all night decorating a ten-foot Christmas tree in an apartment with nine-foot-high ceilings. He didn't let me out of his sight. It was imperfect and ludicrous, and also one of the most loving gestures I've experienced—one that inspired me henceforth to provide equally absurd activities to friends going through something awful.

But most of all, there is Justin. On the day of the unveiling a man I barely knew witnessed my graveside tears and took it in stride, chatted with people who were laser-focused on the role he might play in my life (no pressure), and ran out to grab Wawa hoagies for dinner. That day, I had to choose between safely avoiding another burn or opening up to this quiet introvert who'd proved he'd show up, no matter what, and try my best to do the same for him in spite of it all. So, very nervously, I chose the latter. Who knows—maybe that day I had a guardian angel after all.

Our relationship isn't all easy. I mean, marriage generally isn't easy, but that's a separate book topic that I am certainly not qualified to write. I'm talking about the burden he has taken on of loving someone with a permanent hole in her heart, and my burden of being the one with the hole. It will never be okay that he didn't get to meet my mother, or that the only version of my father he knew was the one who, suffering the loss of the great love of his life, could be downright unbearable in his actions. But Justin was the one who got into the deep muck with me, willing to wade through this mess together and fully engage in a marriage that has four people in it, two of them ghosts.

MEET THE TWINS: GRIEF AND DESIRE

by Emily Rapp Black

The self forms at the edge of desire.
—ANNE CARSON, *EROS THE BITTERSWEET*

After my son, Ronan, died, all I wanted to do was write and fuck.

I didn't try to sleep with my friends, or have drunken hookups with strangers, or experiment with a disastrous threesome in a tiny room at the top of a winding staircase, or spend a hot and furious night with a friend I had long and madly desired in a by-the-hour motel in Bushwick, Brooklyn, a place so seedy it had paper sheets on the beds and no locks on the doors, and it didn't dampen my desire at all. I didn't stay up all night writing, or drive with my laptop literally on my lap so I could write at stoplights, the words spilling out of me.

Why? Because I had already done all of that during the two years between Ronan's diagnosis at nine months old and his death from Tay-Sachs disease at nearly three years old. I believed that the wild work and the wild sex were part of what I called "acting out." During some of this time, I was still married to and living with my son's father; during some of it we were separated. But I wasn't ashamed of the when and where or how of any of it, and although I recognize that this behavior was hurtful to many, I still don't regret it.

The wildness—the writing, and especially the sex—I experienced during Ronan's decline changed me, saved me. Any good lover engages with risk of some kind, and every creator does the same—and to risk was to live.

As soon as I met the man who would become my now husband, Kent, and fell into the kind of great love I had been waiting for all my life, the kind that both flattens and revivifies, he became the target of my wild affections. I wanted him and only him, and I wanted him all the time.

At first it was fun. Kent couldn't cook a meal without finding his pants down around his ankles. A lot of perfectly good steaks lay smoking on the grill, dinners burning up on the stove while we got busy in various rooms or on the kitchen table, or in the enclosed yard of the house we now share together. I wanted sex every which way: in cars, in public (a favorite was a campground outside of Santa Fe), wherever and whenever. We lived large and beautiful and fast during those first months of our courtship while Ronan was still living. We were buoyed by the newness of our connection, our remarkable and almost instantaneous intellectual and physical compatibility, and our ability to talk about anything during the time of Ronan's most precipitous decline, from the mundane to the profound, even in the midst of emotions that ranged from the freeze of panic to the mania of dread.

After Ronan's death, we were relieved, almost ecstatic, because his suffering was over. Watching someone die reinforces the fragility of life, the power of chaos, the endlessness of loss. Sex—the thrill of it, the feel of it, the visceral, writhing nature of it—was the opposite of death. It was life. I needed life.

During this time I was hornier than I've ever been, almost

embarrassingly so. Was this the right reaction? I wondered. Should I have been wearing black and weeping in the dark, or meditating in a stoic fashion for hours on end, in the weeks after Ronan died? Here I was, brimming with desire. I wanted Kent—his attention, his body, his release, his odors and hair and flesh and voice in my ear. I didn't want gentle sex, either. I wanted dirty talk, because it made me feel less like a grieving mother and more like just a woman, a being made up of desires and impulse. I didn't want acquaintances to softly tell me how "sorry" they were for my loss. I wanted to be pinned down, attacked, thrown around a little bit. Pinched.

This was slightly disconcerting to both of us. Of course everybody wants to be wanted, and good sex is one of the great pleasures of life, especially when you love and trust your partner. But this felt different, and we both noticed it. Kent started to somewhat correctly sense, though I wasn't aware of it, that this wasn't really about my desire for him (although just looking at his hands across the dinner table could make me wet, and still can). Instead, this was about my great and terrible sadness, which was a thing I dragged around in my belly, my forehead, my fingertips. I didn't want to feel it. I wanted out of my skin. I wasn't clawing at Kent for connection but for disconnection. In some sense, it was the least intimate we'd ever been. It was not unlike my actions immediately after learning of Ronan's diagnosis, when I knocked my head against a wall until someone made me stop, as if I were trying to force my head, my body, my reality, into a new world.

In my earliest sex education classes, in a cold church basement, I was taught that sex in marriage was only good when sanctioned, and that good meant morally good, not literally good, as in ecstatic orgasms. Sex outside of marriage was wild, indecent, and for bad girls only. We were encouraged to learn the difference and act accordingly. For the longest time, I did just that.

But grief changed me, the love of my son changed me, my love for Kent changed me, and all of this changed how I experienced desire—both creative and erotic—because desire itself changes us, offering a glimpse into a new person, a different possible self.

Grief alters us, body and mind, by splitting us in two. It is the only way to live with it and not be destroyed by it. The knowledge of what you have or had is pressed against the knowledge that you will lose it or have lost it. Grief sex, if it must have a name, is not, as some romantics would have you believe, the moment of your transcendence, but a deliberate escape, which is less ecstatic and far more desperate.

Just as we lose in grief, to love is to lose an essential boundary of the self. So my reaching out in the interest of disappearing was a legitimate expression of desire. Proof that you can be annihilated—in love, in loss, and yes, in sex—is also the same proof that you can go on living. This is why the Greeks envisioned desire as a kind of melting, a dissolving of the known world in service of creating a new one.

Desire is the shattering, uplifting knowledge of the distance between where we are forced to come from and where we must go. Of course it gives rise to sex, which can move us through the boundaries of any experience by lifting us into a new one, one that is different each time. You move, you change, you come, you rise. But you also don't always see yourself clearly. By revealing so much, so quickly, to so many, I had muted my responses to true intimacy. Instead of looking at myself or another, I just wanted to become lost in the body so I would be free of the mind. It is wild, it is delirious, but it is not sustainable.

During those years of my son's slow unraveling and my tumble into real love with my now husband, my heart felt stupid and stumbling, and all I wanted was sex and art. Now, two years out, I can see that what I wanted, both then and now, was this: the heart unmasked, its bare face the tiniest flag.

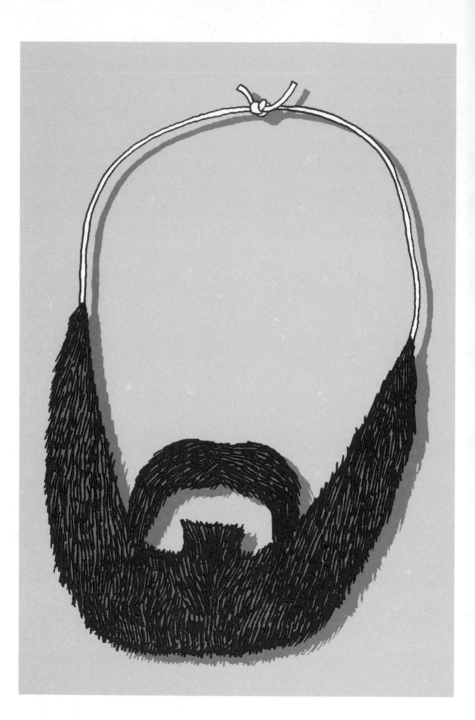

ARE YOU MY PAPI?

by Mathew Rodriguez

In 2011, I lost my father to an AIDS–related illness, and I lost my virginity to a man I barely knew. I also moved to Manhattan's Washington Heights neighborhood, where the men appreciated my curvy body, and where I stumbled to find my footing both as a modern AIDS orphan and a sexually liberated young queer.

To lose my father right after college graduation made the world expand into a maelstrom of frenetic energy. I was catapulted, in quick succession, into the world of work, the world of sex, and the front of the family line.

Sex, gay sex especially, is filled with Freudian familial language. It's all "Spank it, daddy," and asking whether I've been bad. You get called "baby." Or, if he's Latino, we might call each other Papi.

The first person to call me Papi was my father. To be young and Latino and to be called Papi is to swallow chicken soup.

My relationship with my father was defined by distance, both physical and emotional. He moved to Cleveland from our home in New Jersey after he and my mother divorced in 1999. I was only ten years old when, one Monday afternoon, my father moved out of my home and my family of four turned into a three-person operation. I spoke to him on the phone on Sunday evenings. The calls diminished in frequency as I grew older, and completely disappeared during my college years. I had to learn that his love for me existed in the negative space of things we didn't say to each other.

Sometimes, I think about the maxim "Daughters marry their fathers." It speaks to the desire to find a man we trust, even if it's a partner for the night. We want to feel his trust—we want for it to be sturdy and familiar, like a knit blanket or macaroni and cheese. If daughters marry their fathers, have I been trying to date my dad?

I know my father had interests. He loved to dance and played the guiro, a wooden percussion instrument he stroked with a comb to keep a beat, in a band with his brother. But everything beyond what we needed to know about each other as father and son went untold. He never shared his HIV status with me; my mother told me only as he became sick and edged closer to death. My father was a decades-long heroin addict who received his diagnosis as I was growing inside my mother. I never really came out to him as gay, even though I've been out since age thirteen.

With the men I date, I want to know everything about them. I want it all at once—a spiritual data dump. If something were to happen, if they were to get hit by a car on the way home from our first date, I could say, "I knew him."

My dad was a gentle, forgetful man. He'd scramble to recall facts, like a child trying to capture an elusive lightning bug. In mid-October he'd ask if I needed someone to bring me out trick-or-treating that night or what Sunday in November Thanksgiving would fall on.

He could cook a meal for four in thirty minutes while dancing. He would spin my mother and stir a pot of beans. He would make water soak into a grain of rice at a rate that defied physics.

In a sexual or romantic partner, I seek out someone who indulges me, like my father did. My father would feed me—a fat little boy with a sweet tooth—a daily after-school snack of Oreos, and on report-card day he'd give me six or seven or eight of them as a reward.

My father, like any father, wanted to teach me how to ride a bike without training wheels, to show me where to put my hands, where to fix my eyes, and how to anticipate when to brake. I got a black and blue that day. I slammed into the chain-link fence across the street from our house. I don't remember his reaction, but I know, with his help, I continued to ride. And I'd go on to have another accident, when I decided to ride the bike down the stairs of our front stoop. Once again, my dad was there to pick me up and bandage me.

I met Ricardo,* an older Mexican man, at an LGBT conference. He filled me up with tequila sours, and we shared a sweet night in my hotel room. Ricardo did not look like my dad, but he did have a beard like his. He spoke Spanish like him. He was older like him. He had HIV like him. And, for that one night, he treated me preciously.

Ricardo was connected. He knew people from many movements and many struggles. He thrived in conversation. My father was chatty to a fault and loved human interaction. Once, my mom recalled to me, on a road trip that brought her and my father through Arizona, he met someone he knew in a desert rest-stop bathroom.

Ricardo laid me down on my hotel mattress. He taught me how to touch him, where to put my hands on him, and where to fix my eyes; he requested they stay locked on his as we began.

*   Ricardo's, Evan's, and Steve's names have been changed.

I see Ricardo in Facebook pictures at other conferences. He meets other writers, other men, other people with dads, dead or alive. I wonder if they touch each other, what they teach each other.

There are other older HIV-positive men who I ask to pay me attention. Evan disappears for months at a time. I don't know if he's okay, but this doesn't bother me: when I was young, my father disappeared at times to feed his addiction, but always returned. On Father's Day, I sometimes call Steve, a blogger who is also a recovering addict. When I speak to him, I discuss my life in ways I would if my father were still alive. Mostly, I talk to him in hope of some guidance.

Even with a father around, a bike-riding lesson can produce an inner thigh with a big purple blotch. Now—other men, other blotches, other lessons. The yearning for human connection, whether two hours or a few sweet months, is the desire to be taught, to be shown new things, to hear new stories, to get a slightly widened worldview.

My dad didn't know me as a sexually active, dating adult stumbling through twentysomethinghood. Maybe that's for the best. But I know he would've loved my willingness to crash.

WHAT'S GOOD ENOUGH NOW

by LaNeah "Starshell" Menzies

I sat on the new couch with that familiar breakup hole in my stomach, telling me that this was the end, while my boyfriend's voice echoed throughout our newly renovated apartment, crescendoing in volume as though he were desperate to awaken my soul. As he spoke, I realized I was only half listening. The other half of me was thinking, I've got to get this album finished; arguing is a waste of time. So I blurted out, "If we are going to break up, then we should just do it." I knew by the look on his face that I had crushed him.

A week later, he moved out.

He was convinced I didn't care. He couldn't understand how I wasn't feeling as though life were over, as though I had to call his cell phone obsessively in the days that followed our breakup to tell him how we had to be together, how I couldn't live without him. I knew that I could.

Three months earlier, on the heels of five years together, we'd moved into a cute little apartment just across the George Washington Bridge from Manhattan. But long before the moving trucks pulled away, leaving our two sets of dishes under the same roof, our relationship had been suffering thanks to an old worry of his: he felt I didn't love him, or at least couldn't express that love.

Funny thing is, I loved him more than anything. Cheesy, I know, but it was the kind of romance that shows you the future, the sun, moon, and stars, when you look into someone's eyes.

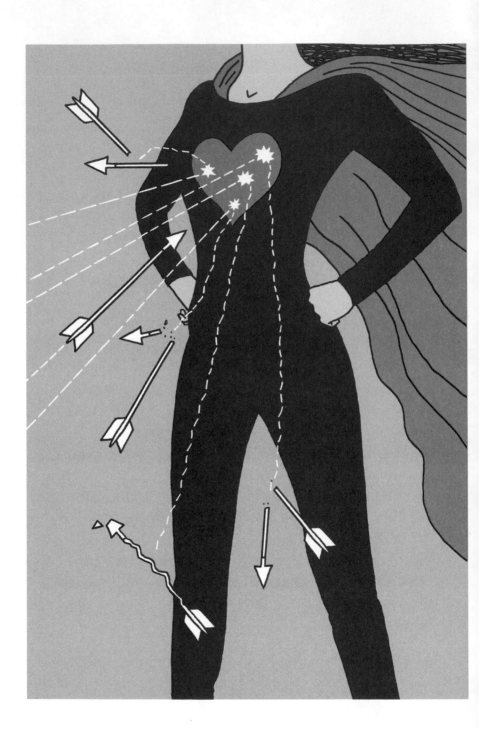

We took long walks at Shed Park and shared every thought imaginable inside the gazebo where we'd carved our initials. We drove to the beach for ice cream because we agreed that ice cream always tasted better at the beach. He was the only person who could walk into a room and know by my tearful expression that I'd been watching Lifetime.

When we ended things, a lump in my throat formed as I realized everything I'd miss about us. But the end happened because I couldn't focus as much time and energy on him and "us" as on my career. I'd spent my whole life trying to get to my current reality, working with some of the biggest names in the music industry. At that moment, my record contract was more important than starting a family.

The breakup was devastating to me. But softening the blow was the knowledge that he'd still be here—"here" meaning living and breathing. That was good enough for me.

When my sister left, she was no longer just a phone call away. She'd been gone for real since she was fourteen, when she took her own life. We'd been joined at the hip from the day I was born until the night she died. And since the moment we found her, I've wondered why she didn't wake me up in my bedroom, right next door to hers, to tell me how desolate she'd been feeling after an early teenage breakup, to tell me how she was contemplating leaving us. I never got to convince her to stay. There would be no more gossiping about boys or laughing at our brother's quirks or arguing over sharing ramen noodles. Ever.

With that perspective, I came to feel that if someone leaves but they're still alive, it can't be that bad. But it wasn't until that moment in the home I shared with my boyfriend—when my reaction to that last argument drove the final nail into our relationship's coffin—that I understood the emotional rewiring I'd undergone when it came to matters of the heart.

I've been vaccinated against the worst depths of loss. I could still experience all the emotions of the breakup, but not at the magnitude where it impaired my functioning and my rational side, the way it used to. I'd miss the little things. But because I knew he was aboveground, just a text away, I knew I'd be okay.

Meanwhile, I had no clue whether my sister was okay.

At first I thought this dynamic had something to do with this particular boyfriend, the first since my sister's death. But the one that followed inspired the same sentiment, and the one after that, too. I never feel dependent on my relationships for emotional stability or happiness. Friends and romantic partners have categorized me as "cold" because I don't cry after arguments or beg them to stay in my life. But I believe I will always feel okay living without someone, in a way that others cannot understand.

If the whole point of getting into a relationship is to fall completely and madly and utterly in love to the point where you feel like you can't live without someone, but you know that you can, are you able to love completely? After my first breakup, before my sister died, I was devastated. It felt as though someone were ripping my heart out of my chest for months on end once the security of that relationship was gone. It's different now—and to be honest, it's liberating. It's my new superpower. Anyone who goes through losing someone in their life the way I did deserves a superpower, right?

The thing is, though, all superheroes have to give up something precious to retain their gifts. For me, it's been the ability to grow happy and healthy long-term relationships. I haven't quite figured out how to balance my strength with the fact that my partner may need me to feel like I can't survive without him. And I don't know how my story ends, because I don't know if I ever will.

TABOO TIMES TWO

by Alice Radosh

What cannot be said will be wept.
—SAPPHO

"We've been lied to," Bart said. I rolled over on my side and saw that my husband of almost forty years was grinning. "It's not supposed to be *this* good when you're *this* old."

He was right. Our whole generation *had* been lied to. Holding hands, tender hugs, and a peck on the cheek were supposed to be the acceptable acts for older couples still in love. Anything more intimate than that was either unacknowledged or grist for cartoons and stand-up comedians—funny at best, but more likely kind of disgusting. Bart and I never bought into that stereotype. We were septuagenarians now, and the sex was still fun. It bound us together.

When Bart was diagnosed with multiple myeloma in his mid-seventies, we were both stunned. He had always been strong, athletic, energetic, and healthy; but now the cells in the marrow of his bones were being destroyed by cancer. Within a few months, our hikes up the Catskill high peaks were replaced with quiet walks along the stream near our house. A few more months, and those walks were replaced by visits to doctors. Eighteen months after diagnosis, Bart died.

Friends and family from around the country and Europe came to mourn together. The loss was enormous, and it was not mine alone. Night after night the house was crowded with people who hugged me and cried along with me, who packed my freezer with casseroles and offered to sleep over, should I want the company. Sympathy cards jammed the narrow box at my rural post office, and more than a hundred stories filled Bart's memorial website—stories from colleagues at the college where Bart taught, from squash partners and friends at the local table tennis club, from total strangers he tended to as a volunteer EMT, from a heartbroken granddaughter. Loved ones called daily to check in, and my adult children urged me to come for an extended visit.

Bart's death brought into sharp relief all of the ways our lives had been inextricably intertwined. Gone was the person who shared my pleasure in (and anxieties about) our children and grandchildren. Gone was the partner who slept next to me on the ground as, year after year, we ventured farther into the Canadian wilderness on our canoeing trips, who read Hesse aloud to me, who smiled over at me during a concert when the cellist played the opening notes of our favorite Brahms quintet. Gone was the man I marched alongside to end the Vietnam War, the sous-chef who raved about my cooking, the person with whom I loved discussing books and movies and the news.

But not until the immobilizing despair of those early months of grieving abated was I blindsided by the realization that the sexual intimacy Bart and I shared was also gone for good. I was unprepared for the shock and the depth of this loss. This felt far more essential than things like concerts and canoeing, which were things we *did* together. This was about who we *were* together.

I called this feeling "sexual bereavement," and immediately

understood that this loss would not be easy to share with family and friends. Despite the recent spate of best-selling books, popular blogs, and talk shows "discovering" that older people enjoy sex, I soon realized that the taboos around sexuality are still strong and entrenched. We're already not supposed to talk about death in polite company. Pair that with sex, and you've got a double taboo.

When I tried to bring it up with friends, I felt I was trespassing on other people's privacy. Awkward statements about the absence of intimacy in their own marriages for the last ten years and various versions of "Who cares about sex anymore, anyway?" were quickly followed by "Want another cup of coffee?" One good friend, a therapist, told me I was "brave" to bring this up. By far the most commonly offered antidote to my feelings of sexual bereavement, though, was suggestions from well-intentioned friends that I set up a profile on a senior dating website. But I didn't want a new partner. I wanted the decades of shared humor and pillow talk that were critical to sexual enjoyment, the appreciation of bodies that had aged together, the understanding that develops over a long period in an enduring sexual relationship. I wanted Bart.

I started to search for confirmation that my feelings were not inappropriate. What I found instead was a culture of silence. I read Joan Didion's and Joyce Carol Oates's classic memoirs about mourning a beloved husband. They are lauded as unflinching, but in their combined nearly 700 pages, there is no mention of the type of sexual bereavement I was experiencing. The unspoken message, as I received it: Keep your mouths shut about sex.

I turned to self-help books for widows, and found that there, too, discussions about missing sex were pretty much nonexistent. These books urged me not to confuse missing touch (acceptable) with missing sex (misguided). Missing touch didn't have anything to do with sex, I was told, and could be replaced with massages, cuddling grandchildren, and even going to hair salons to get shampoos. Clearly, they didn't know what Bart was like in bed. This loss wasn't something a hairdresser could handle!

Calling upon my training as a research psychologist, I launched headfirst into a research project on this doubly taboo subject. A colleague and I created and mailed a survey to 150 older women, asking how often they had sex, whether they enjoyed it, and if they thought they would miss it if they were predeceased. The survey touched a nerve. We got an unheard-of response rate of 68 percent and set to work analyzing data, reviewing academic literature. Just as I suspected, the work provided a surprisingly good counterbalance to collapsing into a pool of tears. What's more, it taught me that I was no outlier: the majority of the women surveyed said they would definitely miss sex if their partner died, and most said that, even if it felt awkward, they would want to be able to talk to friends about this loss.

That study was published in a peer-reviewed journal, and life continues for me. My dog and I go out in my new one-person canoe. My friends come over for dinner and rave about my cooking. The loss of Bart has a permanent place in my life, but it is surrounded by a full and happy existence.

And the sexual bereavement? The great thing about good friends is that they are convinced you're a "catch," and that any man would be lucky to have you. When I laugh and ask,

"Know any nice left-wing, single men over sixty-eight?" their faces go blank. I reassure them that I'm not lonely, but I don't rule out the possibility of meeting someone. I even have the start of the personal ad I might place one day: "The love of my life and my canoeing/hiking partner died four years ago. Looking to replace the latter."

THE PROMISE

by Mattie J. Bekink

Four days after the birth of our daughter, my husband, Victor, and I walked down the bright white hospital hallway outside Amsterdam to learn her fate. Would she live or die? Would she be brain-damaged or not? I was a thrum of terrified and optimistic exhausted energy, trying not to cry. Sleep-deprived and consumed with worry, I was also emotionally frayed and physically fragile after an emergency C-section. The night prior, in the NICU, I'd kept my hand on her precious newborn body until dawn.

Victor held my hand in the hallway and stopped briefly. "We are walking through hell right now," he said. "And there is no one I would rather be walking with." I nodded and we continued.

Our daughter, Elouisa, died in our arms later that night.

Victor was outwardly calm during our daughter's few days. He'd been so composed throughout the panicked emergency surgery ending with Elouisa's limp body being pulled from mine that doctors asked whether he had medical training. Victor focused on information—facts, details, possibilities—and shared it with family and friends. I spent my time clinging to hope. Victor returned home to our two-year-old son nightly. Alone at the hospital, I'd call him, my breaths barely breaking through the sobs. He'd manage to calm me down and encourage me to try to rest.

Much later, Victor revealed he knew we were about to receive bad news in that bright corridor. He had recently passed one of the doctors who reviewed our baby girl's case. The doctor had looked away. Victor allowed me to remain hopeful until the very end, staying strong during her life because I could not be. Only afterward did I realize how much energy it must have cost him to put forth that strength during our time in the NICU.

Leaving the hospital was a blurry mixture of rain and tears. Everything felt obscured. I stared at the droplets slipping down the car windows, the indistinct headlights on the highway, undone and unsure about how we could continue our lives. I turned to Victor and said, "Our daughter just died in my arms. Now what?" Even as I asked the question, I knew we'd be answering it for a long time, and in complex combinations: together, with our son, and individually. I didn't know how we'd manage that.

It was soon clear that Victor and I grieved differently. Our energy and emotions ebbed and flowed. Rarely were we in sync. Sometimes I wondered if we were experiencing the same loss. The following months saw us frequently walking through isolated hells, two loving parents separately grieving the loss of our baby girl, bereft and desperately nostalgic for a future that would never be.

That first night at home—and repeatedly over the course of several days—we gathered our family and friends for a meal around a long, candlelit table. We went through several cases of the excellent red wine we'd brought on our move from Milan to Amsterdam, carefully saving it for special occasions. (We drank it all in the week after Elouisa's death.) Victor told everyone he was so proud of his "beautiful, strong wife." Those words were difficult to hear because I was devastated, bewildered, wondering whether I was at fault, and caught in the magical thinking of grief, still trying to reason my way to a different outcome. Then he looked everyone in the eye and promised we wouldn't let this destroy our marriage. He looked at me and said this would not destroy us. I looked at him and promised the same. "I want to ask each of you to help hold us to that," he said. Those with us around the table tearfully and solemnly agreed.

I didn't appreciate the prescient wisdom of this request at the time. But the commitment we made to each other in front of our families and closest friends that night became more important than our marriage vows. We were determined to not lose each other in our grief. That required learning to respect our different processes and give each other the space to weather our own storms. It was not easy.

I needed constant motion. Once, a friend told me I didn't need to load the dishwasher because others could help with such mundane tasks. I explained that actually, I did. The act was strangely critical to my keeping it together in that moment. Nights were torturous, sleep impossible. Moving kept me going. Victor was the opposite. He slowed down, stayed still, slept. I couldn't understand that.

As time went on, I looked at Elouisa's pictures. Victor did not. I framed one in our bedroom. He didn't want a physical reminder of the most painful moments of his life, but as difficult as it was for him, he allowed me to keep it there. I write about our daughter and our loss to order the chaos of my shattered heart. He doesn't read much of it. When people ask us how many children we have, we often give different answers. To me, the passing discomfort I may cause to strangers matters less than my pain when I don't mention her. Victor doesn't feel disloyal in not mentioning her to strangers. He doesn't want to let just anyone in, sharing Elouisa only with those who have earned her.

Amazingly, our son Tuur noticed these different grieving styles and responded accordingly. With the emotional intuition of a toddler, he'd often know I was about to cry before I did. He'd place his little hands on my cheeks, look into my eyes, and whisper "Baby" or "Don't cry, Mama." I tried to be emotionally present for him and did not mask my feelings. Victor's grief was less visible. His weeping was internal and private; mine was in the living room, at the table during breakfast, as I cycled Tuur to nursery school. Tuur saw that, and at first spoke more to me about his sister than to his father.

During my darkest moments I felt the full weight of the commitment we'd made. I blamed myself for Elouisa's death. I succumbed to feelings of failure. My body, tasked only with seeing her safely into this world, had failed. I spiraled dangerously and depressively into an absolute sense of worthlessness and failure. I nearly wanted my marriage to fail, in order to feed and satisfy the thought-demons consuming me. But our promise wouldn't allow me that. I could let myself down, but not Victor and the friends and family who had borne witness to that promise. So I worked through the pain and slayed the demons again and again and again with all the strength I could muster, through counseling, community, ritual, reading, and writing. Victor and I kept our distance and embraced each other as needed, even when what the other was experiencing was incomprehensible.

Elouisa died on Thanksgiving, as if to remind us there is

still much to be thankful for. Nonetheless, I found weddings, baptisms, birthdays—anything celebrating life's milestones—painful. If I smiled my way through the ceremony, I sobbed on the way home. I'd find myself at the center of the dance floor, a vision of carefree bliss, but aching inside for all I'd never see our daughter do. At one wedding, the boisterous band forcing us to shout-whisper in each other's ears, I wept on Victor's shoulder and told him of my deceit in these moments. He understood, of course, but he said we were tough and pointed out what I couldn't see: the pain of losing Elouisa was so great that we were now free to be unafraid and to be stronger, braver, more loving, to simply be more. Her death could rip us apart, or it could bring us closer.

That moment sealed a fortitude that is invisible to anyone outside our marriage: that we can be strong together and live a bolder, better life. What we share is more powerful than our different griefs. We know the pain of parenting pure love. Early on, we'd vowed not to let our marriage be destroyed by our daughter's death. Now, we choose to stay together with purpose.

GUESS WHO'S (NOT) COMING TO DINNER?

Surviving small talk after a loss

By Rebecca Shaloff and Modern Loss

IDENTITY

Who We Were
And Who We've Become

INTRODUCTION

by Gabrielle Birkner

My mother and stepfather showed up unannounced at my office around six thirty on a Wednesday evening, with what my mom termed "the worst news you're ever going to hear."

"Dad," I said, doing the process of elimination in my head.

I was twenty-four and unmarried. I'm an only child, and I didn't yet have children of my own. My mother was standing right in front of me. Who else could this "worst news" be about? I searched her face for answers, expecting, I suppose, for her to tell me something about a heart attack or a freak accident. My dad took chartered flights between Sedona, Arizona, where he lived with my stepmother, and Phoenix, where there was a larger airport. I was always worrying about whether those little planes were safe.

"They were murdered."

They.

Murdered.

I remember sitting under the fluorescent lights in the stairwell that connected the lobby to the Stamford, Connecticut, newsroom where I worked and asking questions to which my mom didn't yet know the answers. Specifically, who would have done this and how and why? My dad and Ruth had only recently moved to Sedona, but had quickly established themselves in civic and cultural life there. Ruth, an accomplished public speaker, presided over the Sedona Toastmasters Club. They both joined the local community boards and were active in the Jewish community. They'd shown me the progress on the new synagogue building when I was there five months earlier for Rosh Hashanah, the Jewish New Year.

That Rosh Hashanah, I had stood between my father and stepmother and recited the liturgical poem famously read on the holiday: "On Rosh Hashanah it is inscribed, and on Yom Kippur it is sealed: how many shall pass on, and how many shall be born; who shall live, and who shall die; who in his time, and who before his time; who by fire and who by water; who by sword and who by beast; who by hunger and who by thirst; who by storm and who by plague; who by choking and who by stoning . . ."

Who?

How?

Why?

Back at my mother and stepfather's house, where I spent that night, I remember fielding endless phone calls, from family, friends, faith leaders, and reporters covering Sedona's biggest news story in years. The February 20, 2004, edition of the *Sedona Red Rock News* led with the headline "Double Homicide in Sedona" and contained a thoughtful editorial calling my dad and Ruth "the type of people who define community." That same edition contained news more typical of what goes down in Sedona: efforts to protect local trees from bark beetles, a proposal to widen a local roadway, and, in honor of National Pet Dental Health Month, a column titled "Caring for Pets' Teeth Is Critical." Just two weeks before the murders, the *Red Rock News* had carried a letter to the editor that my father wrote about a recent charrette session. "My hat is off to the [Arizona Department of Transportation]," that letter concluded, "for being open-minded and listening intently to everyone's feedback. We are making real progress in visioning a road that we can all be proud of and will keep Sedona beautiful."

I remember waking up the morning after my mom and stepfather had shown up to deliver the news, and for a fleeting moment before I opened my eyes, thinking that, *phew*, this was all a bad dream. Realizing that I was in my clothes from the day before, that I was in my adolescent bedroom, was hell.

This was so far from anything my twenty-four years and ten months had prepared me for.

I had grown up in relatively safe and cosseted suburban communities. I had graduated from Northwestern. My parents were divorced, yes, but both of them had been happily remarried for more than a decade. I never wanted for anything of import, and I had not previously experienced the loss, or grave illness, of anyone in my immediate family. Like many of my peers, I was living in a crappy apartment, paying my dues at work, going out with assholes from dating websites (before dating apps existed), and laughing about it all over drinks with friends. And then, without warning, I was swept into adulthood by medical examiners and mortuaries, by police, prosecutors, plea deals, and probate, by a pain for which I had zero point of reference. Neither did my peers. Most hadn't lost a parent, let alone known anyone who had been murdered. While friends' lives seemed to continue apace, mine had become unrecognizable. They were who they'd always been, and my new and unwelcome identity was that of The Girl Whose Family Was Murdered.

"One might expect that the families of murder victims would be showered with sympathy and support, embraced by their communities," the journalist Eric Schlosser wrote in his 1997

Atlantic article, "A Grief Like No Other." "But in reality they are far more likely to feel isolated, fearful, and ashamed, overwhelmed by grief and guilt, angry at the criminal justice system, and shunned by their old friends. America's fascination with murder has not yet extended to its aftermath."

I was feeling all of that, though I'm incredibly thankful that most of my friends expressed a genuine desire to be there for me. One of my colleagues, Jon—not knowing what to do and not wanting to do nothing—arrived on my doorstep with bagels. My workout buddy, Melanie, addressed and stamped all of my sympathy acknowledgments. Lindsay, my closest friend from my semester abroad in Paris, brought me stacks of celebrity weeklies, and at my request timed me on their trifling crossword puzzles: "Newlyweds' _____ Lachey," "_____ in Translation, starring Bill Murray," "Paris Hilton's BFF," "Nicole _____." Cindy invited me to tag along on her family vacation to Hawaii. Annabel, heroically, met me in Sedona, to help me prepare my father and stepmother's house for sale. My friends mostly came through, and many did so in a big way. But understandably (and thankfully), they could not relate.

When I returned to work two weeks after the murders—after the double funeral and after the joint shiva, and after zoning out to more daytime television than I had watched in years—one of my editors pointed me toward the nonprofit organization Safe Horizon, whose Families of Homicide Victims program offered a biweekly bereavement group. It was there that I found my tribe, among a handful of wise, empathic women (and one man) with whom, on the surface, I had little in common: not faith, race, generation, or relationship to the deceased. But they understood me—implicitly, yes, but also because they listened to things that my friends could not. Like specifics about the crime, which prosecutors said was committed in "an especially heinous, cruel or depraved manner," and details of which had been making their way into press reports.

Every other Thursday we'd meet, for a while in the community room on Manhattan's Upper West Side and, later, for years, in a church basement in Harlem. Over takeout, we'd share our stories, and the unique emotional and logistical by-products of losing someone to homicide. The group's facilitator, Theresa, a preternaturally calm middle-aged woman with gray dreadlocks and a mellifluous baritone, was so focused on bearing witness to our pain that it would be months before I found out that she had lost her own brother, Kenneth, who had been shot to death years earlier.

In 2005 I traveled with several members of my support group to Kansas City, Missouri, for the annual conference of the National Organization of Parents of Murdered Children. Alongside some three hundred other relatives and friends of those who had died by violence—founded by parents, the organization is not just for parents—we listened to keynotes from mental health professionals and law enforcement officials, and participated in workshops with titles like "How Much Did My Loved One Suffer?" and "Ask the Medical Examiner." Conference-goers had traveled from all over: Chicago, Little Rock, San Bernardino, and the Bronx. Many wore T-shirts and buttons bearing the smiling faces of their murdered children or parents, siblings or friends, and donned red rubber bracelets with the words "Someone I Love Was Murdered." I wore two bracelets. On the last night of the conference, there was a slideshow featuring photographs, names, and dates—birth and death—of those who had been killed. Those in attendance were given electronic candles, and told to switch them on when their loved one's picture appeared on-screen. There were so many victims that the slideshow went on for over an hour.

Those bimonthly dinners in Upper Manhattan and those annual conferences, held in a different American city each year, provided a rhythm to my life, and maybe even saved it, those first few years. No pressure to move on, to talk about something less of a bummer, to suppress the burgeoning gallows humor that made so many others uncomfortable. No pressure to untangle who I was from what had happened to me. These fellow travelers understood that there exists a pain so profound that it becomes embedded in your psyche, your personality, maybe even your DNA.

But grief wasn't their whole identity—they were bankers, social workers, actors, executive assistants, mothers, grand-mothers, and aunts—and they taught me that it didn't have to be mine either. We provided for each other a safe place to talk about the unspeakable, and to talk about other things and other relationships. In their company, I could acknowl-edge that some of what plagued me had existed before the murders, that some of my personality traits were heightened by the trauma but did not result from it. I may be The Girl Whose Family Was Murdered, but I was, am, and will be more than that, too—for worse, for better, and forever.

FOUR LITTLE WORDS, ONE BIG MEANING

by Michael Flamini

"I am a widower."

Those are four words I never imagined myself saying. Not at my age—not without a plane crash or a terrorist attack taking one of us out.

Instead I lost my partner, Gary Lussier, to liver disease. He was a former dancer, handsome with a wicked sense of humor and a way of embracing the world that would shame most people. He didn't get to embrace the world for long enough, though. He was fifty-two and I was fifty-three on the day I walked out of NewYork–Presbyterian Hospital/Cornell Medical Center, dazed, confused, and alone.

He died less than twenty-four hours before he might have had a successful liver transplant, slightly more than three days after I rushed him to the hospital, more than a year after his illness began to manifest itself, and about a quarter century since we had joined our lives. Even though I was well past fifty, I found myself in the I'm-too-young-for-this-to-happen category.

And of course there was another complication: I was not married to Gary, even though we had been together twenty-four and a half years. Though we had no legal document to govern it, ours was as true a union as any other. We had the emotional support of our two families and a large group of friends. I had the support of a slew of coworkers who understood what I was going through. Gary had the benefit of being

treated at a top New York hospital. And I had the rare luxury of being able to consider my place in the world free from the family legal battles that plague some spouses, the worries about the quality of care, and, given my company's health insurance, the financial concerns that can be life-shattering for those left behind. In other words, we were lucky.

In the days after his death, I began to ask myself, "What am I now?" I was no longer a "partner." I searched and searched for a word that defined me. Finally, I settled on the most obvious and yet, for me, the most problematic word: *widower*. In choosing it, I set myself the task of understanding its meaning.

I was also trying to find the courage to say it out loud.

Of course, *widower* implies "marriage," "husband," "deceased wife," and—in the past, at least—"heterosexual." We weren't married. I am gay; we referred to each other as partners. The first time I said it out loud—"I am a widower"—I was alone in my apartment. The silence was so loud, it threatened to crush me.

When that sentence broke the isolation I'd been living in, I knew I had found a word that would take me forward—but one that would provoke surprise in others.

Did he say "widower"?, I imagined people thinking at cocktail parties. "I didn't know they were married . . . ," they might say, in private, when they took off their pearls or undid their ties. Worse might come from hatemongers I didn't even know, but knew were out there. The question obsessed me: How could I call myself Gary's widower and be true about it?

For me, the ability to say "widower" came down to the question of what the word *marriage* means. We've all been taught that marriage refers to the moment when two people profess vows of love before a governmental or religious authority, rings are exchanged, documents are signed, and the couple runs off to happily-ever-after.

Then there's the Stephen Sondheim definition of marriage as "the little things you do together" in the song of the same name. We certainly had our fill of those throughout the years: not just Thanksgivings and Christmases and Easters or trips abroad or weeks on Ogunquit Beach in Maine. No, we had more than that. We had almost a quarter century of eating pizza while watching television, having dinners with friends, arguing about how best to do the laundry, having a bang-up row in public, commiserating over each other's daily work woes, and celebrating each other's triumphs. So in that way, we did indeed have a marriage. Through millions of small acts, private and public, we were life partners.

There is, though, a deeper meaning that one finds a few rungs down from the first one or two definitions of *marriage* in most dictionaries. It's a more private definition of *to marry*, one that is less concerned with ceremony and legality than with the intimacy and commitment between two people: "to take as an intimate life partner by a formal exchange of promises in the manner of a traditional marriage ceremony." Had Gary and I done that?

Over the years, every night, we said "I love you" to each other before falling asleep. Were those not exchanges of a mutual promise renewed each day? I think they were. But were they enough to pronounce us married? Did we have some deeper and more formal promise? In looking back, we did, though no clergy or justice of the peace was present.

We met when a legal marriage between two men was unthinkable. During our time together, we heard the revolution-ary roar of "We'll live together unmarried!" from both straight and gay couples. But now that marriage was actually possible, I had begun to think about how wonderful it would be to have a husband, someone to call my own, someone defined by a word that could not be mistaken for a business associate: *husband*, not *partner*. Just thinking of those words made me feel different: stronger, safer, and—in a corny way—a man in love.

When in 2011 the gay marriage law was finally passed in New York State, where we lived most of the year, we were at our weekend home in Massachusetts, where gay marriage was already legal. It was a beautiful day, and we were in the gar-den, weeding. Gary seemed to be on the mend after his initial diagnosis and treatment. I had felt a strong are-we-going-to-get-married? vibe from him since we heard the news that we now legally could. There, among the boxwoods and my gar-dening shears, I knelt on one knee and said, "Gary, will you marry me?" He was shocked. Frankly, so was I. He said, in a typically Gary way, "Well, I don't see a ring . . ." And then, to my surprise, he said, "No . . . not until you get me a ring." I was crushed. I had never asked anyone to marry me before, but there it was: "No."

Not long after that day, Gary's health began to spiral down-ward again. The incident was pushed aside by multiple hospi-tal stays, the imperfect weekly calculation of his place on the liver transplant list, the day-to-day monitoring of weight, at-home visits from medical workers, frantic expeditions to spe-cialty pharmacies, and, most wrenchingly, the ups and downs of watching the person you love most in the world become in-creasingly and dangerously ill.

My marriage proposal remained buried in our garden until about an hour before Gary began to die. He was in the ICU, his liver failing, unbeknownst to me. He was drifting in and out of consciousness. During one lucid moment, he grabbed my hand, pulled me to him, eyes wide open, staring straight into mine, and said, "I do!" with startling vehemence.

I was speechless; but since I was his chief cheerleader on the road to transplant, I said, "Oh, no, you don't. . . . We'll do this right once you get your liver." He laughed a little. If God or the idea of God has to do with love, I like to think that he or she was present when that vow was made; if true love has ever made itself manifest, it was in that moment. We finally had our formal ceremony, and I clasped his hands tightly. An hour later, the massive hemorrhage that ended his life began, and he lost all consciousness.

Months later, I told a friend that I wished I'd said, "I do, too!" and he said, "You did, on that day in your garden."

I now understand that we were, indeed, married in many ways, and so I have come to say "I am a widower" with confidence, if with little joy. It's not a nice thing to have to say. It puts people off or—even worse—makes them want to take care of you when you least need it. That statement's message is "I lost my spouse, but I am still alive. I'm standing on my own two feet and intend to go on living for as long as I can." It means you have freely given a significant part of your life to someone who is now gone, and that you are alone. It also now, thankfully, has less relationship to gender preference. As Wendy Wasserstein wrote, "Love is love. Gender is just spare parts."

How, then, do you say "I am a widower"? It has nothing to do with age. Young or old, you say it plainly, like saying "armor," knowing that nothing else can ever hurt you as much as your spouse's death. You say it in the full knowledge that the union you had with your deceased spouse was as deep and as rich and as true as any other. You say it with remembrance, and most of all, you say it with love and pride for the spouse who has passed on—that singular, unforgettable human being who taught you, truly, how to love and to be loved.

"I am a widower."

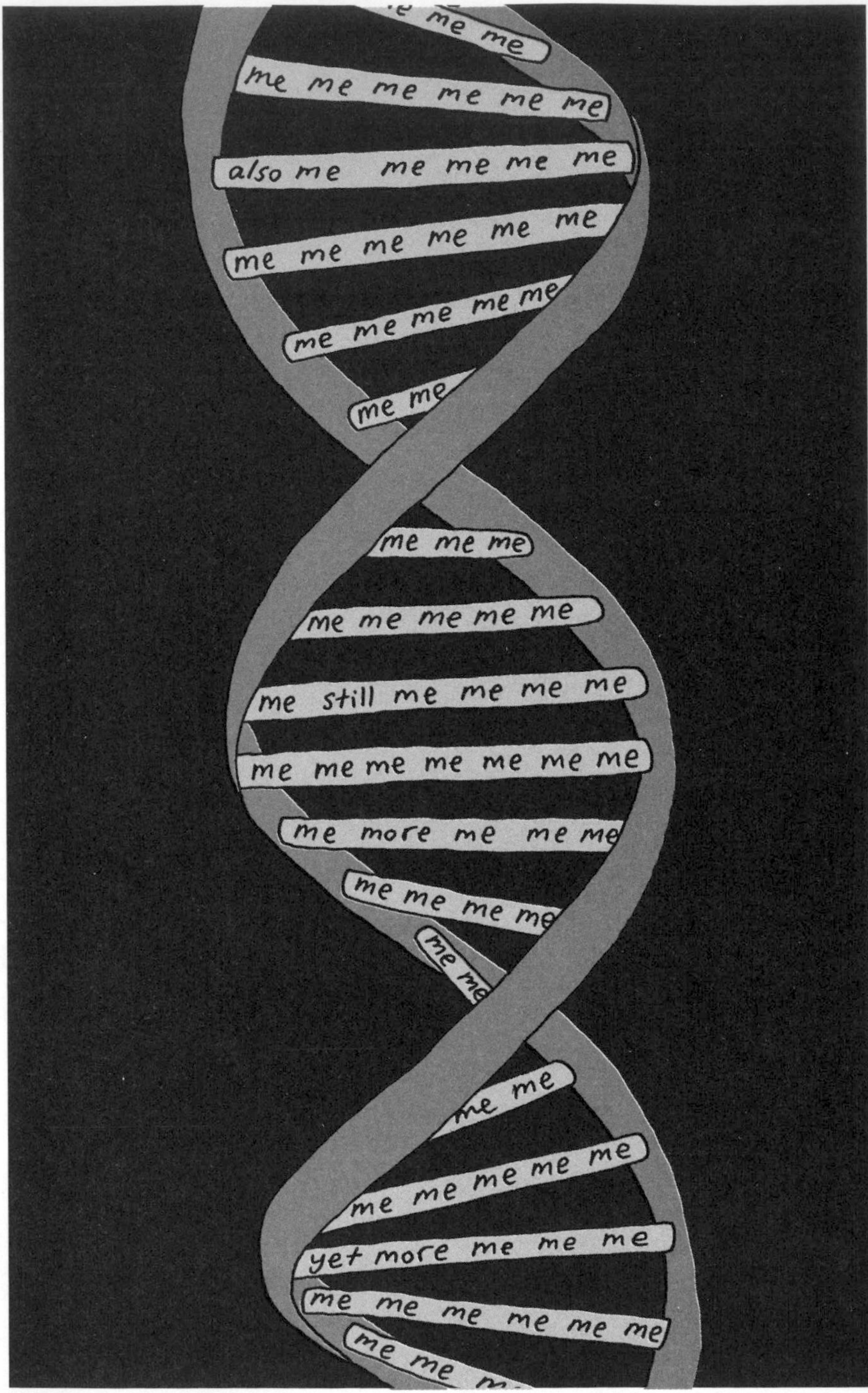
me me
me me me me me me
also me me me me me
me me me me me me
me me me me me
me me
me me me
me me me me me
me still me me me me
me me me me me me me
me more me me me
me me me me
me me
me me
me me me me me
yet more me me me
me me me me me me
me me

DAD-DIE ISSUES

by Yassir Lester

It's the middle of 2014. I don't remember the date. My phone rings.

"Hey, Yassir. It's Mom."

"How are you, Mom?"

"I'm good. But I have to tell you something."

"Okay . . ."

"Your dad is dead."

"Ha ha, makes sense."

"And he died nine years ago."

"What?"

I'll rewind.

I am the product of a single-mother household. My brother and sister and I all have different fathers, which, let me tell you, made for lots of fun answering the resulting questions in small-town Georgia. I never knew my father and never cared to find out about him either. I'd seen two pictures of him: one of him scowling through his mustache, and another of him scowling through his mustache and leaning on a red convertible. I tore up the first picture. I don't know why. It just seemed like something a person haunted by their absent father should do. It felt right in the moment but had no motivation behind it. Or maybe I'm lying to myself. Maybe that was the first time I allowed myself any sort of emotion regarding my father.

Those two pictures may be the most information I have on the man. Everything else I know about my father is informed by things he told my mom, but it's not like the dude was super honest. He claimed to work in computers. I know he was Palestinian, and the only reason I believe that is because if he weren't, Yassir would be a weird name choice for a baby. He also claimed his family was back in Saudi Arabia. I have no clue if this was true, but it did worry my mom. For a number of my grade-school years she would give my brother and sister and I passwords that people would have to say to us if someone other than she were to pick us up from somewhere. Mom was very worried about us being kidnapped by any of our fathers, which is funny because they literally wanted the opposite.

That's it. That is everything I know about my dad. Three stale, generic facts about the man that's half responsible for my being alive. If you were on a date and these were the pieces of information your guest decided to share with you, you'd immediately get up and never talk to them again because they were so boring.

So I didn't focus on having complicated feelings about an absentee dad I never met. But that's not to say I didn't take full advantage of blaming my shortcomings on not having one around the house. When I didn't make it onto the fourth-grade basketball team, I cried to my mother that if I had a dad I'd be a better player. She let me know pretty quickly that I just didn't have any dribbling skills and I should practice more, dad or not. I learned to change a tire by seeing someone else do it. I had no idea how to make a Windsor knot on a necktie, so I watched a YouTube video. YouTube could single-handedly raise the fatherless children of this country, and it probably is already doing so.

From time to time, my mother would google our fathers to

see where they were. In this particular instance she was actually looking for my sister's father, but she randomly decided to pop on over to another search and see what my dad had been up to. The answer was nothing. Because, you know, he was dead.

Here's where it all became confusing. Death brings up so many feelings, thoughts, and conversations. Plans to be made. Legacies to cement. I had none of that. To find out someone you don't know but are tied to genetically has been dead for nearly a decade, you'd think there'd be a moment of sadness or deep contemplation. Nope. Zero.

Though I'd never met my father, I'd done all the mourning and grieving I needed to growing up, whether I was conscious of it or not. I felt relief knowing he was gone. To be honest, I'd always feared he'd reach out to me, and out of sheer obligation for his half of contributing to my existence, I would have to go to lunch with him. I *hate* meeting up for lunch if I don't have to. Also, what would we talk about?

"Hey, Yassir, good to meet you."

"Good to meet you too, I guess, Dad? Should I call you that?"

"I have no idea, Yassir. I left six weeks after you were born. Anyway, have you seen *Breaking Bad*?"

The more I thought about it over the next few weeks, the more I found myself genuinely elated that my deadbeat dad was actually, you know, dead. There were questions I had growing up that went unanswered, and now that was no longer a concern. The only answer I truly needed ("Where is this dude?"), I had.

In 2014, finding myself fatherless once again, I smiled. There was no need to wonder about this nebulous father out there and what parts and traits of him I got, because it truly didn't matter anymore. I was the same person I'd been moments before I found out about his passing. And for the nine years he was dead without my knowledge. And the twenty-nine years before that where he was surfing or whatever and pretending he didn't have a child in the world.

I find that so much of who we think we are is clearly our parents. You can only live for so many years under the rules of another before you absorb some of them into yourself. As we age, we slowly turn into our parents and sometimes share their politics and religion. Laugh at the same jokes. Read the same books. My mother and I love the same music. We share a smile. There are many things we have in common. There are also many personality traits and thoughts and dreams within us that couldn't be more opposite. I used to wonder if those came from my dad. Now I like to think, "That's just me."

THE DEAD-BROTHER CODE SWITCH

by Rachel Sklar

Hello, nice to meet you. I'm the girl with the dead brother.

Ugh, was that a downer? Sorry. Let's try it again: Hello! I'm the girl with the dead brother!

Yep. Still awkward and depressing. It just hangs there, silencing everything else. Because how can you make small talk after that?

And, Lord, sometimes you just want to make small talk. Sometimes you want to say absolutely nothing of importance to people who don't know anything about you and thus have no reason to think you're anything other than, well, just a girl.

When you're the Girl with the Dead Brother, that's a nice vacation. Especially when your brother dies when you're eighteen, weeks before you graduate high school and leave behind your bereft brotherless house for university, and a new world that doesn't know you share parents with a dead person.

How did he die? you're wondering. The question hangs in the air because there are so many awful possibilities, and it's impossible for your mind not to leap to that question immediately, even if you're too polite to ask. So fine, I'll go there. I found him in the garage on a sunny Sunday afternoon in May, sitting in the front seat of his car. There were two cars in the garage. Both were running.

It's not natural for a young person to die. It's a tragedy. It's wrong. It upends everything you know, everything you rely

on and take for granted. The world is not safe. Your family is not forever. People end.

And when a young person dies, it's news. Everyone knows. And when it's your brother who dies, leaving behind you and your sister—his twin—it's everyone you've ever known, because you all lived with your parents in the house you all grew up in, around the corner from the public school you all went to and the park you all played in. So many people got to the shiva on foot, not because they were religious but because they were five minutes away on Banbury and Sandfield and Sagewood and Tanbark and Cheval. We were on Bamboo. You knew which house it was by all the kids spilling out over the lawn. If you'd added red Solo cups, it would have looked like a fairly decent party.

My family didn't talk about things like "identity," but ours had shifted dramatically. And publicly. Our nice happy nuclear family was now grotesquely abridged. And everyone knew it. Suicide has an extra dark, heavy layer of awfulness to it, because there's the unavoidable question: Why? Not the unanswerable, inscrutable *why* of "Why me? Why her? Why him? Why us?" that accompanies tragedy that comes without agency. It's the perfectly reasonable question of "But why did he do it?" with a hefty side of "Who missed the signs?" "Who said the wrong thing?" and "Who ought to have known?" It's the unavoidable undercurrent of blame.

Fair or not, guilt and shame are part of the package, bundled in like some lower-tier movie channel that you end up getting because you already pay for HBO. That car crash . . . that tumor . . . that freak accident—if no one could predict it, then no one could stop it. But suicide is different, because surely those closest to him ought to have known. Right . . . right?

Girl with the Dead Brother had extra oomph as Girl with the Dead Brother Who Killed Himself, and all the bundled assumptions that went with it.

So, man, did it feel good to meet people who had no clue about any of it.

My university was two hours away and a big feeder school from my community, so it had the best of both worlds: the support system of people who knew of my bereavement, and the wide, anonymous beyond filled with the sweet blankness of people who didn't. I was able to code-switch back and forth from Dead Brother Girl to Student Paper Girl, Student Council Girl, Debating Club Girl, and, yes, Frosh Fifteen Girl.

The transition wasn't seamless. Wherever I was, *I* always knew that I had once had a brother, and now he was gone. That year was a rocky, muddy, unwieldy one as I grappled with all the usual college issues (friends! boys! grades!) along with my own delightful cocktail (grief! guilt! shame!). Anonymity can cut both ways. It is profoundly alienating to be surrounded by sloshy drunk people as inside your head is blaring *Wait! Stop! How can you party when my brother's dead?* and even more alienating when alongside that thought you can't also help but think, *Does this toga make me look fat?*

(News flash: togas make everyone look fat. It's a bedsheet. Even the fitted ones only fit beds.)

News spreads, so sometimes my reputation preceded me. One hot summer night on a sceney roof deck with friends, I was all big hair cascading down over my favorite red-wine stretchy top, letting some guy chat me up—because why not.

It wasn't going to happen, but the attention was nice, and I was still learning how to talk to people I didn't know in bars.

Perhaps he sensed I was unimpressed, because suddenly he leaned in for the kill. "I know who you are," he said, shifting closer. "I know about your brother. I'm here if you want to talk."

My face flamed red. I felt like I'd been caught, my cover blown, my carefree alter ego unmasked. He'd changed the game from casual to serious, looking to bond over the emotional response he'd demanded from me. I felt like it was my obligation to respond—he'd asked, it would have been rude not to—and so I answered this random person's questions about finding my brother dead in the garage, while around me the carefree rooftop people enjoyed their carefree night.

As I branched out further from the community where I was known, that sort of thing happened less. I moved through college and then law school and then moved to New York (aka the biggest toga party in the world), and I figured something out: as you grow up into an adult, no one knows your baggage unless you share it.

If you weren't the one who died, then you eventually have to figure out how to keep living. And part of that is figuring out what kind of access you want others to have. They're not invited into the shower with you in the morning, and they're not invited into how much money you have in your bank account, so why should they know about your life? Even if the question seems innocuous, if they ask "Do you have any brothers or sisters?" you don't owe anyone that answer. You get to decide. Sometimes that feels great. Sometimes that feels lousy. But you are allowed to put yourself first. That is the privilege of the living.

But it is not an absolute privilege. That's why you haven't heard about the rest of my family. (Obviously I can't out myself as a bereaved person without outing them to anyone who knows us, but what they decide to share is up to them.) But anything you need to know about my family is contained in that one sentence: "If you weren't the one who died, then you eventually have to figure out how to keep living." It's been twenty-five years. We're here, we're together. Life is good, even and still and despite.

Life is great, actually. Because recently I had a baby. She is an amazing and miraculous gift—she would be anyway, but I'm a single mom, so my nuclear family is her nuclear family. When my brother died, he turned us from a family of five into a family of four. Now, twenty-five years later, she's turned our family of four into a family of five.

She is named for him, of course. When people ask about her name, I don't always share its provenance. *She's named for my dead brother. No pressure!* The "no pressure" part will be up to me—because now I'm not just the girl with the dead brother, I'm the mom of the girl with the dead uncle.

As I write this, I am exactly two decades older than my brother was when he died. If I met him now, I would think he was a kid. (Though for the record: a tall, handsome, smart, funny, kind, wonderful, earnest, generous, loving, awesome kid.) But I can only think of him as my older, wiser, sagacious elder, especially since I know he would love me using *sagacious* because he loved words like that. I still wonder what he'd do, imagine what he'd say, and try to do him proud.

I still know a whole lot of the people who spilled out over our lawn at that shiva twenty-five years ago. I see them on

Facebook or at weddings and bat mitzvahs or randomly on the street when I take my daughter back home for a visit. And wouldn't you know—anonymity is nice, but introducing my daughter to people who knew her uncle is even nicer.

They don't need to ask where she got her name, because they know his.

MAKING PEACE WITH MY MOTHER'S WHITENESS

by Amy Mihyang Ginther

In the fourth grade, a boy in my class called me the N-word. I was pretty confused, since I am Korean American. My mom, she wasn't confused; she marched into the principal's office to stick up for me and to demand that my school take appropriate action. Mom was a warrior when it came to her transracially adopted children.

After she died of lung cancer in August 2008, I moved to Seoul to teach English and reconnect with my biological family, and I was eager to become involved in the city's vibrant Korean adoptee community. There I met others who had grown up in the West but were now creating lives for themselves in the country of their birth—marrying Korean nationals and raising families, opening small businesses like bakeries, and politically organizing for adult adoptees who wanted access to their records.

Only in Seoul did I realize how unusual my upbringing was. Sure, I grew up in a predominantly white town in upstate New York, but there were other Korean American adoptees in my hometown. By contrast, many of those I met in Seoul had grown up in complete racial isolation in the United States or in "progressive" European countries like Denmark, France, and Germany. As we exchanged stories, I realized that my mother was unlike many of the others' white adoptive mothers, who were often remembered as insecure about their fertility, their identity, and their transracial relationship to their children.

I met adoptees who settled in Korea for personal reasons: the chance to live abroad, or the opportunity to connect with their biological family. I also met those who were doing so for political reasons: rejecting outright their life and families in their adopted countries. Some of them were estranged from their adoptive parents. In Seoul, I joined an adoptee-led reading group, and what emerged was a macro view of Korean adoption that centered around forces of misogyny, poverty, religion, neocolonialism, and racism. It was a dramatic departure from the more sentimental, mainstream narrative that adoption is an individual act of altruism.

This dynamic may place adoptees at odds with their adoptive parents, many of them unwilling to wrestle with the idea that their sons and daughters may have been unnecessarily separated from their first families. Tensions are often played out and examined at adoption conferences between adoptees, adoptive parents, and those who work in adoption and post-adoption services, in Facebook groups, on Twitter, and in other comment threads online.

As I began to engage in these spaces, I felt increasing pressure to reject not only white adoptive parents as a group but also my own parents, very specifically. But my body was still full of grief, my brain and heart so consumed that I was physically exhausted and experiencing short-term memory loss. I had just bathed my mom's brittle body, fed her ice chips, and watched her last, shuttered breaths escape from her chest.

I began to draw on my years of training as an actor, and how I've learned to make space in my body for contradictory sensations and experiences. I thought about this a lot in relation to adoption—refusing to accept a binary that pits adoptive parents like my mother against emancipated or radical adoptees. So I have created room for my ideologies, the social justice work that I do, and my love for my mom to coexist. I feel her sense of pride when I am my authentic self in my teaching, my performance, and within adoptee spaces. I can see my mom as part of an oppressive force, but it does not diminish my admiration for her. Nor does it lessen my grief.

I realize that the type of person my mom was makes it easier to justify this. She would remind us that families would come in all shapes and sizes, and she would vehemently correct strangers when they assumed we were Chinese or Japanese. When people would gush at how lucky I was to be adopted, she would insist, "No, *we're* the lucky ones." When the bullying in kindergarten began, we approached my teacher about coeducating my classmates about Korea and my adoption. I was too young to realize that she was acting as an ally, empowering me to be the authority of my own adopted identity.

Others have watched their white friends and family grow defensive when we bring up issues like transracial adoption, white privilege, the exclusive nature of white feminism, and cultural appropriation in pop culture. My mom's belief in me made me exactly the type of person to fight for the right to be heard. And I choose to believe that, had she lived, she would continue to support the work that I'm doing, no matter how uncomfortable it may have made her.

JUST SAY UNCLE

by Michael Arceneaux

"Fuck that faggot."

My dad was in the midst of one of his drunken stupors. The kind that went on and on into the night until he finally decided to shut the fuck up, go to bed, and actually stay there.

My dad is maybe five-eight on his tippy toes, 170 pounds dripping wet, but he is the living embodiment of a Twitter tantrum thrown by Chris Brown. He has his moments, but he's not exactly a ray of sunshine and has never had any qualms about sharing his anger—no matter if it comes at the expense of your sanity.

Per usual, my mama made sure to try and negate everything that had just flown out of my dad's mouth. "Don't listen to him, Michael. Daniel wasn't gay."

Yet most of the things I learned about my parents and other family members came from one of my pops's drunken rants.

My mother was the one who explained my uncle Daniel's death to me, when I was six. She told me he died of something called AIDS. Or, in kid-friendlier terms, he was gone from this place and relocated to heaven. Jesus was there. Ideally, you want to die and be able to kick it with Jesus or something.

My sole memory of Uncle Daniel is his funeral mass at St. Francis Xavier. There, inside a quaint Catholic church on the south side of Houston, I accompanied my mother to the front of the altar and started to sob hysterically after looking into Daniel's open casket. I was six, and there was his dead body lying in some box. It seemed like the appropriate thing to do given the occasion.

I learned what a faggot was in the days following the funeral.

"Faggot!"

"Faggot!"

"Faggot!"

And on and on my dad went about what a faggot his dead brother was. How sick he was as a man to lie down with another man. That only punks loved the way he did. Why his death was his fault. It wouldn't be until years later that I learned that Daniel was not only a gay man but also a heroin addict. Now, my father has his own battles with addiction, as do some of his other brothers. But Daniel's greatest offense was bigger than drugs; it was about who he had sex with.

I was a child who inherently knew there was something different about me. And Daniel's death birthed a paranoia that followed me well into adulthood, because it was the moment I realized I was a faggot. It was the moment I saw that I was different, and that the consequences of that could be harsh.

Daniel died not long after I had finished kindergarten and started noticing that I had far more fun with boys—especially during naptime, when I could never nap—than I ever did with girls. Imagine a child who liked touching boys in "funny" places below their waists learning that men who like other men can die from that attraction. Imagine learning at such a young age that you are less than the others who liked the opposite sex; that you are worthy of being despised; that not even familial ties can spare you from the disdain your purported deviancy has earned you.

Obviously, sex is supposed to be about joy, and most learn that through time and experience. But I only knew sex in terms of reproduction for straight people, and certain death for many others. Sex became tainted to me years before my hormones ever kicked in—and once they did, I felt conflict, repulsion, and fear. I shied away from sex into my twenties, and when I lost my virginity, I did so with shame. There have been times when I went into a panic after a sexual act, falsely believing that I hadn't been as safe as I should've been. You could have put me in a full-body condom, and still I might've told you that it wasn't enough.

Even brief moments of pleasure were erased by the memory of my dead gay uncle in a casket. I hesitated to embrace any facet of myself that constituted being gay: the sound of my speaking voice, which sat higher than those of most boys around me and could easily translate to sissy. Or the way that I danced, which screamed feminine and gay-gay-gay. I still remember the day someone said I "danced like a faggot." It was meant as a compliment, but all it did was trigger my anxiety about being marginalized the way my uncle was or mocked like the caricatures of gay men I saw on TV shows like *In Living Color.*

When I was twenty-one, I finally decided that I couldn't keep fighting a losing battle. It was not about how my parents would react. I didn't care if some of my friends did not understand. I needed to stop running from the truth. I was tired of forcing myself to feel an attraction that never felt as natural or rewarding as the one that had long been innate. I was tired because I traveled thousands of miles away from home to effectively start over, only to make the same mistakes as my parents and those around me: keeping secrets, denying the obvious, and bottling up emotions. I was tired because I knew my life deserved more than tiptoeing around a closet. People have always acknowledged my honesty. But what kind of honest person lies about his very core?

Once I did come out to myself, I didn't miraculously become a much more secure person—it happened little by little. I learned to accept the things about myself that I could not change. I accepted that the things that bothered me most about myself were not worthy of my shame. I realized that the people who projected their prejudices onto me had their own shortcomings.

I've only discussed my sexuality once with my father. He asked if I was "funny," and at the time, resentment wouldn't allow me to share any private part of myself with him. I knew that he knew, but I also understood that not admitting it directly would hurt him more. So I didn't answer. He never asked me directly again. Years later, I found out from my sister that he actually defended me to other relatives, saying that he just wanted me to be happy. Our relationship is complicated beyond my sexual orientation, but I have learned forgiveness—and I do know that in this instance, saying that he loves me and wants me to be happy is the best he can do. I accept it. My mother still struggles with it for religious reasons, but at this point, that is no longer my concern. She listens to Jesus; I dance with boys to Beyoncé.

Now I'm in my thirties, and I've mostly conquered my fears. I've made peace with the reality that HIV is not a death sentence. I dance often and gleefully. I don't care how my voice may sound to others; I know that what I say is what matters most. I do not allow myself to be bound by anyone else's pre-conceived notions about who I am and what that means.

I simply define myself as I see fit.

I am the gay uncle to two beautiful nieces. I have made sure that the ignorance of my parents has not carried over to them. They do not fear for my life—they're just happy that I am fully living it. I am not a faggot to them. I am Uncle Mikey, who they want to be happy with another boy. Uncle Mikey is just Uncle Mikey. Not an abomination. Not a victim. Not someone who has to hide who he is.

I may not have really known Daniel, but in every area of my life, I try to live for him and for those who never had the chance to exist exactly as they are without burden. I don't know where he is now, but I hope I have made him happy for how I've done it.

SURVIVOR GILT

Creative ways to use what's left behind instead of banishing it to storage purgatory.

By Stacy London

Grief isn't tidy. But it can be innovative and transformative. It's OK to not deal with "things" right away. Time and distance bring new ideas for honoring someone's memory through material items.

Wear anything that's your personal style as is. Make other objects work for you, or recreate them into something completely different. Take your time. You'll know when you're ready to dive in.

Some work best in their natural state:

The 70s are always in!

- TRY ON THE CLASSICS BEFORE DOING ANYTHING DRASTIC. NINE TIMES OUT OF TEN, THEY'LL COME BACK INTO STYLE.

Store things the right way:

- REGULAR PLASTIC BAGS DEGRADE SILK, FUR, OR WOOL GARMENTS OVER TIME.
- CASUAL CLOTHES GO INTO BAGS THAT SUCK EVERYTHING FLAT. NICER STUFF? BREATHABLE GARMENT BAGS INSIDE A PLASTIC BIN.
- REPEAT AFTER ME: <u>NO CARDBOARD BOXES</u> (UNLESS YOU WANT PET WATER BUGS AND ROACHES).

Consider all your senses when it comes to keepsakes:

- SMELLS CAN BE A POWERFUL MEMORY TRIGGER. WHEN YOU'RE REALLY MISSING GRANDMA, TAKE THE SWEATER SHE KNIT THAT SMELLS LIKE HER OUT OF AN AIRTIGHT ZIPLOCK BAG AND WRAP YOURSELF UP.

- BACK UP IMPORTANT VOICEMAILS.

Hi, it's dad. Just calling to say...

- FRAME A FAVORITE RECIPE. MAKE IT ONCE A MONTH. IF YOU DON'T COOK, MAKE IT TOGETHER WITH A FRIEND WHO DOES.

DAD'S SIMPLE SHEPHERD'S PIE

Don't be scared to wear the damn jewelry:

- NOTHING GOOD EVER CAME FROM LEAVING A DIAMOND NECKLACE IN A DARK BOX. PIECES FALL OUT AND CAN BE REPLACED. LET YOURSELF TRULY ENJOY WEARING SOMETHING FROM THE PERSON WHO LEFT IT FOR YOU.

- ARE YOU A TINY PERSON WITH AN OUTRAGEOUS COCKTAIL RING? TAKE IT FOR A TEST RUN. YOU NEVER KNOW.

- CAN'T STAND A VALUABLE ITEM? MELT IT DOWN AND CREATE SOMETHING ELSE.

Fabulous, darling!

Repurpose and reinterpret:

Sometimes things just need a hem. Other times, it's clear they just weren't meant for you to wear. In that case, completely change the piece. Its legacy lives on. You're just giving it a new life.

- CONSTRUCTIVE AND CONSCIOUS TAILORING CAN MAKE SOMETHING USABLE AND MODERN.

- GIVE AN OLD ACCESSORY A NEW ROLE.

- REPLACE PARTS.

DYE

Make some art:

- CONVERT SHOES INTO BRONZED BOOKENDS.

- DISPLAY KEEPSAKES ON A WALL.

- TURN YOUR DAD'S OLD T-SHIRTS INTO A QUILT OR PILLOW.

- REPAINT FURNITURE IN A BRIGHT NEW COLOR.

- SEW LEATHER GLOVE PIECES INTO A PATCHWORK DESIGN ON A CANVAS BAG.

INHERITANCE

Property Of:

INTRODUCTION

by Rebecca Soffer

According to family lore, my dad fell in love with my mom the moment they met, in the summer of 1972, when she interviewed for a temp clerical job at his advertising agency. (He didn't hire her, claiming later she'd have been an awful secretary.) He'd missed the mark in his first two marriages, which resulted in three sons much older than me, but with my mom he finally figured out married life. They spent thirty-five years together traveling the world, amassing a huge network of friends, and embarrassing me throughout my adolescence by happily dancing cheek to cheek whenever we passed a sax player in Rittenhouse Square.

My dad was deeply traumatized for months after losing the love of his life in a sudden and violent accident. And so, of course, was I. During that time, neither of us could bring ourselves to go through her belongings. This was my first encounter with the many knots that form with all the stuff, trivial and critical, sentimental and surprising, valuable and not, that loved ones leave behind.

My mom's closet, a place where I once made gleeful discoveries of things like her ivory-leather jewelry case and red disco-era stilettos, became a place where everything was for the taking, and yet none of it seemed okay to have without her. Instead I left it all intact and became chief curator of the Museum of Shelby. I lovingly preserved hundreds of her items as though they were ancient Greek artifacts. Her registration form for a beginner's bridge class she'd repeated at least five times. The soft pink bathrobe with one unused Kleenex in the right-hand pocket, which I stored in my closet and would later wrap myself in whenever I just couldn't even. And the bar of glycerin soap my cousin gave her one December that proclaimed FUCK in suspended multicolored letters, an object that sparked the family exclamation "Fucksoap!" when life got tough.

Clutter, maybe. But clutter that mattered.

As the only daughter, I was automatically charged with dealing with the "female" stuff like clothes and shoes and personal papers. I didn't have unilateral rights to things like furniture, artwork, and decorations. But I wasn't even thinking about those at the time. My dad was still living in their place, and I wasn't about to start cherry-picking his life apart. More important, my mother in her will simply left everything to him. She was years younger and never thought she'd go first.* I just assumed that sometime, far in the future, we'd work it all out. But reading his will four years later, I was crestfallen to discover his seemingly cruel plan to distribute my mother's items after he died.

But my dad wasn't a cruel person. He was witty and fun. He taught me to love Mel Brooks, tie the pile hitch of a boat dock, and pitch a no-hitter in my middle-school softball games. He revealed the beauty of the best water ice† flavor combination: chocolate on the bottom and cherry on top. My dad wove grandiose bedtime tales about Marvin the Moon Man, took me to see Fred Savage host *Saturday Night Live*, and hired more

---

* If you take anything helpful from this story: FOR THE LOVE OF GOD, WRITE YOUR WILL (AND PUT THOUGHT INTO IT).

† A Philly-style dessert that is thicker than a slushy but thinner than a sno-cone. Oh, and a million times better than Italian ice.

women than men because he knew we're just better. But as someone who grew up poor in West Philadelphia and relied on smarts and charisma to found an international ad firm in spite of having no higher education, he was also a survivor. And one of his survival tactics, especially after my mother's death, was to tell people what they wanted to hear so that he didn't have to deal with the discomfort of their true reactions.

The result: in some cases, we were each promised the same items, which held equal meaningful value to everyone.

Somebody get the fucksoap.

So, after my dad died, what happened to the item I wanted most, the Saarinen womb chair my mother had told me she spent so many comfortable hours in while pregnant with me? Dad left it to one of my brothers. When I asked that brother if he'd consider selling it to me, he claimed a superior sentimental attachment to the chair because our dad and his mom, my dad's first wife, bought it as a couple. And the dreamy painting of four moon cycles that I associated with my dad's magical bedtime stories? I had to make an actual written case for why I wanted it.

All this bargaining was made worse by communication "facilitated" through estate executors and spreadsheets listing the estimated value of each item. This dickering dragged on for more than a year, and it was nauseating. My siblings and I weren't overtly nasty to each other, but we weren't overtly kind. "Be nice to each other," my father warned us all in his will, "or I will haunt you." It was meant to make us smile, but every day it felt more and more like he really was haunting me through his choices—his choice not to choose, mostly, and to let us duke it out ourselves.

Now, it wasn't as if we were dividing up oil fields. This was suburban Philly, not fucking *Dynasty*. In the year after my dad's death I stress-lost ten pounds but regained about a ton in *stuff*; a fruitless bid to make up for my parents' inability to take my unborn kids on camping trips or for weekends down the shore. Did I really need five side tables? Or the ten-by-twelve-foot Persian rug that now blocks the entry to our boiler room because that's the only place we could roll it up and cram it?

My breaking point came over a valuable work of art, a piece I'd been mesmerized by for as long as I could remember. I'd wanted to hand it down to my own children, and supposedly so did my dad, because he once told me so. Yet its fate came down to one word in the will: "Negotiate." My brothers and I argued over whether it should be appraised, who'd appraise it, and whether said appraisal was valid. We argued over whether to sell it or whether one should buy out the others. When all of them, one of whom lives in South Africa, proposed to "keep it in the family" by *literally rotating it from person to person each quarter,** I knew I was done. My father was haunting me, all right, and would do so as long as I obsessed over this process. I felt as though I were en route to a pre-forty heart attack, losing my marriage, or both.

As for my husband, he was desperate for any topic other than the nightly episode of "Can You *Believe* This Happened? No, Really, *Can You?*" He also wasn't thrilled about collecting an increasing number of items that would force us to basically replicate my childhood home.

And so I said "Fuck it," and let it go. A painting, a chair . . . whatever I'd get, I'd get.† And I'd stop fighting for what I didn't.

---

*   Hi, never do this.

†   It did not include the painting.

After the material and financial aspects were settled, I had time to grapple with other sticky wickets in the world of inheritance, ones that are far more nebulous than grabbing a lamp. Suddenly I was the keeper of my parents' private lives, their friendships, and their memories. My own sense of self was forever changed.

For instance, one of my mom's friends sent me hundreds of e-mails chronicling twenty years of their relationship. I wondered if reading them would change my image of her, or if she'd feel violated if she knew I'd done so. Late one night I sifted through a few of them, and soon felt a deep ache in my throat while learning the details of her heartbreak after my grandmom's death, and the demoralization that set in when, after she'd committed to a diet for several months (one I didn't think she needed), her newly menopausal body couldn't manage to lose one pound. If only I'd known then, and had been able to comfort her.

Then came my parents' enormous global community of friends. I inherited them all. I saved address books, added their e-mails to my contact list, and resolved to keep all these lovely people in my life. Soon I realized that just because my parents had a lot to say to them, it didn't mean I did. But over time, with distance from my rawest moments, I've found common ground with some of my parents' closest friends. One threw me an engagement party in San Francisco. Another came to my son Noah's first birthday party in New York. Another has become a professional mentor.

As my parents' only child together, I also inherited the role of family historian. I'm the one who must retain every single detail about everything and pass that on to my children. What if I forget some anecdote that best illustrates my parents' personalities, or a piece of our heritage, or some detail holding the key to a future puzzle regarding my or my kids' health? ("I have no idea if my mother had extreme acid reflux as a baby!" I screamed at my pediatrician, while holding a newborn whose spit-up scenes were straight out of *The Exorcist*.) It's a struggle not to buckle under that pressure, which admittedly I put on myself.

All in all, inheritance is a stern mistress. But when you think all is said and done, it also doles out joyful serendipity.

I got a call six years after my dad's death. A decade-old lawsuit he'd filed against a hotel client in Ocean City, New Jersey, had finally been settled. The payout was a joke, but I also received $1,200 in hotel vouchers, printed out on mint-green paper. I booked a room for the following weekend.

The hotel itself was a craphole. But Justin, Noah, and I spent that September weekend running up and down the boardwalk, riding the Ferris wheel at Gillian's Wonderland Pier, and becoming poster children for the "If you fry it, we'll eat it" ethos. At preschool drop-off the following Monday, Justin texted me a photo of Noah building a long, intricate row of wooden blocks. "He's building a boardwalk," he texted. "Not my idea."

Looks like my parents sent Noah on that memorable beach vacation after all.

ICKY POP

by Sara Faith Alterman

I went through a fairly serious *Law & Order* phase when I was twenty-two, living in Myrtle Beach and working as a bartender at an Applebee's. I felt sad and underwhelmed by my own existence, so when I wasn't slinging frozen mudslides in a spattered green polo shirt, I was home in bed, eating soggy chicken wings and binge-watching crime procedural marathons. I remember one episode wherein a bunch of WASPy, pearl-clutching mourners gathered in a lawyer's office for a reading of a patriarch's will. One of the sons learns he's been iced out of an inheritance, and as he's hulking out, the scene cuts to commercial with the show's signature *dunh-dunh*.

At that point I hadn't yet considered that my parents might die one day, and I wondered if *they* had a will, and if when they died, *I* was supposed to go to a lawyer's office with my brother and aunts and uncles and whoever to find out how much money I was getting, and whether I'd need to either commit or protect myself from a murder.

TV was my best friend for much of my twenties, probably because up until then I wasn't really allowed to watch much of it. My New Englander parents weren't cruel or conservative or religious fanatics. They just wanted to keep my brother and me as wholesome as possible for as long as possible, to shield us from the smut and the creeps of the world—which apparently included Jon Bon Jovi, as I learned when my mother refused to buy me a *Slippery When Wet* cassette. It

was an interesting parenting choice, when you consider that my father was a pornographer.

A jokey pornographer, I should say. In the 1970s he penned a collection of novelty adult books that leaned heavily on double entendre, buxom cartoons, and groaner puns. Those books, they are my inheritance. Because while my friends' dead parents passed on pianos, homes, heirloom jewelry, and retirement savings, my father left me his catalog of body- and slut-shaming works, including his all-time best seller: a large-format paperback called *Games You Can Play with Your Pussy*.

I discovered Dad's books when I was in middle school. Since my parents' efforts to protect me from the world only made me more curious about it, whenever they left the house I'd rummage through drawers and cabinets in search of anything and everything more interesting than my Herself the Elf LPs. One afternoon I scaled the built-in bookcase in our living room, which we called the Duck Room because of its all-encompassing mallard-themed decor, and jackpot: a bunch of paperbacks jammed together in a corner, stuck behind an encyclopedia. I opened *Games You Can Play with Your Pussy*, with its cartoon cat cover, expecting comic strips; so I was super confused to find chapters with titles like "How to Clean Your Pussy" and "How to Care for a Sick Pussy."

The rest of the books were a series, all featuring the same main character, Bridget, who was brunette, apple-cheeked, and very, very large. And that was the "jokey" part, I guess, the idea that a fat woman could be sexy. In one story, Bridget is tied up by her landlord and tickled. In another, she goes for a job interview at a lollipop factory and has to get down on her knees to show the hiring manager how good she is at sucking.

When I heard the garage door rumble—my parents were home now—I scrambled to put the books back on the top shelf. As I did, I noticed that right below the title of the books was "by Ira Alterman." My dad.

It was hard to understand, because my father was not a creep. He was a kind and sweet man who'd had a good run of authoring ye olde porno rags, as you do in your twenties, I guess, and he gave it up when I was born. He had a vanilla corporate job at the same company for thirty-plus years. We played soccer in the yard and drank cartons of chocolate milk together whenever he drove me home from ballet class. These books, which I returned to many times over the years, taught me about sex, and I'm ashamed to say, they turned me on.

We never, ever talked about it.

Which is why it was so strange when, decades later, Dad called to say that he'd lost his job, and he was going to start writing his books again.

"What books, Dad?" I asked, pretending.

I spent the following year fielding bizarre sexual material from Dad. Rambling e-mails about sex positions, links to images of entangled body parts, printouts of new manuscripts with titles like *The Naughty Bride: An Indecent Wedding Night Guide* that he expected me, now a professional writer, to critique and refine and help him market. It was wildly out of character.

Dad was diagnosed with early-onset Alzheimer's a few months later. His doctor told me that Dad would probably start saying and doing inappropriate things, that I shouldn't take it personally because it's just a hallmark of the disease.

We only talked about it once, in a moment of clarity, when

he confessed he didn't have any money and was terrified of leaving the family with nothing when he died. He needed to revive his writing career, he told me, because he didn't have anything else of value to leave as an inheritance, just the copyrights to his books. "Don't worry about leaving me anything, Dad," I'd begged. "Just don't leave."

But he did leave, two days after his seventieth birthday. And now I'm left with a cardboard box of Dad's books. They're currently nestled above the hanging rod in my baby boy's closet, next to outgrown baby shoes, battery-powered toys that tinkle that sort of horror-film kiddie music, and another box filled with broken Christmas ornaments.

The irony of this "inheritance" is that it's worthless in every sense. The books hold no financial value, and they don't add anything to the greater cultural, literary, or sexual discourse. There's no sentimental value for me. The only sentiment I feel is: Ew. I suppose, in that sense, Dad's crippling fear about leaving me with nothing of value came to pass.

I'm not sure of my next move, or if I even need to make one. Copyrights eventually expire; unpublished works can stay forever so. I do need to move the books a little farther out of reach of the baby, who is growing at lightning speed into a nimble little boy who will no doubt climb every climbable surface in our house. I'm not hiding the books to protect my son from smut or creeps or from seeing naked women, though. I'm just not ready to have the proverbial birds-and-lollipops conversation. But there *will* eventually be conversations—about sex and consent and the strength and beauty of the female form in every shape and size. Even though my inheritance is a pussy, I'm not.

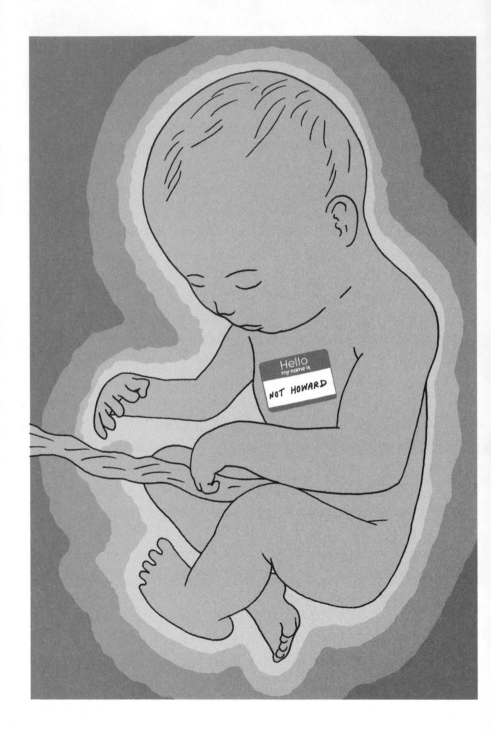

HONEY, DON'T SCREW UP
THE NAMESAKE

by David Sax

"How about Henry?"

"Too popular."

"Hugo?"

"It reminds me of Hugo Chávez. What about Hadley?"

"Ugh, it sounds like a line of outdoor furniture from Maine. Here, look at the list, what's wrong with these: Haim? Hiroshi? Hardeep? Huxford?" I turned to my wife with a cautious smile and a deep Japanese bow. "How about that, Hiroshi Sax?"

We were deep into the second trimester of pregnancy when the question of naming our unborn child of undetermined sex really began gathering steam. Other friends who were pregnant at the same time had already locked down their top three choices, like an NBA team securing draft picks, while we were floating along toward B-Day without so much as a single decent option. Our situation wasn't that different from many other expectant couples, but we both felt the added pressure of legacy, which made the search both easier and vastly more complicated.

My wife's father, Howard, had passed away two years earlier. He was sick at our wedding and died, at age fifty-nine, a week before our first anniversary. Howard was a larger-than-life figure: an exceedingly kind and generous man, an eccentric hippie who greeted strangers with hugs and lectures on alternate consciousness. His death was the first outside of elderly grandparents in both of our immediate families, and now, with his inaugural grandchild growing inside my wife, the expectations our baby had to fill were substantial.

"Are you in there, Howie?" my sister-in-law asked into my wife's belly, the first time she came over after hearing the news. Her brother, who had become more religious since his father's death, referred to the baby as the *neshama*, Hebrew for soul. There was talk of the baby healing the family's wounds, of the circle of life looping around, and even a few open suggestions that the baby was Howard's reincarnation. Before our fetus even developed bones, it was tasked with delivering my relatives from the burden of their grief. No pressure.

At first, we thought the task of honoring Howard would make naming the baby easier. After all, we had automatically winnowed down our potential choices from twenty-six letters to one, streamlining the process and saving months of fruitless list making. But as we flipped through the baby name books and websites and clicked on the custom name-picking software my wife had bought, we soon realized that honoring Howard in the Jewish tradition of naming a baby after a deceased loved one was going to be trickier than we thought.

H is not an easy letter for names. It offers great options if you are Indian or Japanese, but for two contemporary Jews, it offers a choice between the ultrabiblical (Hadassah, Hepzibah, Hulda) or new-aged bubbly (Happy, Harmony, Holiday). We'd toss these names out into the air, jokingly addressing the baby with each one, asking it to kick if it liked Hadley or stay silent if it objected to being called Helga. Unfortunately, the kicks always came late at night, when my wife was trying to sleep. This baby wasn't playing the name game. After a month of this, we realized we were getting nowhere. In the meantime, the heat was on: as the due date approached, relatives, friends, and even barely familiar acquaintances seemed to pester us increasingly about whether we had a name picked out.

"We've got some ideas," we'd say, with a smile, as a cold panic shot down our spines.

During those long, frustrating nights, as we circled round and round the same selections, I wished we were part of a culture where the naming process was automatic, like Anglo-Saxons ("Howard Jr. is off playing cricket, can I take a message?"). We toyed with the idea of just coming out and naming the baby Howard if he was a boy, but then my wife realized a second later that calling her father's name out to someone suckling at her breast, or crapping on her floor, was going to make life unreasonably awkward.

After months of frustration, we slowly moved away from H for the first name, vowing instead to honor Howard with a middle name. It was liberating. Now there were twenty-five other letters to choose from. We began focusing on names we wanted, names that would reflect who he was rather than what he was called. Eventually, my wife found one she liked: Noa. She was a biblical character who is regarded as one of the first feminists, and Howard had always insisted that his daughters get equal treatment and opportunity in this world, especially in their religion. Her middle name would be a riff on Howard's Hebrew name.

Luckily the baby was a girl. Because if we had a boy, he probably would have been called Hiroshi.

And when little Noa came out, wriggling and screaming,

my wife's family did indeed seem to find some sort of peace with their loss. The baby brought them immense joy, but all the talk of reincarnation, of her embodying Howard's soul, of Noa acting as his living legacy, quickly faded away. She was her own person, they realized, descended from Howard and hopefully embodying his best qualities, but she would grow into her name, just as she grew into herself.

A year later, Kate Middleton gave birth to her royal son. "It's a boy!" I yelled downstairs to my wife, who was awaiting the news.

"That's good," she said. "At least they don't have to name it Diana."

THE ACCIDENTAL ARCHIVIST

by Spencer Merolla

Things do not exist without being full of people.
—BRUNO LATOUR, *THE BERLIN KEY*

When I was a teenager, my parents died a few years apart, and as I went through the rituals of laying them to rest, well-meaning people assured me that I would "always have the memories." But almost immediately those memories started to fade. First their voices, then their smells, the punch line to one of my dad's stupid jokes; and after that weird period where I thought I saw them everywhere, I found that the images in my mind of their faces had lost their crispness.

In grief we forget, and it's terrible. I would forage in my mind for details, only to realize that there were fewer and fewer to be found.

There were the memories, which I couldn't seem to hold on to, and there was my parents' stuff, which I could actually hold: a half-empty jar of moisturizer my mother used to soothe her radiation burns, new polo shirts that my dad bought but didn't live long enough to wear, a Post-it note with a phone message on it—the last thing my father ever wrote.

Death turns everything into an heirloom.

Getting to know my parents better was no longer a possibility, but like an archaeologist, I could investigate their belongings for answers to questions I hadn't thought to ask when they were

around. Letters sent to my grandmother chronicle my dad's adjustment to leaving home; a business card tells me about his first job out of school; a snapshot of a handful of scraggly perennials shows me the pride my mother took in the humble beginnings of the garden I knew so well. And like the curator of a tiny and very specific museum, I could comb the archives for whatever selection of items seemed most relevant to my station in life at the time. I took up running in college, and I trained wearing my mom's jacket. I polished my shoes for my first office job with my dad's shoe brush. I pried the backs off the picture frames and replaced photos from my childhood with pictures from my travels. I cut up my mother's wedding dress for an art installation. Surely my parents would not have wanted me to feel bogged down by their possessions, but neither would they have wanted me to forfeit the comforts to be had in keeping them around.

At times, however, the sheer volume was overwhelming. My first apartment (not to mention a storage unit I rented) was full of the kinds of things no twenty-one-year-old would own. My slowness to whittle it down felt like a character failing, an inability to part ways cleanly with the past or successfully integrate it into my present. But I was plagued with guilt, and sometimes regret, at parting with their things; there is a kind of emotional violence in detaching from the past after having been untethered from it by fiat.

Cultural expectations also fed into my dilemma. Despite the trendy infatuation with paring down one's belongings to only those items that "spark joy" (per the internationally renowned Japanese organization guru Marie Kondo), certain strongly held beliefs persist about what should be kept in this scenario—"good" china, a passport, a wedding gown, a valuable painting. Virtual strangers have expressed horror at the idea that I might do anything with these items other than store them indefinitely, compounding my fear that I might someday look around and realize I've done it all wrong. So I lived with, and paid to store, a motley collection of objects, which felt like too much stuff and also like never enough.

With each successive move through adulthood, I have managed to edit my permanent collection. I have a few regrets, like the dress I wore to my mother's funeral, which she had taken me to buy several weeks before her death. I couldn't bear to wear it again. But it was also the last thing she ever gave me. It sat untouched in the dry cleaner's plastic for a few years, until finally I donated it to Goodwill, where it would be just another black dress with no clues to its provenance.

In the last few weeks of her life, when everything she told me took on an outsize importance in my mind, my mom explained that it was important to preserve bad memories along with the good ones. She might have wanted me to keep that dress. But like so many other things, I won't ever know.

Just as grief is open-ended, so too is my relationship with all this stuff. I have come to embrace my roles as archaeologist and museum curator: their creative component, their imperative to make sense of objects with complicated histories. All this clutter—what the minimalism evangelists would have us throw out—offers new opportunities for connection with my parents, long after their perfumes and punch lines have faded.

A year ago my husband and I moved into our first home with a door wide enough to admit my parents' kitchen table. The table is too large for the narrow room in which it sits. It's bulky and awkward, but in its own way, it fits.

UNDER THE HOUSE

by Julie Satow

If a place can symbolize the missteps one makes in the confusing period that follows a shocking death, then my family's home in Vermont is the poster child.

The property, a sprawling edifice that stands alone atop a hill overlooking Lake Champlain, is usually empty. It's not really a home in the traditional sense, having become, over the years, a family warehouse, the place where we keep our most painful memories.

The house is about as far north as you can go before crossing into Canada—close enough to Montreal that the radio often picks up French stations. It was rebuilt some years back on the footprint of an older home that had been there for a hundred years, and inexplicably, it retains the creaky, hollow bones of its predecessor. My parents furnished it quickly, with a smattering of leftovers from previous family moves and a hefty helping of my high-school watercolors. There are still remnants from the prior owners, who ran a bed-and-breakfast out of the house, such as fake ivy vines crawling across shelves and an empty, oversize aquarium that was once filled with tropical fish.

My parents purchased the house in the months following my younger brother Jed's suicide. I remember clearly the despair I felt when they told me they were going to buy it. We'd spent the weekend in a small hotel in Essex, Vermont, swimming in the pool, exploring the area, and looking at houses for

sale. In those dark days my family would often leave town to-gether, as if holing up in some new place could distract us from our anguish. I argued in vain against buying a place up there. It was too far and too cold and too impractical.

During those terrible months, my parents stuck to my sur-viving brother and me like an octopus suctioning its tentacles to a rock in a strong current. If they let go, they thought they would float away. My parents bought the house as equal parts refuge and insurance that we'd always stay with them, unlike our younger brother.

The first thing we did after buying the house was to truck everything that had been Jed's from New York to Vermont. When you're young—Jed was twenty—you don't normally have an inheritance to leave beyond your physical stuff. Into the subterranean basement went his bulky hockey bag stuffed with dirty jerseys and black skates; garbage bags filled with Dave Matthews and Led Zeppelin concert T-shirts, intro-to-psych textbooks, and English papers. We parked his enormous SUV beside the snowblower and the bikes, and for nearly two decades it has stood there, its black paint now covered in film, its engine now rusted out. And still, my parents continue to pay the car insurance.

From the start, my older brother and his family used the house the most. As if he were just an ordinary homeowner, my brother invited friends, swam in the lake, and barbecued large summer dinners beneath the orange sunsets.

I mostly stayed away. I hated the freezing cold lake, didn't know how to navigate the small motorboat we kept there, and as a city girl, felt uncomfortable being so far from civilization. My parents, too, rarely made the drive. My Brooklyn-born father could barely swim, and my mother preferred window-shopping and eating out to fishing or hikes.

Occasionally we came up as a family. Usually it was for New Year's Eve, around the anniversary of Jed's death. One year my parents stayed in their room the entire day, my brother, sister-in-law, and I awkwardly reading in the living room by the fire as my young nephews, oblivious to the significance of the day, played and ran through the halls. But mostly the house sat empty, a ridiculous, oversize storage space for Jed's things.

It is said that homes can adopt a personality. For me this house was a mausoleum. Aboveground the sun shone and the grass was green. But rarely if ever did anyone venture to the basement to see what was decaying down there.

In our way, we've each moved past those terrifying first few years. And while we've all adapted and carried on, the house hasn't changed with us. Jed's things remain stubbornly untouched in the basement; the furniture we corralled ad hoc into the bedrooms remains unaltered. The same blanket covers the bed where I once lay so alone and scared, and now sleep with my husband on the rare occasion when we visit.

You would think we would have just joined together one horrible weekend and gone through Jed's belongings. Confronted those smelly and now likely moth-eaten clothes and books, the pedestrian belongings of a college sophomore. But we have never even discussed it.

We have talked, casually and in passing, about selling the place. It costs a lot to maintain a mostly empty house tucked away in the rural Northeast. There is a lawn to be mowed; there are raccoon traps to be set, electricity bills to be paid, and frozen pipes to be thawed. My parents would welcome the freed-up cash. We all realize how impractical it is. But against all logic, we do nothing.

Recently my husband and I put some savings toward a small cottage on the Long Island Sound, where my husband's family has long spent holidays. In purchasing it, I felt like we were breaking the pact we made when my parents bought the Vermont house—to always stay together, a single-family unit. So I was surprised at how nonchalantly they greeted the news. The intensity with which my parents had once clung to us has dissipated, replaced by the grim acceptance that must come after so many years.

If everyone in my family has moved past the utter darkness that enveloped us after Jed died, then why can't we just tow his car and free ourselves from all his stuff? It may be laziness, but I think it is also dread at having to revisit the rawness of our early grief. So the house in Vermont stands there like an immobile statue to our family tragedy, its contents packed away and set aside. Above there is the appearance of normalcy, while down below, there is Jed's decrepit SUV, its insurance up-to-date, as though the engine would actually turn over, and one day one of us would drive it away.

UNCLE RON

by Kim Goldman

Nine years after my brother, Ron, was killed, I gave birth to my first child, whom I named Samuel Ronald. I was relieved to have given birth to a boy because I had it all planned out. Sam would be the older brother to my second child, who, I hoped, would be a girl. I wanted my kids to have the same age difference as Ron and I did, and I wanted them to be just as close. As it turned out, though, Sam's father and I would divorce, and no more children would join our family.

Thirteen years on, Sam is growing up in a house adorned with pictures of Ron and me. Here we are—Ron is six, and I am three—playing in a bubble bath. Here we are balancing on branches in one of Chicago's forest preserves, my brother leaning over to give me a kiss. We are hugging; we were always hugging. My son is growing up in a house filled with stories about his uncle, like how he pulled me from the wreckage of a near-fatal car crash when I was six days shy of my fourteenth birthday, how he would try to scare away my boyfriends by answering the phone in a scary "dad voice," how he surprised me for my twenty-first birthday—ostensibly to treat me to "my first legal beer," only to lead me to a huge surprise party he'd helped coordinate.

I am forever seeing uncanny similarities between my brother and my son: the sense of humor, the sarcasm, the freckle pattern on their faces, the quiet, introspective personality, so much the same. It always takes my breath away when others tell me they see it too.

Sam knows all about his uncle Ron's life. And he knows an awful lot about his uncle Ron's murder. He understands, to the extent that any thirteen-year-old can, the importance of our famous case and our subsequent fight for victims' rights. He knows Ron's story is part of history—not just personal history, but history books history—and that it remains controversial as it relates to race relations and celebrity justice. He knows that I sometimes leave home so I can speak on behalf of others who have lost loved ones to homicide, but who lack our family's public profile.

Strangers have taken to social media to share their disdain for my life choices in the wake of Ron's death, some even accusing me of exposing Sam to "too much sadness" at too young an age. To me, it seems like just enough. My son shares my sadness not because he knows what it is like to lose a sibling, but because I have taught him what it was like to have one—and now, not to.

We frequently visit Ron at his gravesite. Sam picks out the flowers, arranges the stones on the headstone—a Jewish tradition—and takes his time crafting the perfect message to affix to flimsy plastic sticks that he jams into the rock-hard dirt.

"I miss you. Can't wait to see you," he writes in his chicken-scratch handwriting.

"I hope you are having a good time wherever you are."

And most recently, "The more I don't see you, the more I wish I could."

It's pure, unfiltered emotion stemming from a little human born into a home where tragedy lives. When Sam was younger, he may not have understood what he was saying or feeling on these trips, but as he's gotten older, his comprehension and acceptance of death has developed. He has managed to create a deep connection to another human being he's never met and never will.

He sees his mom and papa on TV and asks if he will one day have to make speeches and do interviews like we do. He wonders how Ron's murder will impact *his* life, *his* future. I don't really have an answer for him—just an honesty about how it has impacted mine, and the choice he will get to make when the time comes to make one.

For a young man who has been exposed to a lot of uglycrying and a lot of yelling at the TV when there is coverage of Ron's famous killer and no mention of Ron, Sam still remains so full of hope. Growing up in a grieving family has been an early lesson in how to cope with pain, how to express emotions, and how to keep moving forward when life throws you off course. Obviously, I would trade any of those life lessons to have Sam's uncle Ron be able to shoot hoops with him on the driveway.

But that's not how these things work.

I wasn't prepared for how my grief would shift, and dramatically so, when I became a mother. What I am learning is that every day, as my love for Sam deepens, so too does the longing for my big brother. I didn't think I could miss Ron more than I already did, but with every milestone Sam reaches, I do. When Sam took his first steps, I missed Ron more. When he entered kindergarten, when he entered middle school, I missed Ron more. When my son fell in love for the first time, when he had his heart broken, I missed Ron even more.

No, I wasn't warned how my grief would change shape after I gave birth. Neither was I prepared to feel so open and so willing to endure it. Because no pain I experience will ever compare to what my brother went through during his final moments. Because there's no love or protective force greater than that of a parent for a child.

I wasn't prepared for my story to be Sam's story, my grief to be Sam's grief, my love for my brother to be Sam's love for his namesake. There's comfort in knowing that this longing for and deep connection to Ron does not end with me.

THERE'S NO WILL. WHAT THE BLEEP DO I DO NOW?

A financial therapist (yeah, that's a thing!) offers help dealing with (and keeping) your family.

By Amanda Clayman

Consider the long-term impacts.

Settling an estate without clear instructions from the person who died can be an emotional minefield, but it happens a lot. People automatically think of money, but an estate is basically whatever your loved one owned and owed when they died. It could amount to just a handful of items, like Dad's baseball trophies. Before divvying things up, consider if your ideal outcome is worth the potential family drama.

Set ground rules.

Let everyone share their goals. Remember, you're in this together—especially when tension arises (and it will).

Remember, people don't have the same view of what's "fair."

Equal division... a need-based system... sending it all to charity? All valid. You can't win an argument when someone defines what's fair differently than you do.

The word "right" is wrong.

Yes, you're *so sure* about your loved one's wishes. But was it in writing? If not, they could've easily said something different to others. THIS IS THE WAY TO BE →

Say no to cliques.

Relatives can form alliances to try to bully decisions through. That's a toxic move when combined with grief.

Mom *ALWAYS* bailed him out when we were kids!

Avoid the family narrative trap.

Arguments can trigger old narratives —especially when relatives are dispersed.

SNIFF! This is... SNIFF! SNIFF! ...important.

Don't edit out the grief.

It's part of the inheritance experience. No outcome from the estate process will alleviate your sense of loss, so allow yourself to go through your emotional process too.

Remember, estate resolution ≠ compensation.

Money isn't love, and it isn't inherently karmic. But that's tough to remember if we feel we've made sacrifices for someone that others haven't.

Call me!

Get help. Please.

Hire a professional mediator to help you work through the process, including navigating practical considerations such as taxes. It's certainly cheaper than the cost of litigation!

DATA

Loss (And Found) In the Digital Universe

INTRODUCTION

by Rebecca Soffer

I was futzing around online at work one Friday afternoon when an e-mail popped into my Outlook stream. "I'm coming up with baked chicken tonight," my mom wrote. "Hang in there. I love you."

Well, that sounded pretty fantastic to me. For starters, it had been a rough week. Also, I was hungry. And finally, I really missed my mom's apricot chicken, considering she'd been dead for more than a year.

Her e-mail was dated May 15, 2006, nearly four months before she died. That was around the same time I'd been in the dumps after breaking up with my longtime boyfriend, conveniently right smack in the midst of "wedding season" among my friends. Gazing at the loving words on my screen, my visceral reaction was to allow myself to be tricked into the possibility that I was actually going to see her that evening. But that was short-lived. There would be no home-cooked dinner. No hugs and kisses and assurances that chances were good I wouldn't end up like Miss Havisham. No Mom. Just more Ollie's Chinese takeout and a handful of digital dust taunting me with happier moments.

Never before had the Internet played such a cruel trick on me. Not even when an early version of Pandora had inexplicably erased dozens of carefully crafted stations such as "Bloody Mother Fucking Asshole radio."[*] But oh, would the Internet

---

[*] An actual song title by Martha Wainwright. (Please, I'm not *that* angry.)

continue to do so. That e-mail, which had bent time and space in its route toward my in-box, was my introduction to the wily nature of the web and its digital cousins, and to the massive wrench that technology has tossed into the grieving process.

Since my parents died, I've had to be on guard against emotional digital sneak attacks. I've declined repeated notes from LinkedIn insisting I *really should* consider connecting with Ray Rosenberg (um, yes, that'd be great to connect with my dead dad, thanks!). Or gotten fleetingly excited when a Google alert indicated new updates on Shelby Rosenberg, only to read a piece on, weirdly, a star male forward on the Yeshiva University basketball team. Or spent hours on multiple devices deleting Mother's Day onslaughts from marketers ranging from the unsurprising (looking at you, Edible Arrangements) to the truly very much so (et tu, Jiffy Lube?).

But if these surreal pop-ups are sometimes funny, especially after some time has passed, they are often shocking and painful. The undead nature of the digital world causes the dead to die over and over and over again, and by extension repeatedly rips off the scabs that strive to form over these deep wounds. And I've had it pretty easy compared to other people I've met through *Modern Loss*. I wasn't the man who could've sworn he was being punked by Google Earth when he looked up his childhood home only to see his dead dad mowing the lawn. Or the woman who spent a few hours offline before learning her dad had died in a car accident earlier that day, and that most of the town had already been talking about it on Facebook for hours. Or the mom who got repeated e-mail reminders from the school district to sign her kid up for kindergarten—the kid who'd died years beforehand.

It's not the fault of the Internet, in its inherent, uncaring existence. It's the way we still have little clue as to how one-off "so sorry for your loss" comments or "sadz" gifs can spark real, live, meaningful action. It's tough to figure out where death fits in among photos of burritos and babies in an unfiltered stream. That stream makes it easy for us to compartmentalize our feelings, and also to forget that grief comes in different guises online. It's not like you just Instagram it with gentle pastels, photos of lost loved ones, and pulled inspirational quotes. Sometimes grief online is in the form of a smiling selfie featuring a sweet pair of new shoes because the person posting it is doing everything they can to keep their shit together. And sometimes it's nothing: just because some people aren't baring their souls on a digital platform doesn't mean they're not in pain.

The Internet taketh away, but it also giveth. And it's giveth me numerous ways in which to find solace and community, and build up my resilience.

For one, the web is an enormous empathy-building opportunity. In a matter of hours, we can provide thousands of dollars to families suddenly saddled with hardships; within seconds, while waiting in line for a cold brew coffee, we can sign petitions to reform bereavement-leave policies. And I wouldn't even be writing for this book if I hadn't been able to help launch an online publication taking on the stigma of loss. That publication is a portal that can draw people out of their isolation from anywhere they have a device, and it is a platform that allows them to bare their grief fearlessly to an audience of strangers-who-get-it, even if they'd balk at doing so in person to their closest friends.

My mom died about the time that Facebook started to take off. So I don't have the benefit of being able to sift through her posts whenever I feel like it, smiling at what would surely have been many social justice awareness campaigns and inadvertent Candy Crush invites. But I've found other places to visit her on Facebook. My favorite is Growing Up Jewish in Northeast Philly, a closed group of more than six thousand enthusiastic members, of which I am one even though I did not, in fact, grow up Jewish in Northeast Philly. This group has become an unwitting support system for me, and a touchstone to her. Do I remember lunches at Jack's Deli, hanging out at the *American Bandstand* studios after school or shopping at Caplan's for Buster Browns? Nope. But it's comforting to think my mom probably did, because those seem like nice memories to have.

I don't have the answer as to how meaningful support can take up as much e-space as LOLcats.* I'm not that smart. But I do know that no "like" can replace a conversation, or a hug, or shared double martinis. So in the meantime, I'll do my best to use the web for good. I'll set G-cal reminders to check in with friends on trigger days and remember they still exist as offline humans who occasionally appreciate a good old-fashioned conversation.

And the uncaring Internet will grind on. I'll keep stumbling upon my dad's terrible AOL joke forwards. A happy old memory will spring up on Timehop. And I'll find myself wishing another ancient e-mail promising apricot chicken would mysteriously find its way to me. Sometimes I'll open these reminders from beyond unwittingly, but sometimes I'll do it with one eye open. Because as much as I hate doing so, I love it. It just hurts so good.

---

*   Nothing against LOLcats. I love them.

MY HUSBAND'S DEATH WENT VIRAL, AND ALL I GOT WAS THIS LOUSY T-SHIRT

by Nora McInerny

When my husband died, it went viral.

As in, his obituary, which we wrote together, was everywhere from the front page of Yahoo! to the *New York Post*. It's a terrible thing to go viral, especially if you've ever read the comments sections on either of those sites, the latter of which is revered for such headlines as "Tiger Pulls Out!" and "Weiner Exposed!" It means that your life—a real, actual life—becomes the kind of meme that octogenarians in Milwaukee share with gusto: here's a fabricated "story" about how Muslims are trying to "cancel Christmas," a listicle of Seven Dogs Who Believe in Jesus, and, oh, your husband's obituary.

Your husband's smiling face is everywhere: in both comforting ways (shout-out to the team at Marvel who actually published his obituary in the pages of his favorite comic, *The Amazing Spider-Man*) and somewhat irritating ones (on the Facebook pages of people who were actually kind of dicks to the both of you back when your darling husband was alive, but who now post about how your husband was "like a brother." I guess they are just dicks to their brothers?).

It also means that you're thrust in front of the judging eyes (and fingers) of millions of keyboard warriors, who decide, quickly and decisively, to fucking hate you. Not because they're all dicks (though some of you are, and I don't care what

you think about the way I smile . . . just kidding, it literally crushes me inside), but because deep under their crusty, troll-like exteriors, they're sad that their loved ones died and the world didn't stop spinning. It didn't make headline news and Facebook feeds, it just . . . happened. "People die all the time!" these people say. "What makes this family so special?"

They do have a point. About my smile, yes, because I do sometimes resemble a horse, but horses are majestic and beautiful creatures, so you'll have to try a bit harder if you'd like to insult me—but also about the fact that people do die all the time. And even though I would strongly disagree, Aaron would tell you that he was nothing special. He hated the word *hero* and the word *fight*. He wasn't fighting his cancer. He was hopelessly outmatched, hoping for a David vs. Goliath kind of situation. Or even better, a Kevin McCallister vs. the Wet Bandits situation, where he could just set up enough traps to get this Brain Cancer sucker to trip over some Matchbox cars, set itself on fire, and eventually get hit over the head with a shovel by an elderly neighbor who he'd always mistakenly thought was a creepy mass murderer. He was hoping for some dumb luck.

To me, it wasn't fair. With all the straight-up horrible assholes in this world, the kind of people who molest children or commit genocide or wear embellished jeans with tight Ed Hardy shirts while smoking menthols, it was *Aaron* who got brain cancer? Really?

But to Aaron, it was perfectly fair. "Why *not* me?" he'd say. "This happened to me because I *can* handle this. And you happened to me because you can handle it, too. You'll be fine. And you'll make sure that our son is, too."

Before Aaron got sick, I was the definition of privilege. I still am, but at least I know that now. Aside from the time in seventh grade that I asked for "the Rachel" but got "the Sixty-Five-Year-Old Woman Having an Existential Crisis after Her Messy Divorce," I'd gotten through life without any sort of actual hardship. My grandparents died when they were old, my parents loved each other, I graduated from college without student loans. I was pretty used to the world opening itself up to me the way I expected it to: on command.

Under a microscope, my husband's illness and death are sad and tragic and terribly unfair, because nice people shouldn't die of awful diseases when they are newly married and young parents. But in the larger scheme of things, we had it easy. Aaron got the treatment he needed, because he had a good job with great insurance, and he worked for a company that cared about him as a person. Every time we visited the hospital, I was confronted by people who had it much worse—whose terminal illness was busying itself by destroying their lives financially and emotionally before finally killing the host. We saw rooms of lonely, decaying people who never had a person to visit them or hold their hand, and waiting rooms where it felt like everyone around us had long ago given up hope. Sure, Aaron had stage IV cancer, but we'd lie in his hospital bed, eating organic, grass-fed burgers from a high-end diner with friends, and feel our hearts break for the man next door forcing rubbery hospital chicken down the hatch, whose only company that night was the cast of *The Big Bang Theory*.

When Aaron died, we had a big old safety net to catch us. Groceries were dropped off on my back step. Our walkway was shoveled every time it snowed. And an online fundraiser had contributions from more people than I've ever met in my entire life. My in-boxes—from e-mail to Facebook—were filled with messages of comfort and love, in languages I couldn't even read.

Beyond our friends and family, we had the love of thousands of strangers surrounding us. They'd found us through Aaron's obituary, which we had written together before he died. In it, we revealed his cause of death as a radioactive spider bite, and his secret identity as Spider-Man, and even included a nod to his first wife . . . Gwen Stefani. What was meant to be one last inside joke from the funniest man I've ever met to the people he left behind was shared around the world by people who had never had the pleasure of meeting Aaron, and never would.

Each of these actions was a small light illuminating a path through this darkness, lit up by people who had been in my shoes, and who cared enough to let me know that I was seen. Not just in a hit-the-like-button-and-keep-scrolling kind of way, but in the oooooh-girl-I-feel-what-you're-going-through kind of way.

"I'm missing both of my arms, but nobody seems to notice," I wrote in my diary a month after Aaron died. There are so many of us walking around limbless and unnoticed, and how do we find each other? The Internet. People share their phantom limbs with me all of the time: the children who died unexpectedly, the husbands who limped along through terminal illnesses, the friends and brothers who took their own lives. They do not all want a response, or an Internet friendship. They just want to be seen—to have another human on this earth know their story—so I treat each one as the honor that it is. I see your broken hearts, strangers. I have added them to my collection.

Aaron's love and death gave me many things: an abiding love for Kelly Clarkson, a passion for Buffy the Vampire Slayer, and the knowledge that I do not have a special bone in my body.

I may not think it's all been fair, but I know exactly how lucky we are. Aaron's death was no more important than the death of anybody else who died that day, people who left the world without fanfare or as a trending topic on Twitter. I'm no more special than other women out there who have lost their husbands and the fathers of their children, who are picking up the pieces of the lives they had and trying to cobble together something new. I don't need to be special. It is enough for me to be alive, to sometimes brush my hair and remember to wear deodorant, to love the people I love as hard as I can, and to remind myself that even the kind of person who leaves a nasty comment on a story about your dead husband's obituary is still a human being with a mother who loves him.

Everyone will lose somebody they love. And I don't say that as a threat, I say it as a fact. Your parents are going to die. Your lover is going to die. The children you don't even have yet, someday they will die. Your barista? Your dog? Your Lyft driver? They're all gonna die someday! Alongside birth, it is the one thing (besides the Rachel haircut, for girls of the 1990s) that we universally experience. It is loss and love that helps connect us through space and time, in this huge human tapestry that spans millennia and cultures and Internet connections.

And that, my trolls, is a pretty long line to try to fit on a T-shirt, but it's still pretty frigging special.

CONFESSIONS OF A GMAIL HOARDER

by Brian Stelter

When I reread his e-mails, I can hear him uttering each word in that unforgettable voice of his.

I think my favorite is from December 19, 2013: "do you miss me? you know you do, bitch."

No one but David Carr could have written me something like that, complete with the *Breaking Bad* reference.

I had left the *New York Times* one month prior for a new job at CNN. David was still at the *Times*, writing the country's most influential weekly column about the media revolution. David was a larger-than-life character. He was almost like a mascot for the *Times*—a living, breathing representation of its journalistic values and ambition and humanity. He was a generous mentor to so many young journalists. And he was the thing I missed most about the newspaper.

David's e-mail updated me on what I'd missed there—some of it was "spicy," as he liked to say, and some of it was silly gossip about coworkers' comings and goings—and rearranged our upcoming dinner plans. Mundane stuff. But his love and his spirit punctuated the sentences, even the misspelled ones. Especially the misspelled ones.

The last one appeared in my in-box on February 11, 2015.

"Am in yer shop. Taping andycoop"

Translation: David was upstairs, taping an interview with Anderson Cooper.

I didn't reply. I just hurried up to the guest waiting area next to makeup. We talked and talked, and when we had to say good-bye, he gave me a big bear hug.

The next night, after moderating a panel discussion in front of hundreds of people at the *Times* headquarters, David headed back up to his office on the fourth floor. That's where he collapsed and died. The medical examiner later said that he had lung cancer, and his death was due to complications from the disease. And now that he's gone, I find myself rereading and finding new meaning from his e-mails. They are a twenty-first-century record of a modern father-son, mentor-mentee relationship. Sometimes they're signed "M'wah." Sometimes they're blank, with only a subject line: "What's the haps?" "Update on your mom?" "U in the shop?" "Read this." The most common: "Call me when you can," with his phone number.

I learned about David's death when I woke up on February 13. Come to think of it, I learned about my dad's death in a similar way—in bed, before dawn, on February 10, 2001. I was fifteen.

One difference was that my mom told me about Dad. She lay down next to me, holding back tears, and tried to break the news as gently as possible. A succession of 150 e-mails, texts, and tweets told me about David. Startling doesn't begin to describe it. My wife screamed when she saw the notifications on her phone. The moment I looked at mine, I knew why. In between all the "I'm so sorry" texts on the screen were the words "David" over and over again.

These people reached out to me directly (while my phone was mercifully on silent) because they knew David thought of me like a son. Now, I don't know if I would have said that so matter-of-factly while he was still alive. He was a father figure, for sure, the closest thing I had to a dad since my own died from heart disease—but did we ever say that aloud? I can't find any trace of it in our e-mails. Really, it never needed to be said.

The e-mails help me remember. The first one in my archives is from 2007 (back when he was still using an AOL account!), just a few months after I had started at the *Times*. I remember feeling intimidated by David. But until I reread the e-mail, I'd forgotten that I got over my nerves and asked him out to lunch.

Over time, the e-mails show us planning SXSW parties. Swapping information about sources for stories. Counseling each other during hairy moments in our personal lives. How to handle a bad breakup. What to say to an editor. Where memories fail, Gmail's archival system delivers.

More than anything, the e-mails leave me wishing for an equivalent digital record of my relationship with my dad. But the only e-mail account Dad ever had was the business one I'd set up for him. Gmail was just a figment of the imagination back then; this was an old-fashioned AOL account accessed via dial-up modem.

David's digital history, on the other hand, is always just a few keystrokes away. As strange as it is to see his Facebook page still online—one of his last posts was about how Brian Williams shouldn't be drummed out of NBC, so his page now looks like a media time capsule—I appreciate it being there. The e-mails, too. A couple of months ago a mutual friend told me she's also been rereading David's messages. She's the one who got me thinking about the value of the digital record.

"I won't ever get rid of them," she e-mailed me. "It makes me feel like he's just on the other side of them."

I have 75,000 Gmail messages and counting, going back ten years. My wife doesn't hoard e-mail the way I do. But she's glad she held on to the one David sent her when I was on the verge of two big life changes: marrying her and joining CNN.

Looking back, I couldn't help but notice this e-mail had no typos or abbreviations. "this next unfolding will be a pleasure to watch, although from a greater distance," he wrote. "and of all the choices brian has made, you are and will be the most important one."

On the evening of the wedding, February 22, 2014, David arrived early at our hotel in Philadelphia and stayed late, taking photos with my family members and beaming with fatherly pride. Earlier in the day, I had sent a love letter and a necklace over to the bridal suite where Jamie was getting ready. Nice touch, right?

Until I recently reread his e-mails, I'd forgotten who deserved the credit.

From Carr2n@gmail.com on February 19, 2014: "Get a little jewel to send over b4 she walks up aisle. Send over With flower girl. That way she always has a lasting totem of that day."

UNRECOVERED

by Meg Tansey

A year after my mother died, almost every appliance we owned broke. I was perpetually overwhelmed and exhausted, and on top of that we were now without a stove or a dishwasher. Our water heater rotted out and poured into the bedroom of a downstairs neighbor. Something mysterious happened in the heating system that caused a waterfall on the main staircase of our building.

My father was an engineer and would have probably blamed something reasonable: wear and tear, or failed igniters. But he was dead, too. Left to my own devices, I interpreted it as both a lesson and a punishment from the universe. This is your life without a mother, I imagined it saying: dirty dishes, cold food, no heat.

There's no way around it, I felt an unseemly amount of self-pity. Around the time my mother died, there was an earthquake followed by mudslides half a world away. Orphans with a lot more street cred than I filled up newsfeeds in the background while I called relatives and made arrangements with the funeral home my mother thought did "beautiful work." I would look at the TV and listen to the condolences and think, you know who I feel sorry for? Those six-year-olds who just had all of their loved ones and belongings swept away. And me.

All of our appliances were replaced, and for a while it seemed like the only thing in our apartment that was broken was me. Until my hard drive crashed. It hadn't been backed up to the new system (yes, the old backup system had been swept up in the appliance purge), and everything was gone. Including the only picture of my mom and me while I was pregnant.

The picture was from our last outing before the baby came, at our usual "city" meeting spot, the New York Botanical Garden. For me, the virtue of the Botanical Garden is that it is in the city, and for my mother and sister the virtue of the Botanical Garden is that it does not seem like it is in the city. We ate lunch and looked at flowers and my sister and I made fun of our mother and each other, which is the main form of communication in our family, and I insisted to my photo-averse mother that the picture be taken. Including travel time, the whole thing took four hours, tops—a perfect family visit.

I was planning a similar trip, the first since the baby was born, when the cold my mother had been fighting took a turn for the much worse. Within thirty-six hours of my telling her "It's almost cherry blossom time," she was in the ICU with pneumonia, "the sickest person in this hospital" as the doctor in charge told me.

To say that losing that photo started an entirely new mourning process, possibly more intense than the first, is both completely melodramatic and true. Before, I had things to do: take care of a baby, make funeral arrangements. Now I had a toddler and an occasional babysitter and all the time in the world to lose my mind. I couldn't sleep. I cried. I blamed myself. I blamed other people. I dragged my laptop to every place I could find; I shipped it off to a specialist who I was told contracted with the Department of Defense. When people warned me that a potential recovery might be expensive, I said words I have never said before or since: Price is not a consideration. I meant it.

Nothing wakes you up to the limits of technology like a month in the ICU, so I wasn't entirely surprised when none of my data recovery options worked. The initial confidence in a professional that is subsequently dashed; the nodding along to overly careful technical explanations that you don't understand and won't remember; the looks on the faces of people who regularly have other people cry on them at work—this was all-too-familiar territory.

How can I sum up my relationship with my mother? I adored her and she adored me and we were very different. But in that picture, with my belly sticking out so far I can't button my coat, we were on the brink of becoming more the same. Motherhood, at least the short-term version of it, the breastfeeding and no-television version—for that, we were on the same page.

People joke about the horror of becoming their mothers, but some common ground would have been good for us. At least, that's what I thought. I'm not naive enough to think that my becoming a mother would negate our differences or solve our problems. But I'm also not so dumb that I can't see an opportunity right in front of me. It was a chance for a new phase in our relationship.

There's mourning the relationship you had, and then there's mourning the relationship you could have had. The relationship future you could have had. The relationships your kids could have had. When I lost that picture, I started mourning the second in earnest, even if I didn't realize it at the time.

The grieving often feel like they have to disabuse people of the idea that grief is a thing that ends—after twelve months, after your birthday, after their birthday. But the mere not-ending of it has never resonated for me in the same way that the constant companionship of it has. Every new job, first day of school, lifetime achievement accomplished—the grief is there. It keeps going and going, and it changes and I change and now I'm just used to it. I'm surprised to be more grateful than not for that most days. I don't need a picture to remind me of the things I had, the things I lost, the things I keep losing.

MEETING PATRICIA, AUNT ESTHER'S AMAZON ALTER EGO

by Joey Chernila

When my aunt Esther died in the summer of 2011, we knew we'd have to deal with her apartment. What we didn't know was that it would mean tackling the floor-to-ceiling Amazon.com boxes crammed in every room.

The job of cleaning fell to my brother, who was living nearby at the time. To reach the two main rooms, he pushed through the boxes stacked along both sides of the hallway. These rooms, too, were filled with Amazon boxes, many unopened. He spent months repackaging unused items, all the while reporting back on the tragedy of all this *stuff*. Why did she need hundreds of pocket calculators? Or dozens of books on beating the odds at the casino?

Why, indeed?

It was only after her death that I revealed to my family that I had known a different Esther. Not the shut-in, muumuu-clad, overweight woman we'd all struggled to love. But "Patricia," who for years had been writing long-form Amazon reviews of everything from books to pocket calculators, ice cube trays, and boxes of sugar. I had secretly been reading and commenting on her reviews all along, and I was her biggest fan.

The first review I encountered by Patricia "A Reader" was in 2007. It was an earnest, paragraphs-long piece about an old picture book. I was reading the review because that very book had just been given to my daughters by Aunt Esther.

She'd always struck me as very self-involved, and we'd only ever had brief conversations in the past, often about her favorite topics: the British royal family and the 1960s soap opera *Dark Shadows*. Mostly she would be parked in front of the TV during my visits to see her and my grandmother in Queens, so we just didn't talk to each other at all.

I didn't know a lot about her life when I happened upon this extra-long book review on Amazon. But the review was so candid, so particular in how it described her childhood, that I was able to piece together the truth using stories my mom had told me about growing up together on 153rd Street, in the same apartment Esther shared with her mother for fifty years. Even then, it took a few reads before I realized that Patricia and Aunt Esther were one and the same. But I kept my discovery to myself, filing it away as just one more strange fact about her.

Here is the opening to one for a single-handed can opener— an item that has sadly long been off the market since this 2007 entry:

I presently live in a "no-pets" building, which has its advantages and disadvantages. The "One Touch Can Opener"—though obviously an inanimate object—can easily be a "pet-substitute," as well as an excellent can opener! For, as it zips around your can, opening it, it makes a nice little "wiggle motion" . . . almost like a fish in the water!

The title of this review is:

"A N D . . . I T . . . O P E N S . . . C A N S . . . T O O !"

Certain obsessions become clear when scanning through the more than 700 reviews posted by Patricia between 2004 and 2011. Among them: *Alien Nation* (the TV show, "NOT the film"); coasters and mugs featuring the British royal family; books on beating roulette in the casinos by use of pocket calculators; pocket calculators; canned fish; and candy bars. After Esther died, these seemingly disparate objects became pieces of a puzzle I could not solve. At least, not without the help of the world's largest online retailer. Why review so many kinds of ice cube trays? Or can openers? I read many further reviews, trying to connect the dots, but to no avail.

It also seems Patricia was either unable or unwilling to purchase many of the items she was reviewing, as evidenced by this late-career review of the film *Lesbian Vampires*:

This movie is full of blood, gore, and lust. (Not that I have seen it . . . I've read other people's reviews.) It has only one redeeming value, in that, (by and large), it must usually keep its viewers inside either their homes or their friends' homes . . . and OFF THE STREETS! . . . I have a very strong suspicion that it insults both REAL lesbians, and, (IF they exist), real vampires as well.

You'd think this review was the pinnacle of her career as an online critic. But Patricia's crowning moment was when she stumbled across a novelty item in the form of a can of Unicorn meat. I can only imagine she came to the item while searching Amazon for other actual canned meats. Patricia is both outraged and disgusted by this product, and does not hold back, giving it two stars out of five:

Now, I am definitely NOT a vegetarian. Yes, I am a proud and happy omnivore (eating non-meat products as well as meat), and even eat . . . VEAL!

However, I draw the line at Unicorn meat! These rare and beautiful creatures, if they indeed do exist, should NOT be killed and/ or eaten! At least, not till we have a good, authenticated herd of

1,000 or so unicorns around! And if this is only a toy, it is still teaching children (and adults), a very bad lesson.

There is considerable debate in the three pages of comments on this particular review as to whether Patricia is writing a spoof review. Patricia baffles her detractors, and in the end she pulls rank on them all:

you can't write over 600 reviews for Amazon, and over three thousand musical pieces—all, alas, presently unpublished—without being sensitive.

The tone of Patricia's reviews is always hopeful, and thoughtful. For me, this is a window into Aunt Esther's world, one that I was rarely privy to in our brief and mildly negative personal interactions. In her first review, Patricia discusses her sometimes-fraught relationship with her more worldly sister, my mother, by celebrating their shared love for a book on class and status. Elsewhere she discusses her childhood, her loneliness, and her desire to be useful, to be needed.

Esther was often alone in that apartment, and in that space, the most mundane objects became useful. Books (even bad ones) became a way to remember her youth and family. Calculators became ways to strike it rich. Teacups bearing the likeness of Prince William allowed for glamorous living. Each thing, no matter how crummy, inferior, and designed for obsolescence, was for Esther a means to share her experience.

Sure, she might have been searching for the perfect pocket calculator. But I think she was also searching to connect with her adoring readers about her discoveries—even if I was the only adoring one.

In the months after she died, I read and reread each of Patricia's reviews. And when I revealed them to my family, they, too, got to know this side of the abrasive woman we'd all found difficult to speak with. It was only during this postmortem literary extravaganza that I could do what I wished I'd done when she was alive: "Was this review helpful to you?" Amazon asked me at the end. Yes. Yes. Yes.

A BRIEF GUIDE TO GRIEFSPEAK

Some language that's probably not used in counseling manuals, but that we think you should know anyway.

Ambiguilt:

Guilt over feeling ambivalence at the death of a family member. Relationships are complex and people aren't perfect.

Anniversary:

A type of day that will forever cease to be identified with happy milestones and instead evoke sharply bittersweet memories related to a dead person. Side effects include pensiveness, tears, and inappropriate outbursts.

Anniversary season:

When multiple anniversaries collide within a short period of time (iterations include deathiversaries, diagnosiversaries, and the entire holiday season). An ideal time for Netflix, spontaneous vacations, and friends who get it.

Closure:

A myth perpetuated by people who don't know what the fuck they're talking about.

Clutterstruck:

The inability to remove dead loved ones' seemingly meaningless items for fear they might later prove to be surprisingly irreplaceable.

RECEIPT

BURGR WORLD

SALE: 02045
MARCH 03 2012
Fries x1
Sooper Dooper
Burger x1
Small Soda x1
TOTAL: $7.21

Comparisons:

Attempts made by people wanting to help you feel better by making it about themselves. (SAMPLE EQUATION: "MY LOSS ≥ YOURS")

DIED LAUGHING

Dark Humor:

What makes you laugh now. May be appalling to others. Ignore them.

Ha ha ha...

Edible Arrangement:

Fruit skewers whittled into floral bouquets. Frequently received en masse, in lieu of actual comfort. May contain a marshmallow at the center.

Sorry...

Freudenschade:

The sting you feel when you see a stranger having brunch with her mother, when yours is dead. Antonym: Schadenfreude.

Ham:

The Midwestern meat of death, often provided to a family in mourning. Variations of ham include casserole, fried chicken, funeral potatoes, baked ziti, Jell-O salads, and sheet cake.

PURE ALL NATURAL SYMPATHY

Kummerspeck:

A German word combining Kummer ("grief, sorrow") and speck ("layer of fat, bacon"). So, yeah, this is literally "Grief Bacon," aka the excess weight gained after a loss.

Lists:

Organizational methods you'll cling to in an attempt to maintain your sanity.

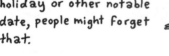

WAKE UP ✓
BREATHE ✓
WASH FACE ✓
EAT ✓
DRINK ✓
SHOWER ✓
GET DRESSED

Monday:

A seemingly innocent day disguised just like any other. But you still feel the loss, and if it doesn't fall on a holiday or other notable date, people might forget that.

Mourn Mirage:

The appearance of a stranger who closely resembles someone who died. May result in your following them several blocks just so that you can be near them (not creepy at all).

Reverse Comfort:

Something you need from others but that others silently expect *you* to provide *them* while discussing this awkward topic. Gentle reminder: not your job.

Sadbooking:

Posting throwback photos of a relative who's died and getting mad at anyone who didn't bother to emoji your status.

Sleep? LOL:

Likely elusive, especially surrounding key dates. (see "anniversary," "triggers," "Monday.")

Triggers:

Whatever takes you back to your dark place. Frequently appearing in such seemingly innocuous forms as found notes, Adele songs, and other Adele songs.

Hi my sweet, can you pick up some SUGAR? D×♡

Ugly Cry:

Heaving sobs, accompanied by a swollen face, active mucous membranes, and running mascara. Known to attack without warning and right before job interviews and first dates.

Wakemare:

The first conscious moments after a happy dream about the deceased, when you remember—yet again—that they're gone.

Yuck yuks:

The combination of shock, relief, and guilt arising from the first time you find yourself doubled over in laughter after a deep loss.

SECRETS

What They Didn't Tell Us,
And What We Aren't Telling Others

INTRODUCTION

by Gabrielle Birkner

My father, Larry, and stepmother, Ruth, met and fell in love while they were married to other people. They divorced their respective spouses, wed shortly thereafter, and remained devoted to each other for the next fifteen years, until their deaths at ages fifty-four and fifty-five, respectively.

I mention their early courtship not to malign a pair of superlative parents, loyal friends, consummate professionals, and law-abiding citizens. They were two people energized by the world of ideas, who spoke frequently about the importance of leaving things a little better than we found them, and who gave of themselves toward that end. I mention it, rather, to acknowledge what has long felt taboo: my father and Ruth, like everyone who has walked this earth, were not perfect.

For years after they were murdered, I felt the need to keep secret anything that wouldn't cast them in a glowing light. I'd tell all and sundry (friends, friends of friends, the owner of the corner bodega, the sales clerk at Staples) how, when I was five, my dad wallpapered every tiny room of the dollhouse he built for me. Or how my stepmother had grown up in rural Iowa, the sixth of thirteen children, and put herself through college, and then went on to earn her MBA. Or how on the eve of my graduation from college, they wrote and inscribed the most perfect poem on the title page of Dr. Seuss's *Oh, the Places You'll Go!* But I wouldn't so much mention that my dad was a bad dancer (#DadDancing was a thing, even before it was a hashtag) or that my stepmother had a corny sense of humor (fittingly, she attributed it to having grown up on a corn farm).

That long-ago marital indiscretion definitely seemed like something I had to keep buried as soon as they were. In death, I felt that they needed to be what no one is in life: flawless. I feared misplaced blame, and worried that the whole tragedy would seem less horrible if it happened to humans and not saints.

Maybe that's because we live in an unruly world and convince ourselves that we can will it to behave. We hear of someone diagnosed with lung cancer and want to know if they had ever smoked. We read about a fatal car accident and wonder aloud if the deceased had been wearing a seat belt, or if they could have done anything to prevent what had happened. We hear about a homicide and begin to make assumptions about the victim's lifestyle.

Even when there is zero possible causal relationship between how someone lived and how they died—what happened to my dad and Ruth could have happened to anyone who has ever hired someone to work in their house, be it a plumber, gardener, or electrician—we seek one out. Even in war, where stray bullets and car bombs kill indiscriminately, people look for patterns that don't exist to justify why some were snuffed out and others were not. As Thomas L. Friedman wrote in *From Beirut to Jerusalem*, his chronicle of the Lebanese Civil War, "I would hear people say about a neighbor who got killed by an errant bomb, 'Well, you know he lived on the wrong side of the street. It is much more exposed over there than on our side.' . . . Or, 'He shouldn't have gone out driving fifteen minutes after the cease-fire started; he should have waited twenty minutes—everyone knows that.'"

But this attempt at rationalization doesn't make the loss less sad; it just makes everyone else feel less vulnerable. At least until their made-up rules are broken.

It was at my first newspaper job, more than a year before my father and stepmother were killed, that I first entered the intersection of Grief and Secrets. My first beat was the "dead beat," aka obituaries. Officially, these obituaries were news items, even if few contained what would be considered news beyond a five-mile radius—the one semi-exception being the obituary I wrote for the guy who played Wilson, the neighbor on the 1990s sitcom *Home Improvement*. Each obituary followed a strict template, which included date and place of birth, and a specific cause of death other than "natural causes" for anyone under age seventy-five. When it was AIDS or suicide or an accidental overdose, families would often ask us to omit that detail—and since the city desk didn't let us do that, some pulled the free obituary in favor of a paid death notice, handled by the advertising department. In the years since then, I've come to understand that secrets complicate grief in myriad ways.

There are the secrets about the deceased that the grief-stricken keep from others out of respect or shame or fear of blame or because there remains a taboo of speaking ill of the dead. In our posthumous retelling, we strike their questionable politics or destructive addictions or debilitating phobias or that the cause of death was a self-inflicted gunshot wound.

There are the secrets the deceased kept from us—those that we'll never know and those that we'll one day find out when we read their will or clean out their apartment or close out their accounts or go through their Facebook DMs. Sometimes these secrets are a boon—$25,000 we didn't know she had, say—but more often they are a burden. As Dr. Amy Cohen, a Los Angeles–based psychiatrist told me: "Secrets are unfinished business, and grief is always complicated by unfinished business."

There are secrets of omission, like when I tell my children about my father, the grandfather they would never know. *He's not alive anymore. His body stopped working.* Sad, but coupled with a sunny coda of "most people live long and happy lives," it's hardly nightmarish. And there are secrets that involve us, our relationship with the deceased, or how we mourn. Maybe we hold grudges or wonder to ourselves if we could have done more when they were at the end of their lives.

I began to challenge my own need for a flawless narrative through my involvement with a nonprofit organization composed of families and friends of homicide victims. At the annual conferences, which draw hundreds of people from across the country, the speakers would explain that it doesn't matter where or with whom the victims lived, or if they had shown good judgment or bad at any point in their lives. They didn't deserve their fate. Full. Stop.

We are imperfect people mourning imperfect people imperfectly. But these imperfections make us no less deserving of empathy and loving expressions of grief.

MY DEAD HUSBAND, THE SERIAL ADULTERER

by Robyn Woodman

A curious thing happens when someone dies: secrets that have been bottled up for too long erupt like a cancerous tumor gone undetected for years. A rumor here and text message there lead to a friend calling one day to ask, "If I heard something really bad about Max,* would you want to know?"

Max and I were together for five years, married for two of them. We lived in South Florida, where I was selling medical devices and Max was an instructor for the nation's largest scuba diving school. His students routinely traveled from far-flung places to complete high-level certifications.

On Thanksgiving morning in 2005, Max went diving with friends at a popular spot near Fort Lauderdale. I waited for him at home, passing the time chatting on the phone with friends and family and sipping my first eggnog latte of the season. All the while, something was going horribly wrong for Max some two hundred feet below the surface of the Atlantic.

The knock on the door surprised me, as did the appearance of Max's boss, who rushed in and asked me to sit down. He had something to tell me: "There's been an accident. I don't know how bad. We need to go to the hospital—now."

I remember saying "No!" very firmly, standing my ground, and then collapsing onto the couch.

During the breakneck drive to the hospital, I frantically

---

* The name of the deceased has been changed.

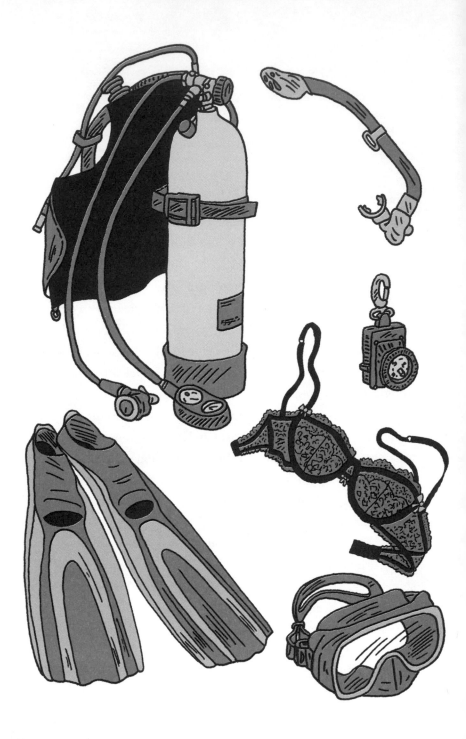

called both my parents and Max's. My mind raced with terrible what-if scenarios. What if he's stuck in a hyperbaric chamber for weeks? What if he emerges from this accident a much less robust version of himself? By the time I arrived, my husband was lying on a stainless-steel table, purple and bloated, water dripping onto the floor from his wet suit. Minutes earlier, he had been pronounced dead upon arrival at the hospital.

His death certificate would eventually read death by drowning. But that declaration didn't even begin to answer my questions about what had gone so wrong.

Every moment of the early aftermath is burned into my memory in slow motion. Family, friends, the diving community, and strangers showed up to mourn Max—and their presence lifted me up.

There's the Max we all mourned and eulogized, and then there was that question: "If I heard something really bad about Max, would you want to know?"

"Yes," I whispered when my friend asked, and then promptly threw up.

The "really bad" thing: Max had many—I mean, many— girlfriends during our five years together, from short-term flings with women from his past to longer-term relationships with scuba students. Turns out he was what you could call a "professional dater" who happened to get married. The truth hurt more than I thought possible, but not knowing was unimaginable to me. And it still is.

Yeah, I know. You're asking yourself, *How could she have been so stupid? How could she not have known this was happening?* I have asked myself the same questions ad nauseam. But here's the thing: most cheaters are caught due to a change in behavior. With us, there was no perceivable change. Max dated the whole time. Add in his frequent work travel, his convenient underwater excuse for not answering calls, and the fact that this happened in the days of relative privacy, before the era of social media, and my shock is relatively understandable. Also, I was a trusting wife. Silly me.

For the longest time, I was furious with Max. I wanted to scream and kick and make him answer for his actions. I even imagined him coming back to life, just so I could punch him in the face. My therapist called my grief process "complicated." *Hello, understatement.*

I had no way to ask Max why or how he could do such a thing. On top of that, I was surrounded by a community in mourning. Until recently, it has been a topic I discussed only privately with my closest friends and family. So I gritted my teeth to make it through one well-meaning conversation after the next. While all of the things I wanted to say were true, it's not exactly kosher to speak ill of the dead—especially to his friends and family, who, I figured, had suffered enough.

Here's the thing, though: Just because someone is dead, that doesn't mean they didn't suck. It just means you're not supposed to talk about it.

It took me six years to forgive Max, and longer to open up about his cheating. It's a time line I am both ashamed and proud of. Ashamed that I carried the anger for so long, and proud that I was finally able to lay it down.

I've come to see Max's cheating like this: It wasn't about me. Max was seeking other women to fill a void inside himself, because facing his demons head-on was more than he could bear. Since first hearing about his infidelities, I have recognized that

Max was battling his own life issues, and I happened to be a casualty of all that. Now my anger has vanished, supplanted by sadness for Max. Letting go of my anger was the best decision I could have made, especially for myself.

Just because someone sucked, that doesn't mean they can't be remembered fondly . . . eventually.

As I wrote this, grief washed over me. I mourned him all over again, smiling through the tears as I remembered the absurd things he would do to garner a laugh. And I recalled the last minutes we spent together that Thanksgiving morning before his dive. I woke up very early with chilly feet, groggily shuffling into the kitchen while he gladly found me some warm socks fresh out of the dryer. Now that I have forgiven Max, I am ready to forgive myself for trusting him and for taking on the shame and guilt of his infidelity—very heavy burdens that weren't really mine in the first place.

PRACTICE IMPERFECT

by Rachel M. Ward

I hate having to tell you my husband died when he was thirty-five and I was thirty-two, and that we'd only been married three years. You might be nodding to yourself in understanding, thinking, It must be retraumatizing for her to have to pass through that moment again and again, to bring new acquaintances up to speed.

How very empathetic of you! Also wrong! But let's focus on how you're a nice person and you're crediting my better angels.

Which is why I am sorry to report: my angels are dicks. Trust me. I hang with them all the time, and they're always doing the right thing for the wrong reason. They sit on my shoulders and whisper, "Guuuurl, just make that sheepish shrug and caaaaaaasuallllly drop the bomb on this poor person."

My angels look the other way as I weaponize my revelation. They cackle as I serve it as a punch line to a rotten joke, a choice I justify based on my late husband's own gallows humor. My favorite is to offhandedly call him a quitter, even though struggling through the last week of his life with an infection that was unknowingly blowing up his heart hardly seems like the easy way out.

It is an unkind strategy, but at least it has the effect of allowing me to coach the recipient of this bad news through the next three minutes of their life: Here is who you're talking to now. Here is how she made a decision not to pity herself, and how that has made her hard to your sympathy. Here is how she exercises control in the daylight hours, because when night falls, joke's on her!

I can't imagine what it must be like to be on the receiving end of this information. Information that, years later, I still— let's face it—refuse to deliver kindly.

I can tell you what I see, as I become the sympathee. The slow bulging of the recipient's eyes. Like the mechanical hunter on a cuckoo clock, in one smooth movement their fore- arm lifting at the elbow to raise their hand to their mouth as it makes a small O. The rest of the phrase that flies out of their mouths like a breath on a punch: "I'm so sorry to hear that." The gulf opens up.

But, also, I *can* sort of imagine what it must be like to be on the receiving end of this information. It's not that no one ever tells me about bad things that happened to *them*. It's just that if I say my bad thing first—and inevitably I will, because I am terrible at keeping things from leaking out of my face, both mouth *and* eye sockets—the dynamic is forever changed.

When I spill my secret first, I become the grief expert, a grief celebrity. I have won the competition of not skill, not strength, but just bad luck. And by then it seems crass—or pointless—to mention whatever trauma you have had.

Divorces, lost parents, childhood pets put down, and the deaths of high-school boyfriends revealed only recently on a trip back home: I watch you reframe these actual tragedies in real time. Your confession either tips back into your throat, like a roller-coaster car that doesn't quite have enough mo- mentum to pile over the hill, or it dribbles out of the side of your mouth, like Katie Holmes abashedly confessing her love to Dawson. (I know Dawson isn't his real name, but I'm not googling "James Vanderwhatever" to check which of the letters in his last name are capitalized and how to put them in the right order. You have to draw a line somewhere.)

I watch that worry work its way across your face, and I get so, so tired. Because being a grief celebrity is exhausting, as I try to find ways to tell this story well and always fail. Even more than that—it's *boring*. I am bored by my own tale of woe. I am over being made an other, over winning this shitty prize. Of having the biggest, saddest secret.

Why *do* these losses always seem like secrets? Why are they always confessions? I managed to luck out a bit—I once wrote a thing that many people in the outer layer of my social circle read, and now sometimes at a party a friend of a friend will say, "Oh yeah, I read your thing, I'm so sorry." And then at least I'm spared The Decision You Have to Make When Evaluating Whether or Not to Tell About Your Thing.

Sure, I could *not* keep it like a secret. I could build up the muscle that would allow me to hold my shoulders back, instead of rounding them around the cavity of my chest, where grief brews up cold and strong. I could be gentler with my revelation, or at least soften the defiance in my jaw. Or I could choose to stop confessing this secret at all. I could boot these bad angels and resign this detail of my biography to the little bulleted list at the bottom, instead of letting it be the topic sentence. I could have T-shirts made.

But I am a coward, and I am sad. So I'd rather change the entire system. I'd rather burn down the entire enterprise of ranking tragedies. And here, comrade, I enlist you. Help me out. When we meet and we get to that point, be there with me too. Tell me about the saddest thing in your life. Let it weigh the same. Maybe we *both* get T-shirts that read "Socialized sympathy now!"

Because when we consider our forms, and the space that deaths, heartbreaks, trespasses, and injustices take up inside us, those traumas can't be measured side by side. We only feel them in proportion to the outline of our own experience.

And that's the secret: everybody's got a shadow inside them. Different name, same scale. Every life has a biggest, saddest thing. I'm just worse at keeping it. You come be bad at it too.

AND THE OSCAR GOES TO . . .

by Catherine Fennelly

I used to be a hairdresser, but now I'm an actress.

Here's a sample monologue from my days, which I spend standing up at a hair salon midway between Boston and Cape Cod:

"Oh, you have two kids? They're seventeen and eight? That's nice. I've got three. Two are in fifth and eighth grades, and the other went to Wake County Community College in North Carolina. He graduated in 2015, and now he's a security manager in Boston. He used to work at Dunkin' Donuts in Braintree, and he was so good at it—honestly, he was at his best when he was pouring coffee for a bunch of regulars. Kids, right?"

I know. It sounds like I'm still a hairdresser. But what would you think if I shared my inner monologue with you? The one that's, you know, true:

"You have two kids? That's nice. I have three, but the oldest one, Paul, died of a Fentanyl overdose. He was twenty-one. Yeah, I knew he was an addict. Yeah, I tried to do everything I could to help him, but my love wasn't enough to save him. He still ended up dying in someone's apartment in Arlington."

My clients don't want to hear any of that. Both the men and women alike want an armchair therapist who's going to focus on "just a trim" or a "number-two blade up the sides and just finger length on top," and forgettable chitchat that can conveniently end right before their blow-dry. So I tell them what

they want to hear. I tell them how proud I am of my son in all that he's accomplishing in life with his hard-earned degree in business management. Not that I'm proud that my son was a kind and loving kid who fought the devil like hell for eight years and lost. Not that I'm a . . . well, what is a word that describes a mother who lost her child?

It's easier making up a story about how my son's life would have been had substance use disorder not snatched it away from all of us, had he not struggled with being bipolar and felt that this world sucked and that he didn't fit into it. Especially for the ladies who sit there with foil in their hair and complain about "all these fucking junkies walking around in the middle of the street."

If I could turn myself inside out, my clients would run for the hills.

You must be thinking, Why doesn't she just take some time off and not deal with this crap? Hike to a remote mountaintop or head to a yoga retreat and try to find inner peace? Trust me, I wish I could stop working to grieve, but financially I cannot. Not everyone has the cash to go to a beach and scream at the ocean. Three days after Paul's funeral, I was back at the chair in all black (a color that for the first time I didn't mind wearing), cutting bobs on nights and weekends. My husband went back to his construction job. We had to pay the rent for ourselves and our two little girls. We're always on the verge of being evicted from our house and our car being repossessed. Grieving doesn't really fit in here.

Sometimes, as I make up this perfect, convenient world for my clients, the guilt slams into me. I wonder if Paul's up there, furious and hurt, listening to my fake chatter, asking "Ma, are you ashamed? Were you embarrassed of me?" And it breaks my heart.

But every so often, someone sits in my chair who gets it. If you're a people person who works with the public, you get a sense of them even before they open their mouths. I know who's not receptive to the truth and who is. Like the gentleman who told me he was going on vacation with his young grandkids and then, distraught, spilled to me that he was raising them because his daughter just didn't have her life together. I knew exactly what he meant by that. Or the kid who pulled up his sleeve to show an angel hugging a crying broken heart that read "Caitlin": his high-school sweetheart who died from drugs. Those are the people who open up, and those are the people I reach. I tell the gentleman I know how he feels, and talk about Paul. I show the kid my own tribute tattoo ("Love you from England to China"—a phrase Paul came up with when he was five, kind of like "to infinity and beyond").

I've managed to reach other people, too, over at TNT Boxing in Randolph. Throughout my life, I've always boxed to help me deal with my anger. And after Paul died, that anger spiked from feeling powerless to save my own son. Here, there is no stigma associated with substance use disorder. Most people who box at the gym are recovering addicts themselves. Here, I let my anger out and beat the crap out of a trainer geared up with a headpiece and jockstrap. Here, I've organized a group of boxing mothers who lost their kids to drugs, who are suffering just like me, and who wake up every morning feeling like they're drowning. Here, I'm just Cathe, Paul's mom, the one with the crazy right hook.

I still have to protect myself at the salon in ways I don't have to at the gym, with my silence or my made-up stories. But whenever I force myself to ignore the next complaint about junkies from a client, I close my eyes and take a deep breath, biding my time until I hit the next punching bag. Because yeah, I may feel broken, black and blue, but I'm still standing, ready to fight.

1937 (ish) — 2013

FOREVER YOUNGER

by Caroline Waxler

My mom was always talking about age—just usually in the context of how a woman should never talk about it.

When Mom died, in 2013, she was either age eighty-two or seventy-five, depending on the source. Over the course of her lifetime she'd give me one number. Others would give me a different one. She'd brush off those messengers as "jealous relatives just trying to be nasty." I never pressed the issue, as I had other things to argue with her about: curfew time, chores, and pretty please could she pay off my credit card debt. Why worry about her age?

My creeping age, on the other hand, was always front and center, particularly as I got older without first bothering to get a husband. When I turned thirty-five, I told her I was planning a party. She was horrified. *Why would you ever tell anyone that number, much less celebrate it? Especially when you're not married?* I brushed off her advice and threw the party, and I brazenly included a photo booth to document the occasion in all its glory.

At Mom's burial, I took a close look at both my parents' headstones. They'd been in place since around the time of my father's death, and I'm now convinced my mom did this premortem to ensure her preferred birth year made it onto the granite. My father's showed his birth year as 1940, which lined up with the fact that he had died at age thirty-seven in 1977. On Mom's was a birth year—albeit not hers: 1937. I'd never imagined that the lie about her age (she was born some seven years earlier) would be taken to the grave. When her birth date was juxtaposed to my dad's, though, the reason became clear. Even in death, my mom didn't want my father—or anyone else for that matter—to know how much older she had been.

After her death I remained as confused—and bemused—as I'd been while she was alive. My first reaction, when I saw the 1937 chiseled in the stone, was to second-guess: *Wait . . . was that actually the right year? Nah, it can't be . . . but it is on her headstone, after all.* My second was to start smiling that she got away with it. If only I'd gone with her to visit my father's grave when she'd wanted me to, I would have had the chance to confront her head-on (as opposed to headstone-on).

The first clue appeared as we were writing Mom's obituary. I called her law school to check a detail that had made it into family lore, that at the time of her graduation she was Columbia University's youngest female graduate. They couldn't confirm that, but they did confirm her graduation date, which was earlier than what I had roughly guessed. Mom never did tell us the year of her graduation, and she would cut out the last digit from any reunion year photo.

Other clues popped up as I cleaned out my childhood home. Like the marriage certificate that had the wrong year of my mom's birth. The last digit of her birth date had been "updated." I know this because I had previously uncovered her original (correct) birth certificate, which she would have had to submit to apply for the marriage license. It was then that I remembered family jokes and stories about my mother's drivers' licenses with various ages, and it occurred to me that this was the cause of some legendary passport drama. The federal government apparently wasn't amused at the inconsistencies in the records, and refused her request for a passport.

While my father initially suspected my mother of having a criminal past ("I have never heard of anybody not being able to get a passport. . . . What exactly did you do?"), Mom attributed the rejection to a clerical error. An intervention by a highly placed law school connection pushed the passport approval through. What we don't know was whether my father was in the dark, or if he really knew the age gap scoop, too, and was just humoring her. Given that he was a brilliant and kind man, I'm going to go with the latter.

But the best-found evidence of Mom's commitment to lying about her age was hiding in plain sight on a little-used bookshelf tucked away in our family home: *How to Lie About Your Age: Sly Advice, plus 60 Years of History and Nostalgia, to Help You Get Away with It*. The book was published in 1979, when Mom was forty-nine—or forty-two, by her own account. It looked never to have been opened. Little wonder, given that by that point my mom could have practically written her own title on the subject.

Though I don't care to admit it, Mom's hang-up has taken its toll on me—especially in recent years. Now, in my mid-forties, the same woman who celebrated thirty-five with a photo booth will go silent whenever anyone mentions age in polite company. After all, I enjoy employment in a workforce that prioritizes youth, and advertising decades of experience is not exactly apples-to-apples with saying you can code. Recently, however, a younger friend startled me by asking my age directly, and I answered truthfully. Immediately, though, I had revealer's remorse, and thought I'd run out of breath swearing her to secrecy.

Maybe it's time for me to crack the spine on that book.

F IS FOR FORGIVENESS

by Haley Tanner

The writer Anne Lamott says this of forgiveness: "Not forgiving is like drinking rat poison and waiting for the rat to die." To which I say, "I'll take my rat poison neat with three olives."

I see Anne's point, I do, but like a stubborn teenager I just don't care to forgive that family member who did not show up to my husband's funeral, who didn't send a card or call or e-mail or text or send a smoke signal or blow a horn from a distant mountain.

This guy, the one I'm mad at, he's not even really that important to me. We weren't close in the first place, but I just *love* being angry at him. I love talking about how angry I am, about how awful he is, how selfish, how terrible it was that he didn't show up. And there's something about Not Showing Up that stays with you. I've met people who can't tell you what they had for breakfast, but they can tell you exactly who didn't make a shiva call twenty years earlier.

It's been five years since Gavin died at age thirty-one. It was cancer. It was awful. It was brain surgeries and liver tumors and metastasis and getting the Very Bad News from the oncologist and me barfing right there in the sink in the exam room from the shock of it. It was worrying all the time. It was trying to live my whole young life in the tiny sliver of hope that exists when 99.9 percent of people with this form of cancer are dead within five years.

But even when the cancer was terrible, our lives weren't: we traveled and partied and made plans and took our dogs to the dog run. The day before Gavin died, we ate fried chicken and pie in his hospital room with our best friends and felt lucky to be in love.

Really, the most frightening thing about watching Gavin die was that I didn't die also. I was very young—twenty-eight—to learn that there exists a pain so profound that it should kill you but lacks the mercy. It will get better, everyone told me, which was the last thing I wanted to hear and the last thing I wanted to be true. I wanted to stay in that place, close to Gavin, close to the epicenter.

I kept breathing, my heart kept beating, and eventually things got better—just like everyone said they would. And because I had already lived through the absolute worst thing I could imagine, I was suddenly afraid of nothing and in a bit of a mad rush to live the life I wanted to live.

I fell in love again—fully, completely, madly in love. I ran the New York City marathon with Gavin's name on my back. I published a novel and went on book tour. I got pregnant and gave birth to my baby in a tub in my apartment. I held my newborn daughter and told her all about my first love, how beautiful he was and how kind.

I still miss Gavin, and I talk about him every day, but I'm not sad all the time anymore. Sometimes my grief is far from me. But don't get me wrong: I'm still actively furious at this one rat bastard for not showing up at the funeral.

Maybe that's because living through Gavin's death made me a bit of an extremist in certain ways. Seizing the day is not just bumper-sticker territory for me. I am aware at every moment just how brief our time here is, and I seize the crap out of it. Also, there is nothing like death to teach you exactly how important your friends and family are—exactly how crucial their love and their mighty presence is. The people who have shown up, they are my tribe. The people who have not shown up, they are not.

Forgiving this rat feels like a betrayal of Gavin in a way that nothing else does. When I fell in love with someone else, that didn't feel like a betrayal. When I gave away Gavin's possessions to friends and family and, finally, Goodwill, that did not feel like a betrayal. But forgiving someone who has not acknowledged Gavin's death feels way worse than it should; holding on to the anger feels way better than it should.

There's a self-help section at the local bookstore that promises that you can fix everything—that with enough hard work, you can heal and let go and forgive and make right every little thing in your life. I find this to be a strange goal. I don't want to work hard to heal anything else, and I don't feel like forgiving. I'm tired of it. I just want to live.

Maybe that'll change one day. For now, though, I feel entitled to my anger, to my rat poison, to whatever my weird wounded psyche wants.

WORK LIFE AFTER LOSS
aka It's OK to cry on the job.

RIGHT AWAY:

Share the news.
Contact your manager and anyone you oversee. Or delegate someone else to do it with whatever details you feel comfortable providing.

Ask for time off.
Check if your company offers bereavement leave, or request personal time off before disappearing for a period of time.

Delegate.
It's unfair, but the work world keeps turning. Clear your schedule, turn on your out-of-office response, and reassign urgent matters if you can.

YOU **DON'T** WANT THIS:

Hey Jenny, what's the ETA on that expense report?

WHILE YOU'RE OUT:

Check in.
Not ready to return after three days or even a week? Consider what would work for you emotionally and financially, and ask your manager. See what she says.

ONCE YOU'RE BACK:

Anticipate the awkwardness.
Some coworkers will get *waaaay* too personal. Others will ignore your loss altogether.

Was it an open casket?

So, did you catch Real Housewives last night?

Expect a few meltdowns.
Find some locations for a break or good cry (the bathroom two floors down, your parked car) and a friend you can contact for support once you're there.

Be gracious.
Your colleagues are bound to have picked up some slack while you were out. Thank them for it.

Check in with yourself.
As time goes by, you might need additional support. Ask for it. If you don't speak up for your needs, nobody else will.

MAKE THERAPY APPOINTMENT ☑

ASK FOR TEMPORARY REVISED WORK SCHEDULE ☑

Pay it forward.
Tell your employer what worked and what didn't about the bereavement policy, if they have one. (Many workplaces don't.) Use your experience to make someone else's easier.

JOURNEYS

Where We've Headed But Not
Necessarily Ended Up

INTRODUCTION

by Rebecca Soffer

Four years after burying my mom and five days after my dad's funeral, Justin and I landed in New Delhi. Going to India was at the top of my husband's wish list, and we'd planned the trip a year beforehand. We weren't seeking some spiritual catharsis; we just wanted to be tourists and have encounters that were far out of our element.

Even though I'd had many healing experiences while traveling after my mom's death, I wanted desperately to cancel our plans. It felt disrespectful to embark on a "dream journey" when my last living parent had been lowered into the ground just a few days earlier. But the rabbi from my parents' synagogue, a chill guy who could easily be taken for a Deadhead, reminded me that after my mom's death I'd regretted not taking more time for myself. "Let's be honest," he said over bagels and schmear during the shiva in my parents' soon-to-be-dismantled home. "If he were in the same circumstances, your dad would have taken this trip. By the way, are you gonna eat that?" He was right: my dad would have never considered *not* going. And, for me, there was nobody alive left to stay for.

The second I got off the plane, I felt like I'd arrived on floor 7 ½ in *Being John Malkovich*. I've lived in and traveled through multiple countries but never felt so out of alignment. To start, the time difference was 10.5 hours. So while it felt like 3:30 in the afternoon for me, it was 2:00 a.m. in New Dehli. The terminal was teeming with vibrant saris, smoke, and a confusing heady brew of KFC, Domino's Pizza, and kathi rolls. It was so crowded that I was actually scared to go into the public restroom, lest I never find Justin again and become a permanent citizen of Indira Gandhi International Airport. The car route to the hotel was shrouded in a deep winter fog through which random things would emerge—a Christmas-lighted rickshaw, a boy carrying a string of marigolds, a cow. It was creepy as shit.

That first day I was too nervous to eat anything but white rice from the Westerner-filled hotel, and I showered with my mouth sealed shut. But then I started to relax, and, dare I say, enjoy myself. We snaked our way through Rajasthan, then down toward Mumbai. In Udaipur, I got sweet-talked into buying pashminas by a shopkeeper who delighted in modeling them on himself while proclaiming, "Fabulous!" I was an enthusiastic Token White Person at a movie theater in Jaipur, where we were asked to pose for a dozen photos with curious locals. And I didn't think twice before eating an entire bowl of stew ladled out by a man who'd just sneezed into the cauldron (to be honest, I kind of regret that decision).

All my senses were stretched to the max throughout the trip. And while e-mails about estate issues and death certificates popped up on my phone, I had neither the time nor the mental ability to ruminate on my losses. I barely even mentioned them to Justin. They just whirled around along with all the other stuff that made no sense to me in India.

Then one day we visited a Jain temple in Ranakpur—48,000 square feet of pure white marble intricately carved into a thousand-plus pillars and dozens of domes. It was completely silent. I walked around alone for the first time since learning about my dad's fatal heart attack, focusing on women's skirts billowing in the wind and the bright stone against the clear sky. A thirtysomething barefoot priest in marigold orange with Patrick Swayze hair approached. He kindly asked where I was from, surely expecting a simple response like "LA!" Instead, perhaps due to that kindness, this was the moment everything unraveled. I melted into tears, hugged him, and told him everything about losing my mother and my father and my unfamiliar new status in this large, chaotic world. He listened in silence, looking at me intently and yet with no judgment in his soft eyes, and lightly touched my shoulder (because probably the hugging was totally off base). Admittedly, that part reads a bit cliché. But it certainly wasn't planned, and I gave in to the moment.

Everything looked bleak when we returned home in early January, the saddest time of year in New York. The city was coming down off its holiday cheer, and the prospect of having to deal with a dead dad and all the ramifications of that was forming a pit in my stomach. But India's unstructured existence, which seemed to fit so much better with my grief, had fortified and replenished me. I was in a dreary New York with a grim chore, yet I felt ready to do what I had to do.

I wasn't surprised by my renewed energy. When I eventually traveled—frequently—after my mom's death, my friends worried I was escaping the inevitable. Many of them assured me that structure was the only way to go. That I was doing the right thing heading back to the daily production of *The Colbert Report*, just two weeks after her funeral, when I was in full-on shock. They said sameness and routine at a job I loved would ground me again, heal me, and reorient me to this brave new motherless world.

But I was unable to think in New York, especially in the television studio, where I fake-laughed at jokes while trying to shut out images of my mother's mangled corpse in my head. When I hit the road during the show's many hiatuses throughout the year, I could finally think clearly.

It was on a sailboat in Bodrum, Turkey, for example, where I decided to break my moratorium on dating and go out with Justin, whom I'd met the night before that trip. It was on safari in Kruger National Park where, in the absence of my most trusted sounding board, my mother, I had a conversation with the elephants outside my hut, and we all agreed it might be time to leave my job. And it was on a road trip down Route 1 from San Francisco to San Simeon where I thought about the people in my life and considered how to maintain only the positive connections. (Coincidentally, that process began the same day I got stuck in the Esalen parking lot after making a wrong turn.*)

While these physical trips jostled me out of my day-to-day, they were outnumbered by the ways I began to feel like a tourist in my new life. One result was a career path I suddenly wasn't so sure I wanted. Nothing will make you mull over your legacy more than having to write a loved one's obituary, whittling an entire lifetime's accomplishments into succinct copy. *Am I leading my best professional life—and leaving enough room for other stuff too?*, the record plays in my mind. *Am I honoring my parents' values by prioritizing projects that make a difference, if even just for a few people?* (Not so easy when one still has to

---

* Sadly, I'm not independently wealthy. I just made some imprudent financial decisions to prioritize these escapes (you don't need to make a Roth IRA contribution *every* year, right?).

cover rent and eat dinner.) *Would they be proud? And will my kids be proud of me when they write my obit one day?*

Another result was reconsidering where "home" is after losing a safe place to return to time and again. A native Philadelphian, I always vaguely assumed I'd move back one day. Now it feels as though I'd be moving back to a faint trace of my family, and, knowing this, the whole world seems up for grabs. That might inspire envy in some, who'd love to be able to change their geographic circumstances, but for me, not knowing where to plant myself or how to decide where home should be has been existential torture. I thought it would get better after having kids, but in some ways it's gotten worse, because the stakes seem higher. Wherever we end up, there will be no trips back "home" to visit Grandma and Grandpa on my side, no way to ingrain the place Mom came from in their identities.

We temporarily tried Austin, where my husband was raised. It's a vibrant and quirky town, but I couldn't stop imagining my son becoming the wrong type of *Friday Night Lights* character and looking at me as though I were some anxious East Coaster (which, let's be honest, I am). We bought a house in the Berkshires in Western Massachusetts after my dad died, in part with some of the proceeds from the sale of my parents' place, so that I could feel like I actually had a physical foundation beyond a tiny and impermanent Manhattan rental. But realistically, we don't know how to base ourselves there full time and make both of our careers work. We considered San Francisco, where I have many relatives, but it feels too far from the majority of my friends. So for now, we remain in New York City, where I've lived for seventeen years, and which, in spite of the still-raw memories of living through the worst of my grief here, and the fact that its cost of living may decide otherwise for us, feels like home more than any other place.

The whole where-do-I-belong exercise sometimes feels like the grown-up version of a game in my toddler's swim class. At the end of class, the kids sit and splash on an enormous yellow foam duck in the middle of the pool. The instructor spins it and sings:

Round and round and round we go
round and round and round we go
round and round and round we go
swimming with Mr. Duck, quack quack
Ready . . . GO!

Then everyone scramble-swims in the direction in which they feel most comfortable. Some parents and kids always go to the same spot. But I, holding my son (who isn't quite swimming on his own), always flail out in a new, random direction. Nomads. Sometimes, as I dart around, it feels as though Mr. Duck is watching me closely, much like the priest at Ranakpur, waiting for me to figure out where to land once and for all.

MY WEDDING GOWN'S LAST DANCE

by Lucy Kalanithi

No woman ever knows the actual fate of her wedding dress.

After the celebrations are over, she has it cleaned of all traces of revelry, pressed, and sealed. She rehangs it gently, perhaps picturing her future daughters, her own hands stroking the dress decades later, or the sexy cocktail getup it could be after hacking off a few feet of organza.

But I'd bet good money nobody imagines wearing her dress in tatters years down the line, while deep in the woods and 6,400 feet above sea level, and with a smile on her face.

Our future daughter, Paul's and mine, was eight months old when we ordered home oxygen for her father, whose body was becoming steadily weaker, racked by the metastatic cancer that was running riot. I rolled the green gas tanks into our bedroom, where, bright as the day I'd worn it eight and a half years earlier, my wedding dress hung in our closet, sealed in a plastic bag for nearly that entire time. I'd worn a red sari for our marriage ceremony, but this—the simple long white dress I'd worn to our reception—was my wedding dress. Paul loved that dress.

Needing oxygen was not a good sign for Paul's health, but it came with a tinge of hope. With that plastic tubing in his nose, Paul would be able to breathe more easily at high altitude. Eight weeks later we'd be at Stanford Sierra Camp, up in the mountains of California's El Dorado National Forest.

Stanford Sierra Camp opens for three months every summer for Stanford alumni and their families, and Paul had worked two full summers there as an undergrad fifteen years prior. In the memoir he later wrote, Paul said that the camp "[concentrated] all the idylls of youth: beauty manifest in lakes, mountains, people; richness in experience, conversation, friendships . . . every day felt full of life." The sixty-odd undergrads who staff the camp wear dozens of hats, cooking meals, acting as janitors, producing skits for the campers (and raunchy versions for themselves), guiding children on hikes, and entertaining the family campers. There are no closer friendships than those forged during the exhilarating and often debauched time staffers share. Every few years postgraduation, they'd reunite there, us included.

Though we knew Paul was dying, we still experienced joy together, and visiting Sierra Camp would certainly bring joy. Both of us were experienced backpackers—though he could no longer hike, we'd revel in the beautiful setting—and even the thought of taking oxygen tanks to altitude made the much-anticipated trip seem somehow more badass, an echo of our treks together over the years, when we'd stuff our hiking packs with xenon headlamps and butane stoves. We were a team then; we were a team still.

But Paul never made it to this reunion. He died, lying in bed next to me and surrounded by family, just a week after we brought the oxygen home. His family, friends—including dozens from his Sierra Camp days—and I were all heartbroken. In the weeks after Paul's death we gathered together, cried, and reminisced. I buried his body, planned his memorial service, and held our daughter close. I also decided I would go to Sierra Camp as his widow—a word that still shocked me, but whose starkness reflected the pain I felt on losing Paul.

When the over-thirty set packs for these reunions, they bring their young children and their travel cribs, breast pumps, white noise machines, and other items not normally found in teenagers' camp duffels. But they still pack their hiking boots, and they always bring "rally gear": their college-dance-party clothes, a key ingredient of Sierra Camp parties. One girl-friend brought multicolored fluorescent cat-emblazoned leg-gings and a pink wig. Another dude brought a prom dress. Paul's brother would be there, and for him I brought a vintage Stanford golf shirt, brightly striped tube socks, and a gorilla suit—all from Paul's closet. For myself, not really knowing why, I packed my sleeping wedding dress.

Camaraderie, music, snowball fights, and reminiscing commenced. The first sunny morning up at camp saw our daughter's first encounter with snow. As she squinted at its brightness, my eyes pricked with tears. I so crushingly loved her and so crushingly missed Paul. He'd adored this place, and he still felt so close it was as if he might have been hiding just behind any of these tall pines. It was almost too much to bear; but it was the only place on earth I wanted to be.

His friends felt the same: Paul was a neurosurgeon and a writer, but aside from his intellect, he was loved for his cre-ativity and irreverence. In tribute to T. S. Eliot's *The Waste Land*, he'd cowritten a comedy sketch called "The Slapstick Waste Land," in which he and a counterpart performed sec-tions of Eliot's masterpiece, yelling "Stirring dull roots with spring rain!" while smashing each other in the face with cream pies and pratfalling on banana peels. It was here that he'd built that skit, while lounging on a wooden deck in front of Sierra Camp's main lodge. On the final night of reunion weekends, the former staffers resurrect those talent-show skits—this reunion would be no exception—and they always close with another well-loved skit that mixes the solemn and the absurd.

In "Water Ballet," eight toga-wearing people glide through a slow choreographed dance to the strains of Pachelbel's Canon in D, their faces serene. They balance silver water jugs on their shoulders, and as the music elicits nostalgia from the audience, they begin to gracefully take sips and spit mouthfuls onto one another, the music and their solemn faces juxtaposing the inexplicability of their actions. It's strangely stirring, surprisingly aesthetic, and pretty goddamn hilarious. They finish by tossing the remaining water directly onto the audience, signaling a night of dancing and celebration. Paul wore that toga many times.

I'd gone through the weekend with my wedding dress hanging unperturbed in my cabin's closet—maybe it had been silly to bring it. But on the last day, I approached a friend with an epiphany: I needed to wear it during "Water Ballet." Paul's closest friends and brother would perform, and midway through, I'd make my way up to the stage carrying a cooler of King Cobra, a horrendous malt liquor Paul had loved. Instead of spewing water, they'd spit that. And instead of drenching the audience, they'd take aim at me.

The skit commenced. Strains of violin filled the room. Midway through, I ascended the stage, solemnly passed out the beer, and stood still among the dancers. When I look back at a video someone was kind enough to shoot on a wobbling iPhone, I'm struck by my pose: arms out, palms up, as if I

am open to whatever might come—a stance of radical acceptance. And that felt right: I was so utterly overwhelmed by
sadness that my only power was to face it authentically, let it
chill me, shock me, drip down my body just as the King Cobra did, and to stand up there in this singular and absurd skit,
which somehow managed to honor Paul even more than his
somber memorial service.

Realizing what I was wearing, the audience leaped to their
feet, eyebrows raised, whooping. Some of them were Paul's
close friends, many of whom had attended our wedding, and
others only knew Paul as a witty prankster thanks to Sierra
Camp lore. We were all spontaneous participants in an intensely
personal and communal ritual of remembrance—one of those
preciously rare moments in which both absolutely nothing, and
yet somehow everything, is sacred.

One of our best friends—a woman who'd been in Paul's wedding party and who'd become one of my closest confidantes—
glided toward me and stoically poured an entire can of King
Cobra straight into my cleavage. I stayed still, shuddering, smiling, and crying. The room went wild. By the end of the skit, I
was drenched, sticky, and sickly sweet-smelling like a college-
party dance floor. My dress, once pure white, was streaked with
amber. The dance party began.

Fifteen years beforehand, Paul had come here as an aca-
demically serious yet wildly funny college student. Twelve
years beforehand, we had met on the first day of medical school
and quickly fallen in love. Ten years beforehand, he'd brought
me to his beloved Sierra Camp for the first time; eight years
beforehand we'd married on the shores of the Long Island
Sound, and seven weeks beforehand he'd died in my arms in a

hospital bed. All those moments somehow converged into one bracing jolt as a tipsy friend careened into me and coursed a frozen strawberry margarita down my back. Journey's "Don't Stop Believin'" thumped into the night. I stepped onto the dance floor.

The next morning, my head pounded after the late night. But my body was relaxed, my eyes just a little brighter. Friends offered to attempt to have the dress cleaned. But I knew no one would ever wear it again. It had served its final purpose: that King Cobra had rinsed my broken heart. Our daughter and I would move into a new future, ensconced by this community, and holding on to Paul in other ways while leaving this dress behind.

WHERE THE HEART NO LONGER IS

by Jacqueline Murekatete

Home is where the heart is, the old adage goes, and it's generally understood to mean the place where those dearest to us are. But when those people don't live there anymore, when they *don't live* anymore, what becomes of home?

For me, home was a small farming village in southern Rwanda. It's where I lived until the age of nine with my parents, four brothers, two sisters, and a large extended family of aunts and uncles, cousins and friends. Mine was a relatively carefree childhood, full of lively family meals, long games of hide-and-seek, and near nightly competitions to see who among us could catch the most fireflies. I dreamed of becoming a doctor. We kids all had big dreams.

Then within a mere hundred days beginning in April of 1994, Rwanda became the site of one of the worst genocides of the twentieth century. More than one million people, the overwhelming majority ethnic Tutsis, but also some moderate Hutus, are estimated to have been killed at the hands of the ethnic Hutu majority. My parents, all of my siblings, and both of my grandmothers were among those killed. My extended network of aunts and uncles, cousins and friends, was also snuffed out in the mass murder.

When the genocide began, I happened to be in my maternal grandmother's village, about two hours away from home. When Hutus in that village began slaughtering Tutsis with machetes, nail-studded clubs, and spears, I found myself on the run with my grandmother, hiding in one place after another, first at a nearby county office for a few days, then for about a week in the home of a Hutu man paid to hide us, before our sanctuary was discovered and I was separated from my grandmother. During the genocide, I watched the people around me being killed, and many times I came within an inch of my life—each time believing that it was my last moment on earth. I ultimately took refuge in an orphanage run by Italian priests, and it is there that I survived the atrocities. After the genocide, I would learn from a surviving uncle that my Hutu neighbors had come and taken my parents, all six siblings, and the other Tutsis in the village to a nearby river, and there murdered them one by one, simply because of their Tutsi ethnicity.

Another uncle living in the United States learned of my miraculous survival and quickly managed to get me out of Rwanda. He would adopt me and raise me as his own. I arrived in Virginia in October 1995 to live with him. There I struggled to cope with the trauma of what had happened to my family, all the while trying to adapt to the new language and culture. I had recurring nightmares about what I had witnessed.

For the next fifteen years I wondered what had become of the setting of my once-idyllic childhood. In 2010, I decided to go back and find out. I was living in New York at the time, where I was in my second year of law school. My friends wondered why I wanted to go back at all; they worried that the experience would be too traumatic for me. But I wanted to learn more about my family's death. I wanted to meet some of the Hutu neighbors who had participated in their murders, or stood by and done nothing. I wanted something akin to closure.

The flight from New York to the Rwandan capital of Kigali took about twenty hours. The whole way there, I doubted my decision. What if the trip proved too much for me; what if it made me hateful or bitter? But now there was no turning back. I stayed a couple days in the capital city, and then drove to my childhood village with an uncle and cousins who were living in Kigali.

As we wound through the countryside, I watched villagers carrying containers of all types of local goods atop their heads—bananas, avocados, mangoes, grains. Some children playing near the side of the road stopped to wave as our car passed. A few hours on, I began to recognize the landscape—the rolling hills, the open-air market. It was like watching a film reel of my early childhood. There, in my mind's eye, were my parents and siblings, cousins and friends. There was my older brother, Jean D'amour, tending to the family cows after school. There were my little sisters, Siphoro and Josephine, drawing water from the nearby well. There we all were, my three younger brothers, too, sitting around the kitchen table eating green bananas with spinach and tomatoes—my favorite!—and singing hymns of our Seventh-Day Adventist faith. There we were, boys in one bedroom, girls in another, telling each other stories until we lost our battle with sleep.

Tears overcame me by the time the car came to a stop at the top of the hill overlooking what used to be our family property. I gazed at the plot below, where our home and farm had been. There was no sign of the house, which I knew had been destroyed almost immediately after the genocide. But I wasn't totally prepared to see it gone, replaced by fields of green vegetables, yams, and cassava.

I looked around at some of the neighbors' children, who had come to take a look at the village visitors. These children, born after the genocide, most likely had no idea that the farm on which they were now standing used to have a house on it that belonged to my family. I felt like a total stranger in a place that had once been the only world I thought existed.

I wanted to scream, to let everyone in this village know that this had been my home, that this land was once my family's, and that my parents had farmed it tirelessly to give their children a better life. How cruel that my entire family had been wiped out—and how unfair that there was no memorial, no sign here proclaiming that they had ever lived.

I checked in with my heart. It was no longer there. And this was no longer home.

FEET, PAIN, LOVE

by Sarah Fox

With each step my feet squished into the soles of my hiking boots. The straps of my backpack dragged my wet clothes across my skin, chafing it with my every movement. My hood hung across my face, and water dripped onto the tip of my nose. I still had twelve miles to go, and I was miserable. There had been two days of rain, but I'd been miserable for much longer than that.

A year and a half earlier I had crawled into a tiny hospital bed in Philadelphia with my boyfriend, Chris. Pressed together by the tightness of the guardrails, I nestled my chin into his bony shoulder and listened to him tell me that there was nothing left to do; his body was rejecting the lungs he had received via transplant two years earlier. It was a week before his thirty-first birthday, and he was going home to die.

Over the next year, I watched his world slowly shrink. He resigned from his job and moved back in with his parents. At first he still slept in his childhood bedroom upstairs, and he could move from room to room. We even managed to eat dinner out at a restaurant one last time. Then slowly he was confined to a wheelchair and the ground floor, and finally to the hospital bed that sat in the living room, hissing and sighing as it changed pressure to prevent him from developing bedsores.

Before Chris died, he gave me a book about a man who walked the Camino de Santiago. This five-hundred-mile hike follows an ancient pilgrimage route through northern Spain

and ends in Santiago de Compostela, where the apostle Saint James is believed to be buried. For more than a thousand years, those seeking a contemplative journey have left their homes to walk this path. A few weeks before Chris died, I sat by his bedside and told him I wanted to hike the Camino. He loved the idea. His greatest regret, he had told me during our last Christmas together, was that we would not get to travel the world together. But that day at his bedside, as he held my hand, he asked me to bring his ashes with me. Three days later he gave me three pairs of socks he had sent his father to the store to buy, two for hiking and one to keep my feet warm at night.

Six months after his death—time spent floating through my days, plagued by a feeling of complete disconnection from family, work, and friends—I flew to Paris and caught a train south to the beginning of the Camino de Santiago. I began in the small town of Saint-Jean-Pied-de-Port at the base of the Pyrenees, along the French-Spanish border. I walked alone, in the stillness of the morning, carrying my eighteen-pound backpack and a tiny metal container the size of a key chain filled with ashes. As the sun rose, I passed farmhouses and heard the tinkling of bells on the cows grazing in mountain pastures. I pressed on toward the mountain pass that would take me into Spain, and at the end of the long day I limped into a stone monastery that opened its doors to the pilgrims streaming down the slopes.

For thirty-four days I woke up and walked. All. Day. I walked through barren plateaus, shaded forests, and endless fields of burned sunflower husks. There were small, peaceful mountain villages and seamy industrial areas on the outskirts of cities. Huge blisters bloomed on my feet, and I covered them with bandages so I could continue. I wore a knee brace and bought a walking stick to temper the shooting pains as I climbed down mountains. At night I would drop my backpack on the ground, massage my aching calves, and stretch my hips. I hadn't set out to make myself suffer. But the angst I had been feeling for so long merged with the physical pain from the walk, and the two became so tightly woven together that I couldn't tell them apart.

I listened when my body told me I needed a break, water, or something to eat. Sometimes it told me I had to stop short of my goal for the day, but other times it allowed me to walk farther than I thought possible. Pilgrims walking the Camino de Santiago mark themselves by wearing scallop shells, the sign of Saint James, and as I walked, it was easy to meet others who were going to Santiago. On the path there were other young people walking with the grief of losing their partners to car accidents or diseases. There were mothers who had lost their children, men whose wives had left them, and people whose lives simply hadn't turned out as they planned. At night we sat around the simple pilgrim meals offered at small restaurants in the villages and shared bottles of Spanish red wines. We had pushed ourselves physically all day, so there was simply no energy left to hold up the emotional walls that keep others from seeing the pain in our lives. We shared our sadness openly. I could say "My boyfriend died" without the conversation ending awkwardly, because everyone who was walking had a similar story.

The rain cleared as I approached Santiago, where the friends I had met along the way were waiting. We had agreed to stop a kilometer from the city so that we could finish our walk together. One of the women had hurt her foot, and everyone switched off carrying her backpack so that we would cross into the city at the same time. We celebrated the end of our long hike in the shadow of the great cathedral of Santiago de Compostela, like so many pilgrims before us. Pushing my body to—and past—its limits had helped me reconnect with myself and with the people around me. I may have started the hike alone, but I finished with others walking beside me. Chris was with me, too.

FROM A PURPLE ROOM TO THE OBAMA WHITE HOUSE

by *Marisa Renee Lee*

I watched Barack Obama's historic presidential campaign largely from the bedside of my dying mother. She had stage IV breast cancer, which was compounded by her multiple sclerosis. It was a pretty shitty time—for both my mom and everyone who loved her.

While I will forever cherish those final months together, I could not help but feel I was missing out on something extraordinary. I was the kid who had held some form of elected or appointed office since the third grade. I was the high-school student who had lobbied for a seat on the local school board to represent my peers. I had started my first nonprofit project before I was old enough to drive. I was young, black, and ambitious. And I knew I should be helping Obama get elected.

Obama spoke of "reclaiming the American dream" during a January 2008 campaign stop in Kansas, the Democratic primaries already under way. He spoke of an America where every child has the same opportunities, of eliminating gaps in access, of ensuring our shared dreams outweigh our petty differences. That night, I sat in my purple-painted childhood bedroom, feeling my own future slipping through my fingers.

My mother—my guiding force, organizing principle, and best friend—died at 5:37 p.m. on February 28, 2008. It was a few weeks after my twenty-fifth birthday, and a few weeks after it became clear that Obama might actually win this thing.

In my grief, I quickly fell out of love with my finance career, with my *Sex and the City* attempt at a New York City life, and even with the breast cancer charity I had started in Mom's honor. Compared with my grief, just about everything else felt silly and mundane.

But what of the ambition that had longed defined me?

"Marisa has good social skills, but demands only the leadership role," my kindergarten teacher wrote on one of my report cards. I have never really understood the word *no*, in part because my mom always encouraged me to try even when failure seemed inevitable. When I was not admitted early to Harvard, Mom—who'd never been to college herself—encouraged me to call the admissions office and find out why. So I did. I was admitted to Harvard in the spring.

When my mom died, my empathic boss knew me well enough to see that I needed to hit reset. He gave me several months to figure out my next steps so that I could earn a paycheck while doing so.

Obama won his presidential bid roughly one month later. The answer became clear: I would go work for him, a pretty ballsy decision, considering I had no connections to his campaign. So many others had sacrificed thousands of hours helping this man get elected and still couldn't get a coveted job in his new administration. It felt like an impossible mission, but didn't the world owe me something for stealing away the person I loved most? And wouldn't that most-loved person want me to go after my dreams? I was, after all, her living legacy. I finally felt the power and strength that comes from seeing death up close and surviving a loss.

With that power and my renewed sense of clarity and direction, I single-mindedly pursued a job in the Obama administration. I'd always been driven, but my new perseverance was beyond anything I'd known before. Nothing could hurt me worse than losing Mom. I pestered friends, colleagues, acquaintances, friends' exes—everyone I thought might know someone who could help me land a job working for the president. Fittingly, it was through my work on the breast cancer charity I started in honor of my mom that I made the connection that got me to the White House.

I headed to Washington in May 2010 to work on the president's financial recovery efforts. Over the next four years I'd hold four jobs between the US Small Business Administration, the White House Domestic Policy Council, and the White House Office of Public Engagement, all focused on crafting and implementing more inclusive economic policies for our country. Instead of preparing financial reports for bankers, I was using my finance background to prepare memos for the president and senior White House staffers on critical business and public policy issues. I was exactly where I belonged.

Seeing President Obama in action was pure magic. I got to watch him fight for the things he spoke about in that speech in Kansas. I also got to watch him poke fun at my father, melt at the sight of my godson (who had just puked on the Oval Office carpet), and argue over football with my husband.

My mother's absence has created a steeliness in me, one that lets me stare down risks and take on assignments that might overwhelm someone with thinner skin. I'm no longer afraid of the "impossible." I'm not easily inundated or intimidated. I hire, I fire, I fund-raise without fear, because I know what real fear feels like. Fear that keeps you up at night, knowing morning will bring you one day closer to being without the person you love. Fear of the day death knocks on the door, and knowing it's your job to help usher Mom between two worlds. By contrast, organizing a meeting for the leader of the free world doesn't seem all that hard.

I was always fiercely competitive and ambitious. But my mom's death has only made me more so—emboldening me to pursue what it is that I want sooner rather than later, because I know how fragile life is, and how short. I wish she were still here today, but I know I am who I am, and where I am, only because she isn't.

ART IMITATES LOSS

by Michael Greif, as told to Rebecca Soffer

Jonathan Larson was inspired to write the musical *Rent* as a response, as a way of honoring some close friends who were struggling with the disease or had died from AIDS. At that time I, too, was mourning the loss of many people I loved to the AIDS epidemic. It was always the best, the brightest, and the most vital who were dying.

There were many other artists who were navigating that terrible terrain and giving expression to our grief and anger and confusion. Plays like *As Is*, *The Normal Heart*, and *Angels in America*, and the novels and memoirs of Paul Monette and David Feinberg, among others, were giving us perspective and helping us to cope or not cope. We were also spending a lot of time in hospital rooms and going to memorials.

Jonathan didn't die of AIDS. Jonathan died of an aortic aneurism connected to an undiagnosed disease or syndrome. There was absolutely no indication that he had anything more serious than the flu. It was completely shocking. Knowing Jonathan, it was very easy for me and the producers to determine that we should continue our plan to present his musical without him so that his voice and vision would remain in the world.

The heartbreaking irony that developed was that Jonathan himself became one of those people whose loss we were mourning while we were performing and presenting *Rent*. The song "One Song Glory" became completely about him and his legacy. "Seasons of Love," which was written to memorialize friends of his, became all about him. The musical's longevity helped to

give me, and I imagine others, an opportunity to mourn him and also to honor him. The effect it has had all around the world and the tremendous influence and inspiration that it has given so many contemporary music theater composers like Lin-Manuel Miranda, like Tom Kitt and Brian Yorkey, like Benj Pasek and Justin Paul, helped address the grief that I felt and the loss of Jonathan to the world.

Working on musicals like *Next to Normal* and most recently *Dear Evan Hansen* also keeps memories of *Rent* and my debt to Jonathan very present. Benj and Justin, the composers of *Dear Evan Hansen*, successfully bridge the gap between popular and musical theater songs, like Jonathan did. The characters in *Rent*, like the Goodmans in *Next to Normal* and the Hansens and the Murphys in *Dear Evan Hansen*, are characters so authentically drawn, so vitally connected to their moment in time, so human and fallible in their mistakes and misconceptions, that they're recognized and closely identified with by audience members.

These musicals share a search for community and family and belonging; they are remarkable because they get people talking about difficult and once taboo subjects. Their audiences are comforted and inspired by how generously and forgivingly the characters treat one another in the most challenging and heartbreaking situations. And I think that's the reason for their extraordinary, long-standing popularity.

PATCHES

by Tanzila Ahmed

Khala pulls me aside and takes me into Nana's empty bedroom. I am jetlagged, having just traveled twenty hours to
Kathmandu from Los Angeles. Khala (my mother's sister)
and Nana (my mother's father) live in a large three-story brick
house with heavy drapes and dark floor tiles in the shadows of
the Himalayan Mountains. The noise from outside—the car
horns honking, the heavy raindrops hitting the leaves of the
mango trees, the prayers blasting on loudspeakers at the local
Hindu temple—makes its way in.

"This is all you have to do," Khala tells me. "These eye drops
here, you give him three times a day. And these pills, he takes
with each meal. And this patch here, you replace on his arm once
a day. Don't forget to give him this patch—it's the one medication that decreases his hallucinations." Then she catches the
panic on my face and pauses. "Oof, you'll be fine," she tells me.

I am in Kathmandu on an adventure in babysitting. For the
next eleven days it will just be Nana and me, alone in the big
house. Khala, who works as a foreign diplomat in Kathmandu,
is headed to England for her son's college graduation. Nana's
health has been deteriorating, and the family doesn't want to
leave him alone, even with the maids, the guards, the drivers,
and the cook around.

As the oldest of Nana's grandchildren—and the one with
the salaried job, who can afford the vacation time—the responsibility has fallen on me. It has also been almost exactly

two years since my mother, his eldest daughter, died. My mother's death was sudden and unexpected, and Nana wasn't able to come out to LA for the funeral or thereafter to visit Mom's grave. The few times I've spoken with him since my mother's death, over a crackling long-distance phone line, we've been unable to communicate. His hearing is faltering, and I couldn't speak without crying.

So instead, I've come to Kathmandu.

"Why are you here?" Nana asks on my first day alone with him. We are next to each other on the one sofa in the sitting room. He spends most of his life on this sofa, napping on his bed, or walking his daily one hundred steps on the balcony. "Is this for vacation, or is it because I'm old?" His voice cracks, self-pity creeping in. I stutter that I had time off from work and wanted to visit. I don't tell him the real reason why I am there. My aunt warned me it would hurt his ego.

My earliest memory of Nana is from when I was five, and we were at a train station in Dhaka, Bangladesh. Though he was long retired from working in the railway system, all the employees would look up and salute him as he walked by. My second distinct memory of Nana is how he taught me to iron with crisp creases—everything in his life had an order and had to be presented in a certain way. He was a tall, broad man, with a thin regal mustache and a close-cropped head of hair. He commanded authority. Now, in his old age, his large body hunches over a bamboo cane. He wears the same wrinkled shirt for days on end as he shuffles from one side of the house to the other.

In the months leading up to my mom's death, she would call Nana daily. She had a stack of calling cards she would buy from the local South Asian market, and every evening she'd sit in the dining room to make her call. I would eavesdrop on these calls sometimes. It wasn't anything remarkable—mainly just "What did you eat today?" But it helped both of them tremendously, particularly following my nani's death.

Mom would tell me how on these calls, Nana would tell her stories of how he would see Nani. Late at night, he would feel Nani's presence in his bed. He'd rush to the wall to turn the light on and see that the bed was empty. He would turn the light off and then feel her next to him again. He stopped fighting it and just accepted that Nani was there. But it creeped out the entire family.

Though I was the one who told Mom to call Nana daily, I didn't take my own advice. I talked to Mom on the phone maybe once a week, and only when she called. On a Sunday in May, Mom and I talked on the phone about how she thought she was coming down with something, and on Wednesday at six in the evening I got a call from my sisters that they were taking her to the hospital. By 1:00 a.m. she was gone, killed by the toxicity of her own blood. I flew down from Oakland on the first morning flight out to my parents' home in Los Angeles. By Friday afternoon, she had been buried at the local Muslim graveyard.

I tried to write to Nana about how his eldest daughter had died. The last time I saw him, we had promised that we would write letters to each other. I started the letter trying to explain the circumstances, but I could never finish it. There was the medical cause of death, and then there was the obesity, depression, and financial troubles that I just couldn't begin to explain.

I was stuck with this idea that when immigrants like my

parents traverse thousands of miles for new lives, as children of these immigrants, our only real responsibility is to keep each other alive. And I had failed at that.

"Do you see her?" I ask Nana tentatively. I have become obsessed with the idea of seeing Mom again. I try to summon her in my dreams, and go to psychics for readings. My little sister felt Mom's presence right after she had died, but for me, the most I can summon is having her as a side character in a dream. If Nana is seeing Nani appearing in the dark, I wondered if Mom has started appearing as well.

His face struggles to understand. He talks about how Nani is by his side every night, how he talks to her. Nana says that Mom is sometimes there late at night as well. He gets lost in his foggy and ungraspable mind. He trails off.

He looks off into the distance and, suddenly, returns. I can tell he is annoyed by my questions. "Is there any use to have these memories?" he says. "Tell me . . ."

Halfway into babysitting, I am going mad. Khala has lured me to Kathmandu and left me alone and isolated, trapped in this house in the middle of monsoon season with an old man losing his mind. I've come to this conclusion that Nana is losing his mind upon closer inspection of his medication. The medicine, for dementia, treats symptoms of early signs of Alzheimer's. He isn't just a cantankerous old man, as my aunts told me before I flew out here. Nana is literally losing his mind. Why didn't the aunts tell me this? I feel completely fooled.

A doctor friend once said that after the age of thirty your brain starts shrinking, and people with dementia regress their memories back to that age. It explains why Nana can't remember me, why he can only remember me as my mother. I would have been fine with a cantankerous old man, but I didn't anticipate how his confusion of me with my mother would make me feel. When he is lucid, he will replay the narratives of death and remember Mom sadly. He will say she died a month ago, and I'll have to correct him, and say it has been two years.

I complain to Khala the next time she calls. I tell her how Nana is seeing things, how I feel trapped in the house, how the house feels haunted. She asks, concerned, if I'm still giving him his patch. She tells me that before they started giving him the patch, Nana's hallucinations were worse. One time he complained about a loud party that was going on in his room—all these people, music and dancing. She went into an empty room.

The patch is tiny—the size and shape of a dime, sticky like a Band-Aid, with the thinness of rice paper and the flesh tone of a white person. My task each night is to carefully pull off the old patch on his upper arm—his skin is so paper thin, mottled with brown age spots, fade spots, and graying hair, that I fear a piece of his skin ripping right off with it—and find a clean spot on his upper arm to attach a fresh patch. His arm is dotted with tiny dark brown scars, where each used patch has been ripped off. This is after the dinner of *maach* and *dhal* and *bhaath*, and Maghrib prayer under the monsoon clouds, and his one hundred scuffled exercise steps with the bamboo cane, and the nightly read-aloud because he can no longer read. And the cocktail of three pills and eight eye drops.

He holds his arm up to my face. "What is this on my arm? Are these scratches?" I examine his faded arm. I don't have the heart to tell him the striations are deep wrinkles, lining his time on this planet.

"Your skin is dry," I lie.

This patch is the medicine that keeps Nani lurking in his shadows and my mom a daughter in his dreams. It keeps the hallucinations to just whispers and the raucous party to just a figment of his imagination. Every night as my nails carefully lift the patch off, ripping my own circle scars into Nana's paper skin, I toy with the idea of skipping this patch so that he can see the shadows crawling on his skin and make sense of the flickering lights. So he can speak to them. Without the patch, would Nani emerge from the shadows? Would Mom walk in from the dreams? Would he be able to hug her? Could he tell her he loved her for me? And then maybe, just maybe, he could tell me what she said?

I wake up in the dead of the night, unable to breathe. A jinn is sitting on my chest. At least, I think it is a jinn, a heavy spirit emanating darkness. My screams are stifled, a force choking my neck. I know that if only I could scream loudly, Nana would be able to come in and save me. My arms are pinned down on either side of my head. I struggle, shaking my head, kicking my legs, trying to shake this thing off my chest. Not a sound is coming out of my mouth.

And just like that, it is gone. I jump out of bed and turn on the lights. I run to the window and see the security guards still standing with rifles slung over their shoulders. The house is quiet except for the ticking sound from the cuckoo clock. Nothing is out of the ordinary.

I try to make myself go back to sleep. Maybe it was a nightmare. But ten minutes later, as I'm drifting into slumber, it happens again, this time with more ferocity.

I no longer question Nana's sense of reality. That night I stay up all night, curled in the fetal position in a corner of the bed, with the lights on, wondering if dementia is contagious.

For eleven days we are Nathni and Nana, granddaughter and grandfather, caregiver and caretaken, pottering around that mansion in Kathmandu, haunted by the ghosts that we brought with us from around the world: me, haunted by grasping at dreams; he, haunted by memories he is unable to remember.

For the rest of my trip, I refuse to sleep in that room, and stay in Khala's bed until she returns. Madness-induced insomnia keeps me up every night, and the lack of sleep makes me fevered and sick. I am incredibly ill until it's time to leave. When the time comes to say good-bye, I cry when I hug Nana. He is crying too, soundlessly. He stands there on the bottom floor, cane in hand, a confused look on his face. I think he knows I am leaving. I think we both know it will be the last time we will see each other. He will die just over a year later. I find some solace in knowing that Nani and Mom are hovering near, to help him until his time to transition comes.

WHAT THEY SHOULD SAY INSTEAD:

ABSENCE + TIME

What Comes Later

INTRODUCTION

by Gabrielle Birkner

That first year after he died, my father still felt incredibly close to the surface of my life. It was easy to remember the sound and cadence of his voice—Southern California by way of the Bronx. I was quick to recall the tune he'd whistle as he dressed for work and the silly faces he'd make when he thought I was being ridiculous. It was easy to conjure up his favorite refrain ("Anything is possible"), or to imagine the advice he would have dispensed in any given situation ("It is not necessary to react"). After all, he had been there for my first steps, my college graduation, and all of the milestones and all of the days in between; he'd been there for almost everything but my grief.

That first year, there were always people around, checking in and telling me to let them know if there was anything at all they could do. Putting aside that it's better to do something than to offer "anything," I did get the sense that they wanted to be helpful and would have welcomed some direction. I received hundreds of letters, filled with colorful anecdotes, from an extended network of friends and colleagues. There were hot meals and house calls and phone calls. There were posthumous awards and trees planted in Israel. There were Jewish rituals that provided, if not meaning in and of themselves, then the time and space to nurse my pain. For a while, my father's and Ruth's cell phones had yet to be disconnected, so I could still call them to hear their voices.

The first year, their stuff was everywhere. I exercised in Ruth's gym clothes and buttered my toast with their flatware and ate that toast on their dining chairs. There was so much stuff that I had to rent out a storage unit on the edge of town. So much stuff that I didn't think much about giving away items, big-ticket and small—and I was secretly relieved when people who knew that my parents had been murdered in their home wanted those things anyway. When people took in their couch or clothes or bedroom set, it felt tantamount to acknowledging that this stuff wasn't tainted and that I wasn't cursed.

That first year, no one judged the size and contours of my grief, and they didn't expect all that much from me, especially while the murder case was still winding its way through the courts. I remember complaining to my friend Molly about how tired, distracted, and unproductive I was feeling. After what I'd been through, she told me, it was enough just to "get up and brush your teeth, and feel proud of yourself for doing it." Conditioner, writing, laundry, bills—all icing.

Then day 366 rolls around, and that somehow becomes thirteen years, and at some point you realize that your loved ones have missed so much more than just your grief. They've missed your wedding to someone they would have adored, and the birth of your children. They've missed the election of Barack Obama, the legalization of same-sex marriage, Facebook, the iPad, what the Internet, of which my father was an early adopter, has become. (He set up a corny e-mail handle for me back in the early 1990s, before it was a thing among my peers, and well before firstname.lastname was standard.)

You realize that their voices don't buzz around in your head the same way they once did. After successive moves, basement floods, and attempts to reorganize your closet, after living with a labradoodle that chewed shit up for two straight years, you realize you don't have all that much left. Your kid is having a hard time, and you're sure that your dad would have known just what to do; thing is, you're having trouble imagining the advice he would have given you. He never knew you as a mother, and never really knew you as an adult, either. By now, you can pretty much forgive everyone around you for forgetting your dead dad's birthday and deathiversary. Getting up and brushing your teeth doesn't cut it.

That first year was the most disorienting. There are a lot of decisions to be made, and many feel like insult to injury. (Pine or mahogany caskets? Brontë or Shelley for the epitaph? What to do with her deodorant, his undershirts, their collection of snow globes? Who gets the wedding china?) But that first year is also the most forgiving.

That first year was traumatic; but what came next—what still comes in waves and iterations, not always anticipated—is more like pure grief. And yet years later, when you're still in a crappy place because of it, you are expected to keep it together. Sometimes I stop and think: It's been so long since I've seen my dad and Ruth, thirteen years long; that makes me miss them more. Even though the expectation remains that the longer they're gone, the easier it will get.

It is no coincidence that Rebecca and I founded *Modern Loss* nearly ten years after my father and stepmother were killed, seven years after her mom died, and three years after her dad's fatal heart attack. Years out, we were no longer ugly-crying on the subway or breaking down to telemarketers who happened to call when we were "having a moment." (Have you ever had a telemarketer hang up on you? It happened to me.) We were working, and we buzzed again with creative energy. My husband and I had a little boy, named for my father, and Rebecca and I were each expecting children with our respective spouses.

Modern Loss wasn't something we wanted to do for ourselves in the earliest, rawest moments of grief. It was an assertion that grief transcends those earliest, rawest moments. It was an acknowledgment of how much we struggled to find writing and resources that spoke to us after that first year, especially once the people around us started invoking phrases like "getting over it" or "finding closure," and became more impatient with our lingering melancholy. It was an affirmation that our losses hadn't kept us from finding happiness, even as we wished that our loved ones were there to see it and share it. It was an admission that yes, the first year is the hardest, except for, in their own way, all the others.

DAVID

by Elisa Albert

You were an astrophysicist. You were way smarter than everyone. You ate absolute trash: chips and Pepsi, Pepsi and chips, the occasional candy bar. You loved Billy Joel and James Taylor and "Africa" by Toto. I called you "Dee Dee" when I was learning to talk. You had bad skin as an adolescent. Puberty was rough on you. You were big-hearted and affectionate and brilliant, like our father. You were angry and dark and brilliant, like our mother. You put up NASA posters all over your room. You hid a terrifically vile stash of pornos under our shared sink—did you think I wouldn't find it? I was eight, much too young for *Hustler*. How my heart raced as I sat on that bathroom floor with those magazines! You liked Douglas Adams and Kurt Vonnegut and Richard Feynman. You did okay in school, but never as well as you should have (me too). You had a terrible temper. You would get consumed by rage, set off by I don't even remember what. Our middle brother would needle you, and recruit me to do the same. "Chernobyl," he nicknamed you, for the way you'd "melt down." I'm so sorry I played along with him. He was terrifically mean, but he was "cool," and I wanted to be "cool" too. You started college as I started the third grade. Years later, your friends told me you felt guilty leaving me behind in the festering pit our family had become. Your concern retroactively warmed my heart. You were right to be concerned, and lucky to get out.

One night, when you were dying in your hospital bed and

I was the only one there with you, I drew the curtains and climbed right into bed beside you. How did I know to do that? I was nineteen years old. I loved you more than I could say. I held you in my arms and rested my head next to yours. You remained unconscious. A machine breathed for you. I held you for a while. I am so, so proud to have done that. To have had that instinct, and to have acted upon it. I don't know how or why, but it made things much easier, later.

At your funeral your best friend wept over your open grave. We all shoveled dirt. Our middle brother put an arm around me while the rabbi spoke. It was so exceptional for him to show me this sort of kindness that I just sat there marveling, waiting for him to withdraw his arm or insult me so I could relax. It was a big showy Tragic Young Person's Death, a crowded and lively shiva. We were the most popular bereaved folk in town that season, believe you me. People pitied us. I didn't like the pity, but I took it, because hey.

Shiva, by the way, is the smartest, rightest, most essential ritual ever invented. An amazing week of parties. Only sorry you missed it. At the end of every raucous night, we congregated over obscene piles of food in the kitchen, laughing about dumb shit people had said that day. People get so nervous around the bereaved; it's amazing. One lady told me it looked like I had gained weight. Another told me I appeared to have lost weight. One woman wondered whether your girlfriend intended to make use of your frozen sperm. Someone else told your girlfriend she was still young enough to meet someone else and have kids.

There was the possibility of taking a semester off from college if I needed to, but I didn't need to. I did wrangle a superior housing arrangement out of the ordeal, if memory serves. And I was aware of my strange, powerful new status: I had been marked by death. A lot of folks steered clear. For a long time, I saw that there were two kinds of people: those who had come into contact with death and those who had been spared contact with death. Obviously it was only a matter of time until the latter joined the former, but in the meantime how clueless and shallow and silly the spared-contact-with-death seemed! How utterly lacking perspective! In a neat inversion, *I* pitied *them*.

"You should write a book about your brother," a friend told me years after you died. It was jarring because (a) you're in everything I've written, and (b) telling writers what to write is dumb. She meant that I should write a schmaltzy memoir about loss and all the profound lessons it taught me. I could repackage platitudes, serve as inspiration and comfort and guide. It would be a best seller. People would live more fully having read it. I think I told her I'd rather suck dick for money, but maybe I just thought it.

When I teach creative writing, I always give students Amy Hempel's story "In the Cemetery Where Al Jolson Is Buried." It's an elliptical narrative about a distracted, terrified woman who can't bring herself to be fully present with her dying friend. She obsesses over disaster and trivia, running circles around the life ending before her eyes. People often have to read it two or three times to figure out what's going on. It's kind of about the opposite of me climbing into your deathbed and holding you in my arms, Davey. It's unbearable. One time in class I started crying when I read the end out loud. Like, I embarrassed myself. Like, I had to say "Okay, why don't we take a bathroom break" and "Sorry, guys, I have some baggage." Once in a while I'll glibly mention that hey, my family happens to be buried in the cemetery where Al Jolson is buried, what a wacky tidbit! They stare blankly at me whenever I do this. Sometimes I wonder if I should stop giving students that story. I think I just want the opportunity to perform this ritual publicly, to be honest. It *is* the most apt story about death I've ever read, but Hempel doesn't have the same readership as, say, Chicken Soup for Whatever Your Problem Is.

I liked *Many Lives, Many Masters* and *Does the Soul Survive?* Some get real pissy about the afterlife when they've lost someone they love, but for a couple years I found thoughts of the afterlife to be extremely wonderful. I don't care if this makes me seem weak-minded or silly. You were an astrophysicist, Dave. You know that energy cannot be destroyed, only changed, transformed.

I have a rad little boy now, and he's a lot like you in all the good ways. He carries your name, and we talk about you all the time. He particularly adores hearing about that practical joke you played at camp one summer. *Tell me about Uncle David and the shaving cream again!* He asks enormous questions about the nature of time and space, and I say that I wish you were here to answer them.

Of late, I've noticed that the street style of cool fashionable types includes these absolutely hideous white Nike high-tops that you used to wear. They were hideous then, and they're hideous now, but they've undergone a mysterious alchemy that makes them cool. Back then they were just ugly and dorky, and I—a snotty preteen—was embarrassed by your sneakers, your utter lack of style. Every time I see those sneakers on the feet of some cutting-edge nineteen-year-old urbane international, I laugh. You were ahead of your time, bro. You didn't give a shit. You were the coolest.

Sometimes when I go running around the lake in the park, I listen to this Death Cab for Cutie album. Usually it wrings out a tear or two, which is exhilarating, honestly, in this mechanized world of ours. It's the only time I actually enjoy running, because I'm using this good strong healthy body (I'm older than you are, now, dude! I'm so much older than you now!), and I like to think I'm using this good strong healthy body for the both of us. In so doing, I'm sending you all of my love. Which, because you're not here, means, I guess, that I'm sending *myself* all of my love, which is pretty nice, too. Schmaltzy, but nice. "The dead: where *aren't* they?" That's the poet Franz Wright.

Our dad can't talk about you without crying, even still. Our mom can't talk about you without getting angry. I say your name as often as I possibly can. Your girlfriend has a husband and kids. We picnicked last summer. I love her, and call her sister. So much has happened since you died. You would have *loved* the Internet, man, oh my freaking god. In a few more years you will have been dead longer than you were alive, which is simply, profoundly, incomprehensibly, absurdly, inevitably . . . just how it goes.

CONSIDERING THE ALTERNATIVE

by Artis Henderson

If my husband, Miles, hadn't died in Iraq four months after our wedding, we would, by now, have two school-age kids, a boy and a girl, and a little house in the country. Miles would be teaching high school, and I would be a writer.

Then again, we may well have been divorced.

Miles and I met in a nightclub in Tallahassee when he was twenty-two and I was twenty-three. He was training to be an Apache helicopter pilot at Fort Rucker, in Alabama, and I worked for a liberal US senator in Tallahassee. Miles was conservative, Christian, Texan. He drove a pickup, owned firearms, went to church every Sunday. I was a Democrat, a feminist, and preferred to sleep in on Sundays. At the time, I didn't view our differences as reasons why our relationship shouldn't have lasted. Now they seem evident.

Still, our relationship worked in such a way that people noticed, flaming with a brightness that stopped strangers in Walmart. There's a photo of the two of us at Miles's parents' ranch in Texas, me sitting in the saddle behind him on his horse, my arms wrapped around his waist. We're smiling in an easy way. How could a young woman who grew up beside the tide pools of South Florida, fiercely wild and independent, have landed there? Love has a strange, beautiful alchemy.

The military told me Miles died instantly when his helicopter crashed in a lemon orchard north of Balad, Iraq. They sent

his body home and declared him "unviewable." I didn't get to hold his hand or touch his face one last time.

I have a hard time describing the immensity of my grief. It billowed up and blocked out the sun. For a long while, I said that grief almost killed me. But there was no almost. I was dead for years, during which my memories of Miles coalesced into a single golden narrative that I refused to question. Even if other people did.

"You'd probably be divorced by now," friends started telling me about seven years after Miles died. "You were still in the honeymoon phase."

I'd protest vigorously. Because on the wall of my brain, I'd been projecting a perpetual highlight reel of the life I imagined I'd be living had Miles survived. Bright children. Beautiful home. Satisfying jobs. Close relationships with our respective families. We'd still disagree about politics, but in a way that we could laugh off. We'd still turn heads at Walmart. But is that really how things would have played out?

We had been together for two years, and our wedding could have waited. But it was important to us that we be married while Miles was gone. For practical reasons, certainly—that way I'd be next of kin if anything happened—but also as a testament that we were in it together. So we held our wedding before he shipped out.

The deployment was to last fifteen months. We knew it was coming—Miles's unit had spent the last nine months getting ready for Iraq—but anticipating a thing and actually experiencing it are very different. A separation like that would have been hard on any marriage, but it was especially hard on our new marriage. And I was beginning to understand in a way that worried me what life as a military wife would be like: the constant moving, the ever-present proximity of a military base with its ring of strip joints and tattoo parlors, the impossibility of having an identity separate from my husband's.

Miles's deployment came in the early years of the war, when we were lucky to get a twenty-minute phone call every two weeks, so we wrote letters to each other. Some were tender. Others crackled with tension, as I vented my frustrations, the sacrifices I thought I was making, and how the spouses who outranked me tried to order me around. I told him I wanted to buy a house in Florida so I'd have a place near my family— and away from the military—to retreat to during future deployments. He accused me of trying to bail. Maybe I was.

After his death, I refused to reread those letters. The sweet ones would hurt my heart, I knew. But more than that, I was afraid the tense ones would threaten the narrative I had built.

Then more recently, I came across old journals I'd kept during the time Miles and I lived together but before we were married. Paging through one of them, I was shocked to see what was written on the pages. There, in my firm handwriting, was all the discontent I had spent years refusing to acknowledge. I was mad about the frequent separations because of training and field exercises, mad about my crappy job as a teacher's aide, mad that I wasn't living overseas, and—worst of all—mad at Miles. My anger, I had decided, was all his fault. Journal in hand, I sat on the floor of my house and read page after page, too stunned to move.

That night I lay awake in bed thinking about the people who had predicted our divorce. For the first time, I wondered if they were right, after all. Had our relationship been destined to fall apart? This idea haunted me through more sleepless nights, until finally I opened up to a group of women I know who have been married for decades.

I told them about the letters, the journal entries. The women looked at me calmly, not at all scandalized, no your-marriage-was-unraveling expressions. They reassured me that the complexity of our relationship didn't negate what had worked within it.

"So your marriage wasn't perfect?" one told me. "That's normal."

Whether we would have stayed together is irrelevant, I realized. I will never know. What I do know is that what we had was real. It was filled with joy and discord. If I want to be able to face into the future—and I do, desperately—then I need to accept both.

THE DEATHDAY-BIRTHDAY

by Nikki Reimer

Year Zero. Birthdays used to be a big deal in the Reimer house. Surprise parties. Complicated scavenger hunts ending in a big-ticket gift. Celebrations spanning a week. For my seventh birthday I got pierced ears *and* a waterbed. We Reimer kids were ostentatiously adored.

The multiple phone calls to my husband, Jonathon, on the day before my thirty-second birthday, were no clue to me that anything was wrong. I assumed a flower delivery or box of cupcakes was headed my way.

Instead, the inconceivable: my beloved brother Chris, my only sibling, had died unexpectedly, one month into his twenty-sixth year. The brand-new Roots leather belt I had bought for his birthday was still sitting in the corner of my living room. I was ostentatious and an asshole.

My birthday instantly transformed from a day of solipsistic, hedonistic glee to the latter half of a hellish forty-eight-hour trigger that I eventually rechristened "Deathday-Birthday."

When I called our parents' house with my flight information for the funeral, Chris's girlfriend, Rena, was the only one who wished me a happy birthday. I was touched that she remembered and glad that no one else mentioned it. I felt ashamed of my former innocence and selfish birthday glee.

Throughout the day Jonathon brought me Ativan and water, rubbed my back, urged me to try to eat. When visitors arrived, he hosted them graciously. A few friends brought cake. I sat and drank vodka with them for a while, but then had to go lie down. In my bedroom I could hear their laughter and tried psychically to cling to it, like when you're drunk and the room is spinning, so you put a foot on the floor to hold on. I squeezed my eyes shut, and their voices kept me tethered to the earth.

Jonathon and I left Vancouver shortly after Chris died, moving back to my hometown of Calgary with no jobs, no home, and no plan. We lived at my parents' house, where every day my husband and mother fought. We were all a bloody mess, lashing out and triggering each other's pain.

Year 1. During the first anniversary of Deathday-Birthday, I attended a two-week writing residency in the mountains, where I began a multimedia elegiac project. I felt guilty for leaving my family together to fight on the first anniversary of Chris's death while I made art in the mountains, but this time to myself felt like a necessity for my spirit and my sanity.

The day before Deathday I traipsed around an old settler cemetery. I'd borrowed an audio recorder, and I used it to record the crunch of my boots in the snow, the clang of an iron gate swinging open and closed in the wind. I read the headstones, many children and young adults who'd perished from the 1890s to the 1920s and '30s. It was not so uncommon for young people to die in those days.

I photographed Chris's buckskin gloves at the base of a tree and wrote a poem that ends, "I am waiting for your gloves to come back to life in my hands." Saccharine. I became Nikki Maudlin-Marie Reimer, Birthday Killjoy of the Future.

I announced Deathday to my new residency friends, and we toasted Chris with expensive Scotch. The next day, a small group of us celebrated my birthday at a fancy restaurant. These small decadent moments felt light-years away from my new painful reality. Over the years I'd be grateful to have spent that first anniversary with artists who didn't recoil from the intensity of my grief like the average relative or coworker.

Year 2. I grew to hate birthdays. My birthday, Chris's birthday, everyone's birthday. Watching siblings celebrate each other's birthdays on social media was the most painful of all. Our younger cousins aged to be older than Chris, and I hated it. Being six years older than Chris, and assuming we would be together forever, I used to count in my head what ages we would be in the future: he twenty-four, me thirty; he thirty-four, me forty. In the wake of his death I lose all sense of time and memory. My mind feels like it's filled with black holes.

I changed my Facebook nickname to "Birthday Killjoy." Once every six months someone will message to ask why my name pops up as a "Happy Birthday" post autocorrect. "It's because my nickname is Birthday Killjoy!" They inevitably find this hilarious, but I am not trying to be funny. I really do want to kill all the joy of all of the birthdays everywhere.

We had a Deathday gathering for Chris at a bar. A guileless couple on a date wandered in and seated themselves, and I couldn't understand why they didn't both immediately drop dead from the ferocity of my hatred. How dare they talk, flirt, laugh too loud? Even when shots were passed around and a toast was raised, they didn't get the hint. I drank about three times more than my limit, the intensity of the emotion in the room too much for me. I got the I-love-you-mans with each one of Chris's dude friends. I hugged them too tightly, kissed all their faces, said I love you I love you I love you I love you.

As if this overbearing affection could have reached him beyond the grave.

For my birthday I spent the day in bed with the sweats,
alternately puking into a bucket or trying to force down dry
toast. I was thirty-four.

Year 3. Jonathon and I had settled into our new reality in
Calgary, painful month by painful month. We'd rented a house
near my work, while he did freelance copyediting from home.
We still missed our friends in Vancouver, our old home, and
our old life every day. The total rupture of everything we'd
known was hard on us both, and although he had limitless patience for my grief over my brother, sometimes we'd fight for
no reason other than stress.

We moved the Deathday celebration to our roomy rented
living room. It was still a bit of a drunken shitshow, culmi-
nating in an improv free-jazz performance with Jonathon on
saxophone and Chris's best friend Marc on furnace pipe, but
it was touching that his friends still wanted to remember him.
All the dudes got the I-love-you-mans with our dad.

I was once again hungover on my birthday. Jonathon
brought me cake in bed. Mom got sick at dinner, and we left
the restaurant before dessert. She puked in the bathroom back
at our place. Rather than giving way to explosive outbursts,
we now tiptoed around each other, not quite sure how or who
to be. I'd gone to extensive counseling and was trying to express my feelings, but my parents hadn't done any therapy. I
kept waiting for them to shatter, though my dad seemed to
bury his feelings in alcohol, while my mom's emotions came
out in sickness and rashes. The prevailing theme of Deathday-
Birthday is excretion.

Year 4. The friend gatherings have ended, and this feels sad, but also okay. Everything feels sad but also okay. Over time the triggers become more manageable, the outbursts smaller. Deathday was a quiet dinner for four at my parents' house.

This year I was the one who got sick. Mom drove me to the doctor to get more prescription meds. We stopped for fancy coffees first, trying to give my birthday a bit of a sparkle.

An envelope came in the mail with two cards from my grandmother, who lives 130 miles away. "Just wanted you to know . . . I'm thinking of you during this difficult time" and "Granddaughter, you're not just one in a million . . . You're a once-in-a-lifetime wonderful person! Happy Birthday." She gets it.

My tolerance for Deathday-Birthday has grown over time. I don't drink as much as I used to. I meditate and read books on impermanence, acceptance, and the nature of pain.

But I'm still the Birthday Killjoy. Just yesterday an old photo in my newsfeed of a friend and her brother stung with the reminder of what I've lost, but the pain is a wave I have learned to ride. Getting older without Chris is never going to be okay, but I've accepted that it's my reality.

"Next year we'll have a party for your birthday," Jonathon tells me one day. "I think you're ready."

"I don't know. We could. We'll see. Maybe."

DOUBLE DIGITS

by Nishta J. Mehra

My grief turned ten last week. Ten is a big deal, you know: double digits. Ten is old enough to do some things by yourself that might have required adult supervision before. Ten is old enough to sound impressive, to have some weight to throw around. Ten gets to stay up later; it gets a bigger allowance.

But ten also means that you're about to be relegated to the gangly realm of the "preteen," which sounds, worryingly, like a medical condition. Grown-ups stop cutting you as much slack. They expect you to "know better."

It's been a decade since my father died, and I get the sense that everyone else feels the time has come for my grief to grow up and move on. No one wants to hang out with my ten-year-old grief. They're tired of it, a little embarrassed when it tries to draw attention to itself. They've humored it enough already, listened to its stories, watched it shed big, fat baby tears. My grief still wants to be held, to curl up in someone's lap, to clutch a stuffed animal and maybe even suck its thumb, but it's too old for all of that now.

Ten years of grief is enough to have learned how to cook every single one of my father's favorite foods, which I serve on Father's Day or his birthday or on my parents' wedding anniversary. Ten years is long enough to have learned that all children's movies inevitably contain dead or absent parents, so it's a good idea to watch them at home and not in the theater. It's enough experience at friends' weddings to pre-emptively position myself in the bathroom during the end of the first dance, because the father/daughter dance will most surely come next.

Ten years means you're no longer worried about how to get out of bed or managing to take a shower or how not to become physically violent toward the next person who tells you that "everything happens for a reason." Your hair doesn't fall out anymore, and the insomnia is gone. Friends and acquaintances have long stopped asking "How *are* you?" with their earnest Hallmark faces on. But you kind of wish they would.

By now, others in my life have joined the club that I occupied for a long time by myself. Though I'm glad not to be hanging out in this clubhouse by myself anymore, it's hardly a place I'd wish on anyone. I feel like the messenger in a young-adult fantasy book, you know, the cryptic being that greets the hero/heroine upon their arrival into an unknown realm? I cannot go with them, but I can unfurl my ten years of grief before them like a coded map, pointing at mountains in the distance, warning of monsters along the path.

It is through them that I realize how long it has been since I let myself be sad. Like, straight-up, no-holds-barred, crying-fit devastated about the fact that my father is dead—still, dead. Ten years ago, I would have balked at the notion that I'd ever have to make time to grieve, that it could be anything other than right in front of my face at every moment of every day. But my life has grown to accommodate my father's absence, to allow me to complete the daily human tasks of living that seemed so impossible at first without him. This is what I was supposed to do, what has allowed me to create a life I'm proud of, a life of great joy, but I actually find myself longing to be, even only just for a moment, twenty-three years old again, in my childhood bed, raw with loss and numb with grief.

For the first few years after my father died, the possibility that he might show up any day, ringing my doorbell and explaining that this had all been a terrible mistake, shimmered around the edges of my daily life, like a dream you can only halfway remember. Before I could stop them, my hands would move to pick up the phone and call him. I'd eat at a new restaurant and think, Oh, I should bring Papa here, my brain interrupting itself just a second too late.

But by now, too much has happened, too much that he's missed. I earned a master's degree. I wrote a book. I got married. I have a son. The fabric of my daily life is so different than it was ten years ago. Other than my mom, nearly everyone I interact with on a daily basis has never even met my dad, which makes him feel *more* absent, not less.

More than anything, I am unable to separate the person that I am today from the fact that my father died ten years ago. His death and my grief have shaped essentially everything about how I move through the world.

The summer my father died was also the summer that my godsons were born: twin boys, dear friends' sons, who I lived with and cared for through my father's sudden and unexpected hospitalization until just a few days before his death. You can't plan richer symbolism than that—if this were fiction, it would seem too obvious—but there I was, surrounded by new life and by death. I woke at midnight for feedings, preparing bottles in a sleepy haze, pacing through the quiet house to lull tiny bodies back to sleep; then I drove, during naptime, to the hospital, punching in the code to enter the ICU, reading aloud to my father, holding his hand, watching him die.

Today the twins are, like my grief, ten years old: long-limbed, scraggly physical manifestations of the time that has passed. How can it be that so much time has passed that these boys are old enough to play on soccer teams and read chapter books by themselves?

Fittingly, they just finished the Harry Potter series, ending book seven a few days after the tenth anniversary of my father's death. I take comfort in the fact that the boys whose new lives buffered me through my first experience with death now know the lessons of that series; that the dead never truly leave us, that scars serve as both pain and protection, that love is the most powerful force on earth.

ACKNOWLEDGMENTS

We are grateful to our agents, Rebecca Gradinger and Christy Fletcher; their belief in this project has never wavered from the moment they reached out to us.

Also to our thoughtful editors at Harper Wave, Karen Rinaldi and Sarah Murphy; Peter Arkle, whose illustrations so beautifully animate the stories in this book; the women of WWDP, from which *Modern Loss* took root; Veronica Goldstein at Fletcher & Company; and to Melissa Baez.

Modern Loss is a stronger community thanks to the support of Awesome Without Borders and the Harnisch Foundation; Rachel Sklar, Glynnis MacNicol, and everyone at The Li.st; Susan McPherson; and Dave Isay of StoryCorps. Thank you, especially, to our talented and committed contributing editors, columnists, and producers, Nicole Belanger, Niva Dorell, Tré Miller Rodríguez, Jennifer Richler, Mathew Rodriguez, Julie Satow, and Meg Tansey, and to every single person who has shared their story of loss with us, both in public and in confidence.

From Rebecca:

Thank you.

To my beloved Brunch Club: Rebecca Ashkenazi, Sarah Blaugrund, Dee Carlisi, Loren Fisher, Kate Friedmann, Dana Gandsman, Hadar Hermoni, Hilary Hochberg Shohet, Tali Rafaeli, Ilana Shatz, and Alyssa Tomback. There's nobody I'd rather ugly-cry and laugh with.

To Taifa Harris, the sister I found along the way.

To Kerry Donahue, my friend and mentor on writing, producing, parenting, and beyond.

To Bruce Patterson, for sensing my resilience long before I sensed it myself.

To my mother's friends, who made the effort: Sandra Gandsman, Sybil Gilmar, Sandra Herson, Judy Leash, and Danice Morris.

To Bev Black, for the Route 1 road trip, and Brett Dickstein, for the Christmas tree.

To Tim Federle: for your wit, your warmth, and your encouragement. You, too, are my dream friend.

To my *Colbert Report* coworkers, who showed up at my mom's funeral in a rented van, I'll never forget your kindness.

To my friends and family who offered creative and business support, cheerleading, patience, and love both soft and tough, frequently over heaps of fries: Melinda and Chris Tarbell, Juliana and Rob Bloom, Ruth Ann Harnisch, Benj Pasek, Kathy Hirsh-Pasek, Jeffrey Pasek, Shaina Taub, Wendy MacNaughton, David Gelles, Rachel Axler, Elyssa Back, Doug Young, Ron Lieber, Jodi Kantor, Jean Vidal, Paul Domencic, and Maureen White.

To Ethan Franzel, for suggesting I build myself a new foundation.

To the ROI Community and Charles and Lynn Schusterman Family Foundation, for supporting people who want to do their share in healing the world.

To Brittney Morello and the Broadway musical theater babysitting scene, for giving me precious writing time through loving childcare while indoctrinating my little boys into the world of Sondheim.

To Ziggy, my furry firstborn: You never made me feel weird for bringing you to my dad's shiva (likely because you can't speak).

To Gabi, for your dear friendship and editorial wisdom.

To Noah and Elliot, for filling my days and nights with more happy energy and unconditional love than I ever thought I'd have.

And to Justin, without whom this book, and *Modern Loss* at large, would not exist. Thank you for this life together in which we still laugh in spite of it all, and for all the journeys and good food we promised each other in our vows.

From Gabi:

Thank you.

To my mother and stepfather, Roni and Allan Lang, for your encouragement and for your loving embrace of grandparenthood.

To my friends and coworkers who carried me through—and beyond—the worst of my grief: Annabel Torrey Raymond, Marnie and Brad Helfand, Sarah Aroeste Blaugrund, Cindy Sher, Susie London, Alexa Weil, Lindsay Feldman, Jessica Levin Amoroso, Melanie Kron, Jacob Berkman, Jeremy Caplan, Molly Jong-Fast, Andrew Polk, Jean Corbett-Parker, Audrey Forsythe, Elissa Strauss, Allison Yarrow, Gina DiLorenzi and the late Albert DiLorenzi, Lisa and John Breunig, Donna and Jonathan Lucas, and Christina Lewis Halpern. I will never forget your kindness.

To Dave and Takako Holland, for taking on one of the most difficult roles imaginable with extraordinary integrity.

To Matthew Strozier and Robert Strozier for pointing me

toward Safe Horizon and Vilma Torres, the late Theresa Pierce, and everyone at the Families of Homicide Victims program, for welcoming me when I got there.

To Dan Levey and his team at POMC, for making crime-victim advocacy your life's work.

To Lucas Wilcoxson and the Sedona Police Department for your professionalism.

To Deborah Kolben, Ami Eden, Jane Eisner, Gary Rosenblatt, and Seth Lipsky, from whom it's been a pleasure to learn, and who handed me tissues when I cried at my desk.

To Laura Sinberg, Liza Percer, Amy Choi, Taly Ravid, and Rebecca Greenfield, whose insights have made this book better.

To the Asleson siblings, who show us all the meaning of family.

To Kay, Jeff and Michele Birkner, Aimee Birkner and Michael Hampton, the late Eva Birkner, Ruth Herman, Nancy and Stuart Siefer (and Rafi), Rabbi Steven Jacobs, Rabbi Joshua Hammerman, Sandra Chernick, and Dr. Andrew Slaby, for your support and care.

To Alana Ain and Rabbi Dan Ain, for your wisdom and loving-kindness.

To Rebecca Soffer, for your vision and cherished friendship.

And to my loving husband, Jeremy Siefer, and our sons, Saul and Hank: you make me happy every day.

NOTES

INTRODUCTION

xxiii One in seven Americans: Comfort Zone Camp with New York Life Foundation, "Exploring Grief's Landscape: A National Research Perspective," 2010, http://www.hellogrief.org/wp-content/up loads/2010/06/CZC-White-Paper-Grief-Research2.pdf.

xxiii As many as 15 percent of pregnancies: Office of Women's Health, US Department of Health and Human Services, "Pregnancy Loss." https://www.womenshealth.gov/pregnancy/youre-pregnant -now-what/pregnancy-loss.

xxiii there are some 23,000 stillbirths: Marian F. MacDorman and Eliza-beth C. W. Gregory, "Fetal and Perinatal Mortality: United States," Division of Vital Statistics, 2013, http://www.cdc.gov/nchs/data /nvsr/nvsr64/nvsr64_08.pdf.

xxiii an estimated 700 to 900 women: Nina Martin, Emma Cillekens, and Alessandra Freitas, "Lost Mothers," ProPublica, July 17, 2017, https://www.propublica.org/article/lost-mothers-maternal-health -died-childbirth-pregnancy.

xxiii hundreds of thousands of Americans are widowed: Diana B. El-liott and Tavia Simmons, "Marital Events of American: 2009," US Census Bureau, August 2011, https://www.census.gov/prod /2011pubs/acs-13.pdf.

xxiii many of them will be younger than forty: Kase Wickman, "Hot Young Widows Club Founder: It's OK to Not Be OK When Some-one You Love Dies," *New York Post*, May 26, 2016, http://nypost .com/2016/05/26/hot-young-widows-club-founder-its-okay-to -not-be-okay-when-someone-you-love-dies.

TRIGGERS: INTRODUCTION

44 "It's so curious": *Letters from Colette*, trans. Robert Phelps (New York: Farrar Straus Giroux, 1980).

45 "There is still a lot I can't bear to know": For a report on the trial, see Larry Hendricks, "Oak Creek Man Gets 2 Life Terms for Double

Murder," *Arizona Daily Sun*, November 2, 2004, http://azdailysun
.com/oak-creek-man-gets-life-terms-for-double-murder/arti
cle_7cf9d717-0dcc-5d03-995a-0263a702edb5.html.

45   death penalty prosecutors originally sought: Larry Hendricks,
"Prosecutors Seek Death Penalty in Sedona Double-Murder Case,"
Arizona Daily Sun, June 14, 2004, http://azdailysun.com/prosecu
tors-to-seek-death-penalty-in-sedona-double-murder-case/arti
cle_22903927-c3cc-5371-9dad-d552a82a73c7.html.

THE BARREN FIELD

71   "Nothing now": W. H. Auden, "Funeral Blues (Stop All the Clocks),"
in *Collected Poems* (New York: Random House, 1976).

TABOO TIMES TWO

106   That study was published: Alice Radosh and Linda Simkin, "Acknowledging Sexual Bereavement: A Path Out of Disenfranchised
Grief," *Reproductive Health Matters* 24, no. 48 (November 2016):
25–33.

IDENTITY: INTRODUCTION

120   "the type of people": Walsh, John. "Double Homicide in Sedona,"
Sedona Red Rock News, February 20, 2004, http://srr.stparchive
.com/Archive/SRR/SRR02202004P01.php.

120   "My hat is off": Lawrence R. Birkner, "A Different View of Charrette Session," *Sedona Red Rock News*, January 28, 2004, http://srr
.stparchive.com/Archive/SRR/SRR01282004P04.php.

121   "One might expect": Eric Schlosser, "A Grief Like No Other," *Atlantic*, September 1997, http://www.theatlantic.com/past/docs
/issues/97sep/grief.htm.

SECRETS: INTRODUCTION

228   "I would hear people say": Thomas Friedman, *From Beirut to Jerusalem* (New York: Anchor, 1989), 37.

F IS FOR FORGIVENESS

251 "Not forgiving is like drinking rat poison": Anne Lamott, *Traveling Mercies: Some Thoughts on Faith* (New York: Anchor, 2000).

MY WEDDING GOWN'S LAST DANCE

267 "[concentrated] all the idylls of youth": Paul Kalanithi, *When Breath Becomes Air* (New York: Random House, 2016), 33–34.

CREDITS

ABOUT THE CONTRIBUTORS

TANZILA "TAZ" AHMED is an activist, storyteller, and politico based in Los Angeles. She is cohost of the #GoodMuslimBadMuslim podcast, which has been featured in *O, the Oprah Magazine*, *Wired*, and *BuzzFeed*. In 2016 Taz was honored as a White House Champion of Change for AAPI Art and Storytelling. An avid essayist, she wrote a monthly column called "Radical Love" and has written for *Sepia Mutiny*, *Truthout*, the *Aerogram*, the *Nation*, and *Left Turn Magazine*, among other publications. She is published in the anthologies *Good Girls Marry Doctors* and *Love, Inshallah*, and the poetry collection *Coiled Serpent*. She also makes disruptive art annually with #MuslimVDayCards.

ELISA ALBERT is the author of the novels *After Birth* and *The Book of Dahlia*, the short story collection *How This Night Is Different*, and editor of the anthology *Freud's Blind Spot*. Her fiction and nonfiction have appeared in the *New York Times*, the *Guardian*, *Time Magazine*, *Tin House*, *Commentary*, *Guernica*, the *Rumpus*, *Post Road*, *Los Angeles Review of Books*, and *New York Magazine*, on NPR, and in many anthologies. She is at work on a new novel, a short story or two, and the Ashtanga primary series.

SARA FAITH ALTERMAN coproduces the acclaimed stage show *Mortified*, which features adults sharing the embarrassing things they created as kids. She's the author of the novels *My Fifteen Minutes* and *Tears of a Class Clown*, and contributed to the best-selling six-word story anthology *Not Quite What I Was Planning*. Sara lives in San Francisco with her husband, son, and a dog she rescued/kidnapped from China.

MICHAEL ARCENEAUX is a Houston-bred, Howard University–educated writer currently residing in Harlem. His writing on issues related to culture, sexuality, race, gender, politics, and Beyoncé has appeared in the *New York Times Magazine*, *Rolling Stone*, *Elle*, *Complex*, *Teen Vogue*, *Ebony*, the *Guardian*, *Esquire*, *BuzzFeed*, and *Essence*, among other publications. Additionally, Michael has lent his commentary to outlets such as MSNBC, VH1, BET, SiriusXM, and NPR. Michael was recruited for the priesthood at twenty; he did a hard pass.

MATTIE J. BEKINK is an Amsterdam-based consultant and writer providing advisory services on institutional strategy, human rights, communications, and China strategy. Her writing has appeared in the *Guardian*, the *Wall Street Journal*, the *South China Morning Post*, and *Scary Mommy*, and on *Modern Loss*. Mattie speaks fluent Chinese, proficient Dutch, some Italian and Arabic—so watch what you're saying around her. Chances are, she understands you.

EMILY RAPP BLACK is the author of *Poster Child: A Memoir* and *The Still Point of the Turning World*, which was a *New York Times* best seller. Her work has appeared in *Vogue*, the *New York Times*, *O, the Oprah Magazine*, *Redbook*, the *Sun*, and many other publications. She is assistant professor of creative writing at the University of California, Riverside, and lives in

Palm Springs with her husband, writer and editor Kent Black, and their family. She likes action and comic-book movies, and the music of Taylor Swift.

HELEN CHERNIKOFF is the news editor at the *Forward*. She created the blog *The New Normal: Blogging Disability*, as well as a food and wine website for *The Jewish Week*. In one of her past lives she was a business journalist endeavoring to move the stock market with her scoops; she is also a rabbinical school dropout. Helen has a master's of public administration from Columbia University and a BA in history and French from Amherst College.

JOEY CHERNILA is an educator living in Great Barrington, Massachusetts, where he hosts Inkless, a live storytelling event. A profile of Joey appeared in the 2015 book *Teaching the Sacred Art* by the Reverend Jane Vennard. His drawings and writings can be found on birthday cards throughout Berkshire County.

AMANDA CLAYMAN is a financial therapist who helps people bring money into balance. She founded the Financial Wellness Program for the national arts nonprofit the Actors Fund, where she pioneered a cognitive-behavioral approach to financial education. She runs seminars and groups for organizations around the country, and is the author of several courses for Lynda.com, the online learning arm of LinkedIn. She has an unhealthy level of fascination with the British monarchy.

RUBY DUTCHER is a writer and recent graduate of Barnard College. Her writing has appeared on *Modern Loss* and in the

Eye Magazine and the *Columbia Daily Spectator*. She lives in Los Angeles with her family and their two dogs, Guinness and Soy Sauce.

CATHERINE FENNELLY is a wife, a mom, a hairdresser, and founder of the nonprofit Let It Out Boxing, based in Quincy, Massachusetts. She's got a killer right hook.

MICHAEL FLAMINI is an executive editor at St. Martin's Press in New York City. His philosophy of how to get along in life, especially when times are hard, is summed up in this quote from Marion Cunningham's introduction to *The Fannie Farmer Cookbook*: "Every meal should be a small celebration." He lives (and dines) in New York City and the Berkshires.

SARAH FOX continued to travel for several months after completing the Camino de Santiago—unexpectedly stopping and falling in love with the islands of the Pacific. Sarah now lives in Guam and enjoys spending her time surrounded by the beauty of the ocean. She is at work on her first novel. When she's not sitting inside at her desk, she spends her time exploring the island the way she knows best—in her worn hiking boots.

AMY MIHYANG GINTHER is a professor at the University of California, Santa Cruz. She has lived, taught, and performed in the United States, the United Kingdom, and South Korea. Her most recent solo show, *Homeful*, ran in London and Atlanta and at the SF Fringe. She has been featured on the cover of the *New York Times Magazine* for her adoptee rights activism and has performed as part of a TEDx in Cheongju, South

Korea. Amy attempts to make ice cream without an ice cream maker and has a strong aversion to street monkeys.

KIM GOLDMAN, the sister of murder victim Ron Goldman, is a longtime victims' advocate and a board member for the National Center for Victims of Crime. She is also the executive director of the Youth Project, which provides free counseling to teenagers. Kim has twice been recognized on the *New York Times* best-seller list, for her books *His Name Is Ron: Our Search for Justice* and *If I Did It, Confessions of the Killer*. Kim recently published two books, *Can't Forgive: My Twenty-Year Battle with O.J. Simpson* and *Media Circus, A Look at Private Tragedy in the Public Eye*; she cohosts the weekly podcast *Broadscast* and is a special correspondent for *Crime Watch Daily*. A single mother, Kim also finds time to manage her son's basketball team and nurture a very healthy shoe obsession.

MICHAEL GREIF directs musicals, new plays, and classics on and off Broadway and at major regional theaters across America. He is currently represented on Broadway with *Dear Evan Hansen* and *War Paint*. Michael is known for his long-term creative relationships with some of the major theatrical voices of the time, including Tony Kushner (*Angels in America, The Intelligent Homosexual's Guide*), Scott Frankel and Michael Korie, and Tom Kitt and Brian Yorkey, as well as major institutions such as the Public Theater and La Jolla Playhouse. He also directed the Pulitzer Prize–winning musicals *Rent* and *Next to Normal*, and has received four Tony Award nominations and three Obie Awards. He holds a BS from Northwestern University and an MFA from the University of California, San Diego.

ARTIS HENDERSON is the author of *Unremarried Widow*, a *New York Times* Editors' Choice named to more than ten Best of the Year lists. She earned a graduate degree from the Columbia School of Journalism and studied in West Africa on a Rotary scholarship. She currently lives in Southwest Florida, where she teaches writing and obsesses over local ecology.

CHAMIQUE HOLDSCLAW is a women's basketball icon, thrice helping the University of Tennessee women's team clinch the national championship. She is a six-time WNBA All-Star, and won a gold medal at the 2000 Summer Olympics in Sydney. Having retired from her playing career, Chamique now advocates around the world to end the stigma of mental illness. In her spare time she secretly practices her fox-trot in hopes of landing a spot on *Dancing with the Stars*.

LUCY KALANITHI is an internist on faculty at the Stanford School of Medicine and the widow of the late Paul Kalanithi, author of the memoir *When Breath Becomes Air*, for which she wrote the epilogue. Lucy completed her medical degree at Yale and postgraduate medical training at the University of California, San Francisco, and the Stanford Clinical Excellence Research Center. She lives in the San Francisco Bay Area with her daughter, Cady, and uses her dual United States–United Kingdom citizenship to justify her love of Scotch eggs.

ANTHONY KING is an Emmy-nominated writer, director, and performer. He cowrote the off-Broadway show *Guten-*

berg! The Musical!, which also ran Off West End in London and is now being performed all over the world. Anthony has developed television shows for CBS, HBO, A&E, and AMC and has written for shows like *Silicon Valley* (HBO), *Broad City* (Comedy Central), *Search Party* (TBS), *Playing House* (USA), *Wrecked* (TBS), *Wet Hot American Summer: First Day of Camp* and *Ten Years Later* (Netflix), and more. He is currently developing a musical version of *Beetlejuice* for Broadway with Warner Bros. He lives in Los Angeles with his wife and two daughters. And he hates cotton balls. Seriously. They're the worst.

MARISA RENEE LEE graduated from Harvard in 2005 and began her career at Brown Brothers Harriman. While working in finance, Marisa founded the Pink Agenda, a breast cancer nonprofit, in honor of her mother, Lisa. In 2010 Marisa accepted a presidential appointment in the Obama administration, where she ultimately served in four roles across the Small Business Administration and the White House. Marisa has served as managing director of the My Brother's Keeper Alliance, a nonprofit dedicated to eliminating gaps in opportunity for boys and young men of color. Marisa is a Green Bay Packers fan. She lives in Virginia with her husband, Matt, and their dog, Sadie.

YASSIR LESTER is a stand-up comedian, writer, and actor originally from Marietta, Georgia. He's written for many TV shows, including *Girls* and *The Carmichael Show*, and most recently starred on *Making History* on Fox. There is a strong chance he is eating Flaming Hot Cheetos right now.

STACY LONDON is known best for her ten-year run as host on *What Not to Wear.* She also worked for the *Today* show for five years as a style correspondent and has been a style contributor to *Oprah, The View, Good Morning America,* and presently *Rachael Ray* and Refinery29. Her book *The Truth about Style* was a *New York Times* best seller. She speaks frequently on the topics of style and self-esteem. Stacy is a crazy cat lady always, but has adopted a dog named Dora who is like a cat, except for the barking.

NORA MCINERNY is the author of *It's Okay to Laugh (Crying Is Cool, Too)* and the founder of Still Kickin and the Hot Widows Club. Nora also hosts the podcast *Terrible, Thanks for Asking.* She lives in Minneapolis with her family. They do this on purpose; please remind her of this in January.

NISHTA J. MEHRA was born and raised in Memphis, Tennessee, in a tight-knit community of Indian immigrants. She received her MFA from the University of Arizona and has taught English, creative writing, and comparative religion at the Emery/Weiner School in Houston, Texas, for the past decade. Her writing has been published in *Guernica, Sugar & Rice,* and *Gulf Coast* magazines. Her second essay collection, *Making Space,* is forthcoming from Picador. Mehra lives with her wife, Jill, and their son, Shiv, who observe the Sabbath with homemade pizza every Friday night.

LANEAH "STARSHELL" MENZIES is an actress, speaker, singer, and writer. Born and raised in Lowell, Massachusetts, she emerged onto the music scene fresh out of George Washington University. She quickly gained recognition as the coauthor of Kanye West's multiplatinum "Love Lockdown" (2008). She followed this up in 2009 with "I Can See in Color," which was featured in the Oscar-nominated film *Precious*. "Birthday Girl," the popular single on Starshell's debut album, has since become the name of the suicide prevention effort BirthdayGirlWorld .com. Starshell's favorite flavors of ice cream are salted caramel, nutty coconut, and butter pecan.

SPENCER MEROLLA is a visual artist whose work investigates the social practices and material culture of bereavement. Her most recent body of work, the series *After a Fashion*, uses repurposed donated clothing that, after being worn to a funeral, has become too emotionally charged for its owner to wear again. She has exhibited nationally, and lives in Brooklyn with her husband and their adorably undersize dog.

ERIC MEYER has been a burger flipper, a college webmaster, an early blogger, and more. In 2006 he was inducted into the International Academy of Digital Arts and Sciences for his work to "inform excellence and efficiency on the Web." He is CTO at Rebecca's Gift, a nonprofit established in honor and memory of his daughter, and cofounder of the interaction design conference An Event Apart. Eric lives with his family in Cleveland, Ohio, which is a much nicer city than you've heard.

JACQUELINE MUREKATETE, a survivor of Rwanda's 1994 genocide, is a lawyer and an internationally recognized human rights activist. She is the founder and president of Genocide Survivors Foundation (GSF), a New York–based nonprofit that educates people about genocides and raises funds to support survivors. Jacqueline speaks widely at schools, NGOs, and houses of worship, and has received awards from the Anti-Defamation League, the American Jewish Committee, the National Ethnic Coalition, and the Imbuto Foundation, among other organizations. She is a graduate of NYU and the Benjamin N. Cardozo School of Law. Jacqueline currently resides in New York City with her husband, Jean-Baptiste, and their young daughter, Ineza, whose name means "goodness" in Kinyarwanda.

AMANDA PALMER, originally a busker, came to prominence as the songwriting and piano-bashing half of the punk cabaret band The Dresden Dolls. She went on to blaze trails in crowdfunding in 2012 with her solo album *Theatre Is Evil* (the world's largest original music Kickstarter to date), which debuted in the *Billboard* top ten. She then explained her philosophies about art, connection, crowd power, and human vulnerability in her TED Talk and best-selling book, both titled *The Art of Asking*. She took the first-place medal for standing broad jump in the Massachusetts Track & Field State Finals in 1986.

ELIZABETH PERCER is the author of two novels, *An Uncommon Education* and *All Stories Are Love Stories*, and of *Ultrasound*, a book of poems on the intersections of medicine and pregnancy. She holds a PhD in arts education from Stanford University, and completed her postdoctoral work for the National Writing Project at the University of California, Berkeley. Despite these accomplishments, she can neither snap nor whistle properly. She lives in Northern California with her husband and three children.

ALICE RADOSH received her doctorate in neuropsychology from the City University of New York. Before retiring to Woodstock, New York, where she splits wood to heat her house, she directed New York City's mayoral Office of Adolescent Pregnancy and Parenting Services. She is the coeditor of a book on women and retirement, and her academic publications include research studies on condom availability programs in high schools. She serves on the editorial board of *Jewish Currents*.

NIKKI REIMER, a poet and nonfiction writer who works in digital communications for higher education, has published two books, *[sic]* and *DOWNVERSE*. She lives with her husband and two cats in Calgary, Canada. Her parents met at a Quicksilver Messenger Service concert in 1971, and it's been mostly rock-and-roll ever since.

MATHEW RODRIGUEZ, an award-winning queer Latino journalist, is a staff writer for *INTO*, an LGBTQ digital magazine, and a contributing editor to *Modern Loss*. He was formerly a staff writer at *Mic* and editor at TheBody.com, an HIV/AIDS news site. A graduate of the master's program in literary reportage at NYU's Arthur L. Carter Institute for Journalism, he is currently working on a memoir about growing up gay in the age of social media. He also hosts a podcast, Slayerfest98, about his favorite thing in the entire world: *Buffy the Vampire Slayer*.

TRÉ MILLER RODRÍGUEZ is the author of *Splitting the Difference: A Heart-Shaped Memoir* and the popular Tumblr White

Elephant in the Room. Her essays have appeared in the *New York Times* and *Marie Claire*, and on MindBodyGreen.com. She lives in New York City and overshares on the Twitters.

JULIE SATOW is an award-winning journalist whose work regularly appears in the *New York Times*. She has also contributed to NPR, the *Huffington Post*, and many other outlets. Her book on the history of the Plaza Hotel is being published in 2018 by Twelve, an imprint of Hachette. A board member of the Jed Foundation, a nonprofit that focuses on the mental health of young people, she lives in New York City with her family. On Monday nights she can be found indulging her passion for *The Bachelorette*.

DAVID SAX is a writer and journalist who writes for publications such as the *New Yorker* online and *Bloomberg Businessweek*. His latest book is *The Revenge of Analog: Real Things and Why They Matter*. David lives in Toronto with his family, which includes the daughter he wrote about in this book, and a son he has yet to make any money off of . . . (yet).

REBECCA SHALOFF is a writer and independent consultant supporting social change organizations with fund-raising and communications. She lives in Washington, DC, where she's in constant pursuit of justice and bubble tea, in that order.

RACHEL SKLAR is a writer, entrepreneur, and feminist based in New York. She writes frequently on politics, culture, and gender, and speaks widely at events and on television. She has written jokes for President Barack Obama. Which is pretty cool. Please tell her daughter that in ten years, when she thinks her mom is a dork.

EILEEN SMITH is a US-born writer and photographer based in Santiago, Chile, where she has lived since 2004. She specializes in essays and stories on travel, food, wine, culture, and language, and is interested in issues of identity, belonging, and place. Her as-yet-unpublished memoir, currently entitled *Thirty-Nine: The Year That Didn't Kill Me*, tells the story of how she faced—at thirty-nine—living to be older than her own father ever was. She firmly believes that pomegranates are nature's apology for the end of berry season.

KATE SPENCER is the author of the memoir *The Dead Moms Club*. Her written work has been featured in *Cosmopolitan*, *Esquire*, *Rolling Stone*, the *Washington Post*, *BuzzFeed*, *Salon*, Refinery29, and VH1. She is a longtime performer at the Upright Citizens Brigade Theatre in New York and Los Angeles, where she lives with her husband, two daughters, and an avocado tree. Her favorite hobby is bragging about having an avocado tree.

BRIAN STELTER is CNN's senior media correspondent and the host of *Reliable Sources*. From 2007 to 2013 he was a media reporter at the *New York Times*. He and David Carr appeared in the 2011 documentary *Page One*. He still has a trophy from winning his fifth-grade class spelling bee with the word *blubber*. He realizes how easy it is to spell this.

HALEY TANNER is the author of the novel *Vaclav and Lena*, a great love story you'd really like. Gavin, Haley's first true love, is buried in the Atlantic. Haley had his ashes incorporated into a man-made reef sunk to the ocean floor in an effort to rehabilitate fragile and damaged marine ecosystems. Haley currently lives in Brooklyn with her partner, Josh, and their daughter, Beatrix. These days when she isn't on the road with Josh's band, Haley is hard at work on a second novel or fantasizing about becoming a midwife.

MEG TANSEY is a chronic oversharer. As the first person in her group of peers to lose both parents, Meg found herself talking to a lot of people about grief. In 2013, that role evolved into her position as the advice columnist for *Modern Loss*. She has an MFA from the New School. A native of Connecticut, she lives in New York City with her husband and two children.

RACHEL M. WARD works for Gimlet Media. She owns many inactive Tumblrs, but her favorite is Ai Weiwei or the High Weiwei. She has worked as a producer at NPR's *Morning Edition* and as a host, reporter, and editor at WXXI in Rochester, New York. Rachel is a native of Columbia, Maryland, just like Jayson Blair and Michael Chabon. Seems about right.

CAROLINE WAXLER is a journalist, comedy writer, and critically acclaimed author of the investing book *Stocking Up on Sin*. Through her company Harkness Hall, she is the editorial director for some of the most memorable conferences and festivals in New York, Los Angeles, and London. She is obsessed with both the Revolutionary War and ghost-walking tours, but has yet to go on one of the latter that covers the former.

ANNA WHISTON-DONALDSON is the author of the *New York Times* best seller *Rare Bird: A Memoir of Loss and Love*, which chronicles the raw early grief of losing her twelve-year-old son in an accident. It was selected as one of *Publishers Weekly*'s Best Books of 2014. In her writing, speaking, and teaching, she explores themes such as community, faith, vulnerability, and survival when the life you expected to have didn't pan out. She blogs at An Inch of Gray. Anna has never had a cup of coffee, but would gladly meet you at Starbucks.

ROBYN WOODMAN is a women's success coach and a writer who lives in the US and Italy. She spends her time encouraging others to live the best versions of their lives through private and group coaching, as well as offering curated travel experiences. She's currently working on a memoir chronicling her experience as a young widow who discovered that her husband had been a serial cheater, with a focus on the unexpected— and often hilarious—personal growth that followed. When asked why Robyn usually responds with "Why not?" Robyn never says no to an adventure.

ABOUT THE AUTHORS

REBECCA SOFFER is the cofounder and CEO of *Modern Loss*. A former producer for the Peabody Award–winning *The Colbert Report*, Rebecca is a nationally recognized speaker on the topics of loss and resilience. She is a Columbia University Graduate School of Journalism alumna and contributes regularly to books, magazines, and other media. Rebecca lives in New York City, the Berkshires, and various deadline caves with her husband and two children.

GABRIELLE BIRKNER is the cofounder and executive editor of *Modern Loss*. She is a graduate of Northwestern University's Medill School of Journalism and writes regularly for national newspapers and magazines. A journalist and digital content strategist, she has served as managing editor at JTA, director of digital media at the *Forward*, and features editor at the *New York Sun*. Gabrielle believes in keeping it real—even in Hollywood, where she lives with her husband and two children.

ABOUT THE ILLUSTRATOR

PETER ARKLE is a freelance illustrator and Scottish. He lives in New York City, where he spends most of his time drawing for magazines and newspapers (his work has appeared in almost every magazine you can think of). He recently drew portraits of fifty black cats for the book *All Black Cats Are Not Alike*—written by his wife, Amy Goldwasser. He does not need to draw any more cats for a while. See more of his work at peterarkle.com.